SEVENTIES SPOTTING DAYS
AROUND
THE EASTERN REGION

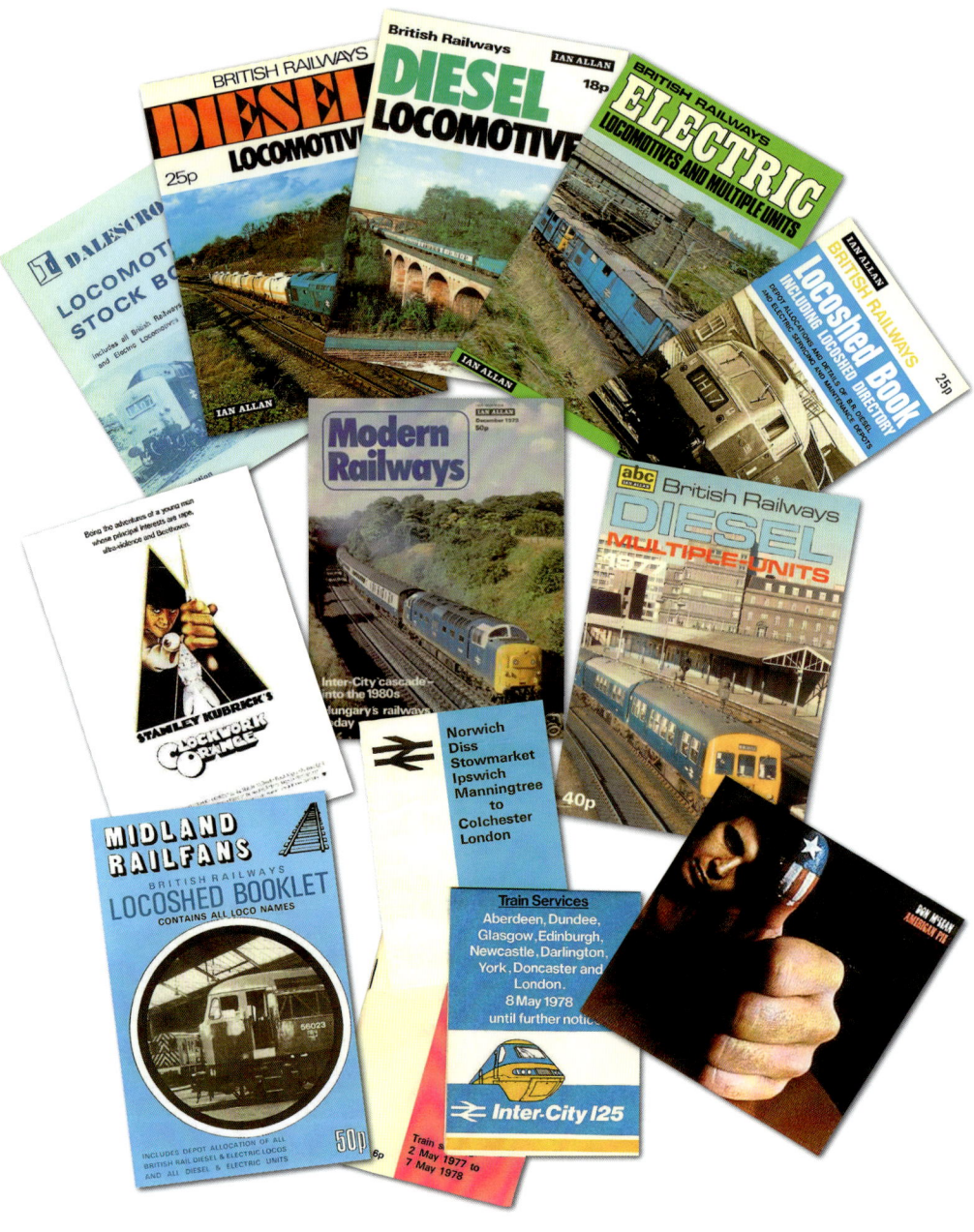

SEVENTIES SPOTTING DAYS
AROUND
THE EASTERN REGION

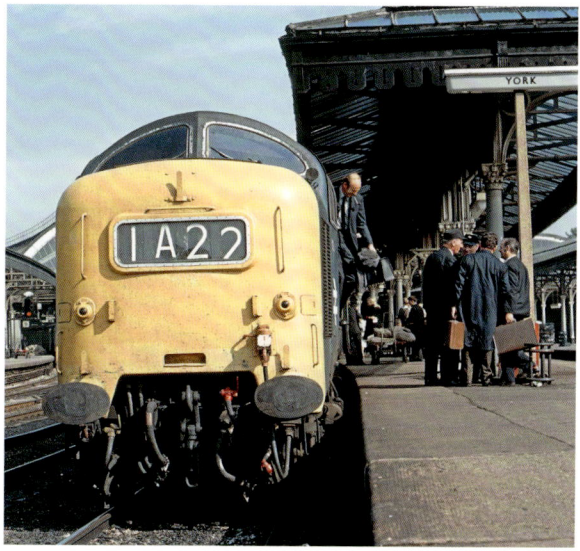

The brief stop at York allows passengers to alight and disembark,
also for the crew to change over for the onward journey aboard
Deltic No. 9012 *Crepello* in 1972. (Strathwood Library Collection)

Kevin Derrick

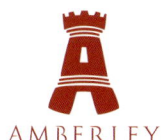

AMBERLEY

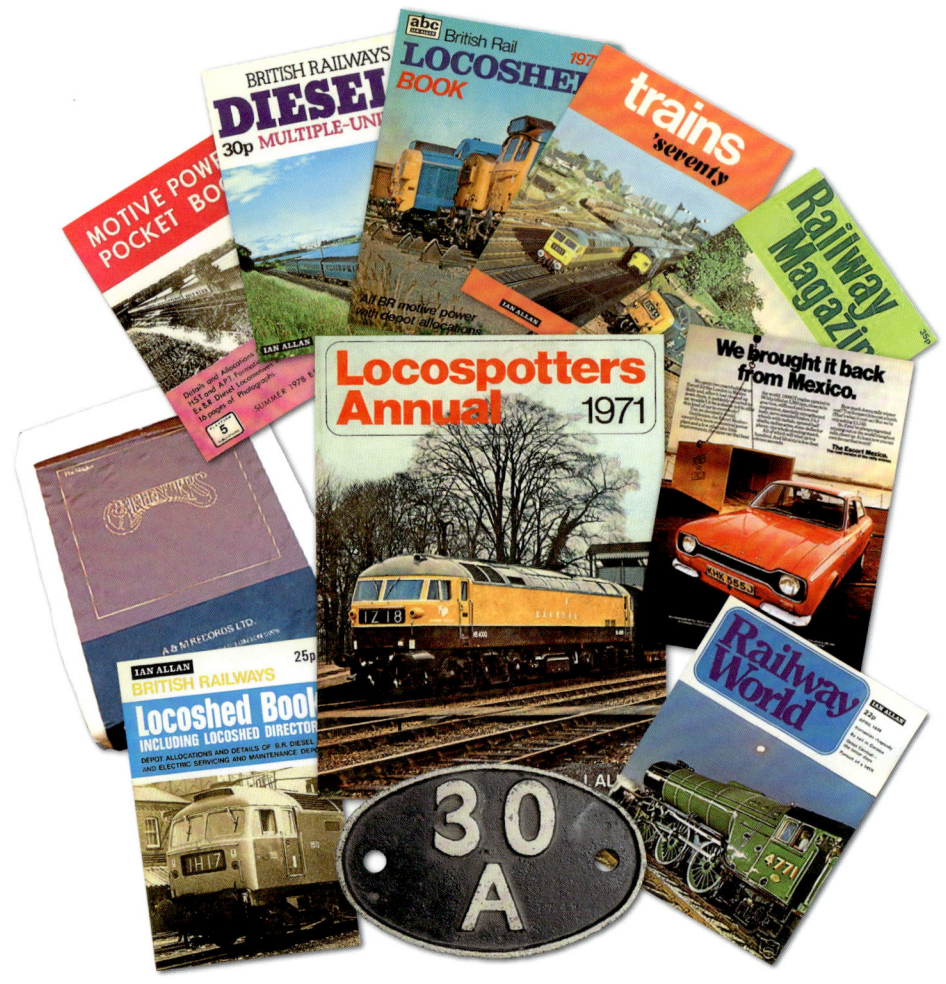

First published 2016

Amberley Publishing
The Hill, Stroud
Gloucestershire, GL5 4EP

www.amberley-books.com

Copyright © Kevin Derrick, 2016

The right of Kevin Derrick to be identified as
the Author of this work has been asserted in
accordance with the Copyrights, Designs and
Patents Act 1988.

ISBN 978 1 4456 6069 1 (print)
ISBN 978 1 4456 6070 7 (ebook)

British Library Cataloguing in Publication Data.
A catalogue record for this book is available from
the British Library.

Typesetting by Amberley Publishing.
Printed in the UK.

Contents

Introduction   6

Stopping off at York   7

Heading for Stratford   14

East from Woodhead   21

Doncaster Days Out   28

ECML Southern Stretches   39

The Preservation Scene   47

Exploring East Anglia   51

North East Amble   62

Shunter Tales   71

Days and Nights on the Cross   78

Specials   85

Crossways in Yorkshire   89

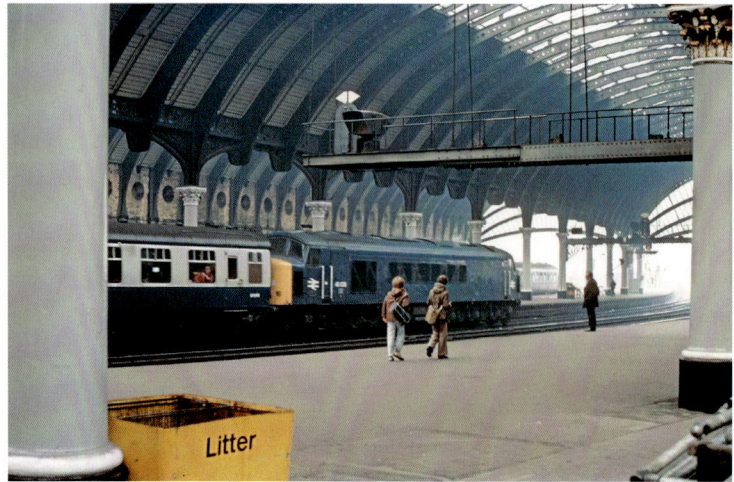

A sobering thought, perhaps, is that these two young lads at York in October 1975 will now be forty-plus. Back in their spotting days, all of the 193 Peaks were still listed in the latest *Locoshed*, which would have cost 40p, twice the price of the 1972 edition. Such was inflation even for young lads. (Eric McBrine)

Introduction

Within this volume of *Seventies Spotting Days*, we take a journey around the Eastern Region and back along memory lane. A region of many contrasts perhaps, from the built-up nature of industrial Yorkshire and the north-east, through the rural services on East Anglia to the glamour of the East Coast Main Line and the Deltics. The byways and branches of Lincolnshire and East Anglia had felt the edge of Beeching's pruning-saw in the sixties. So much so that the viability of what remained had to be questioned. Meanwhile coal and petroleum products still generated much by way of freight business across the region at the beginning of the decade.

Electrification would escape from the former Great Eastern routes to the former Great Northern London terminus at King's Cross and then steadily northwards from the end of the seventies. Meanwhile the Deltics' reign on the ECML would be called into question as the new High Speed Trains began to reduce even their timings on the major expresses.

Among the peculiarities of the Eastern Region was the large number of shunters retained during the decade. Among these were the unique trio allocated to Tinsley, as well as the curious adaptions into snowploughs from withdrawn examples. The region had a fondness for Class 03 shunters that was not shared by the other regions who preferred Class 08s or so it seemed. A few of the many surplus shunters found their way into industrial use across Yorkshire and the North East in a number of National Coal Board uses, including a host of Class 14s.

Once again we will take this opportunity to recall various characters and events from the time, whether they be musical, sporting, recreational, fashion, television, radio or news headlines to help us relive those perhaps carefree seventies spotting days as we travel back in time.

Kevin Derrick
Boat of Garten

Stopping off at York

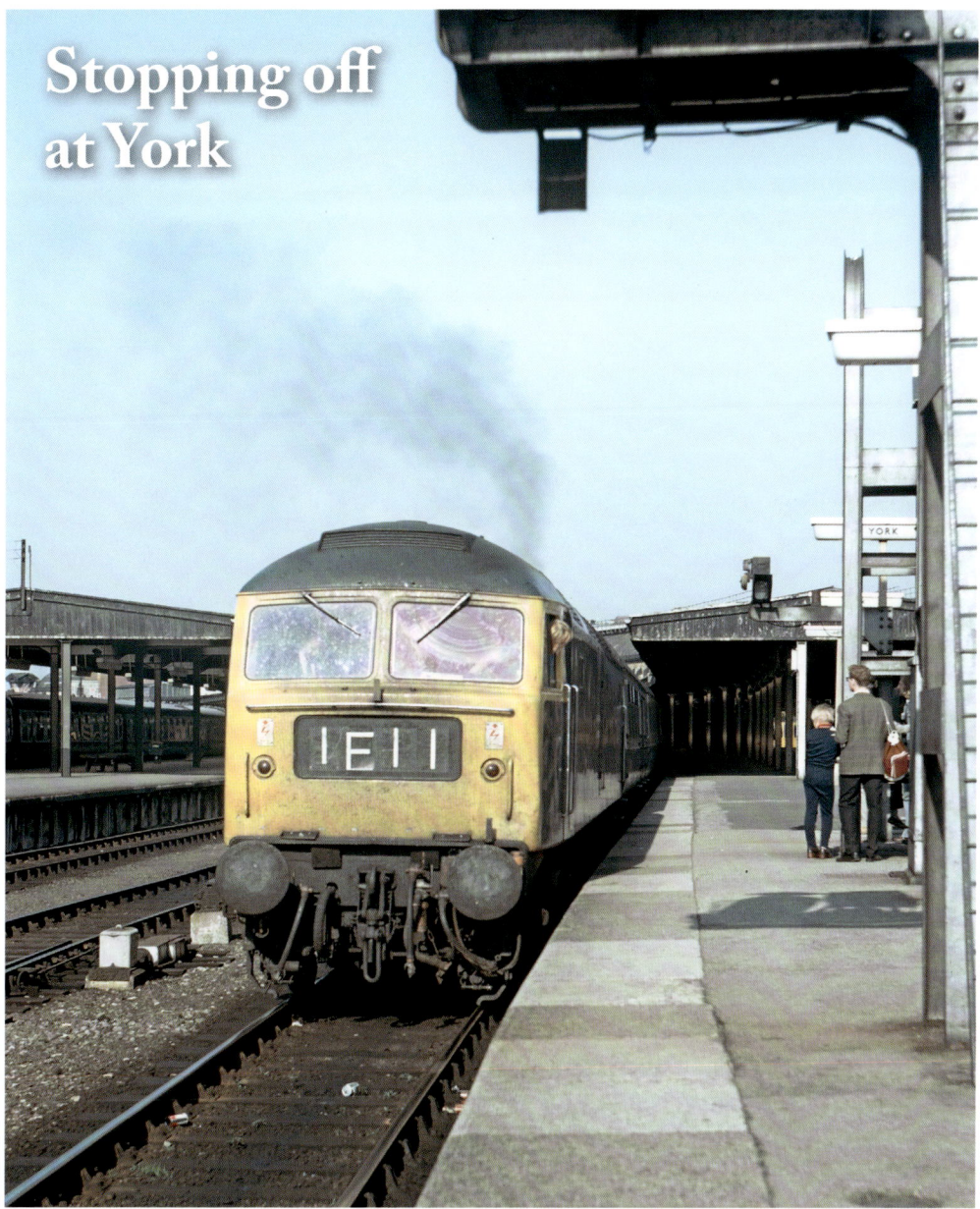

Getting away from the brief stop at York on Saturday 14 September 1974 we find No. 47401. This had been the first of her class into service in the region on 28 September 1962 as D1500, when allocated to 34G Finsbury Park. In the month before this photograph we had seen the opening match of the new football season between Liverpool and Leeds in the FA Charity Shield at Wembley. No doubt most of us will recall the brawl between Messrs Keegan and Bremner on the pitch rather than the game itself. (Roger Bradley)

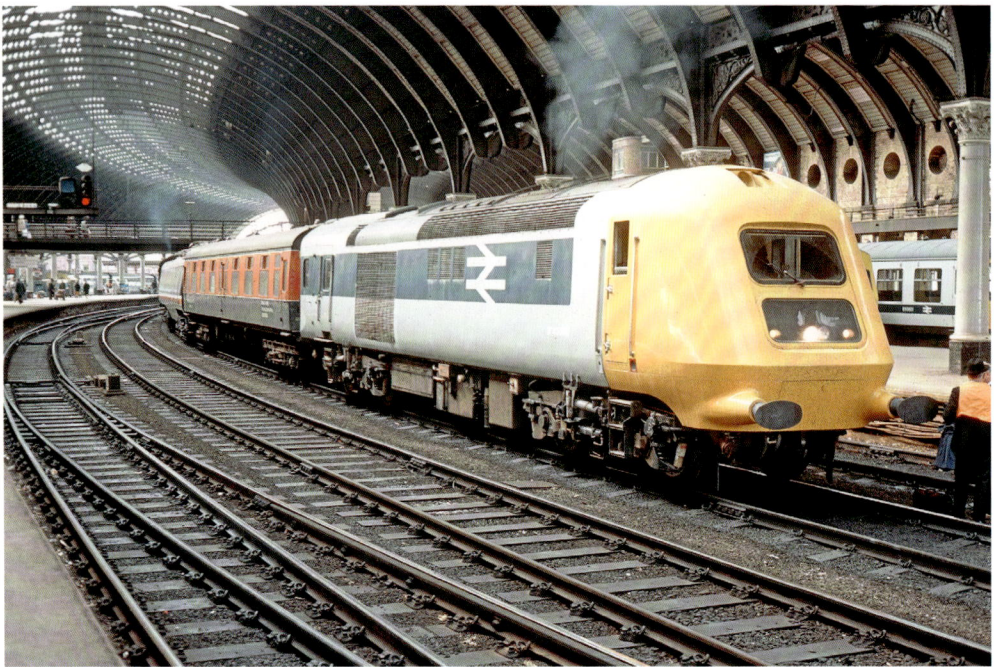

The long level section of line from Darlington to York was often used by BREL to conduct high-speed tests on what was known as the racing stretch. Out for the day in September 1978, we find HST prototype Class 252 car W43000 at the head of another test train. (David Williams)

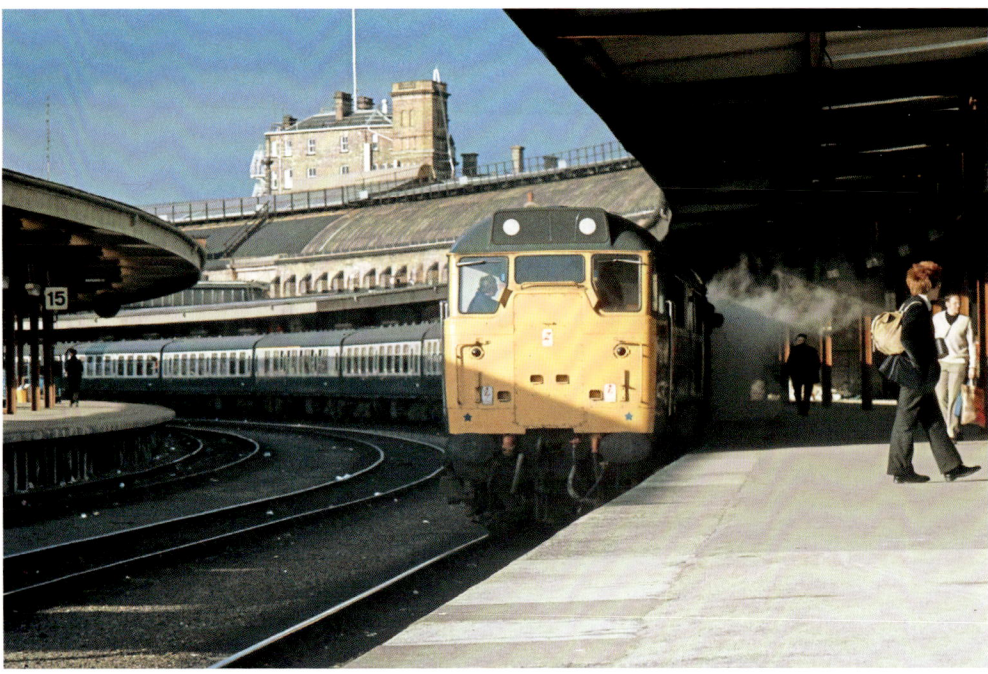

On 16 April 1979, No. 31127 had charge of a York to Manchester service. The Class 31 had enjoyed a couple of spells allocated to York during the seventies, but was now based at Immingham. (Sid Steadman)

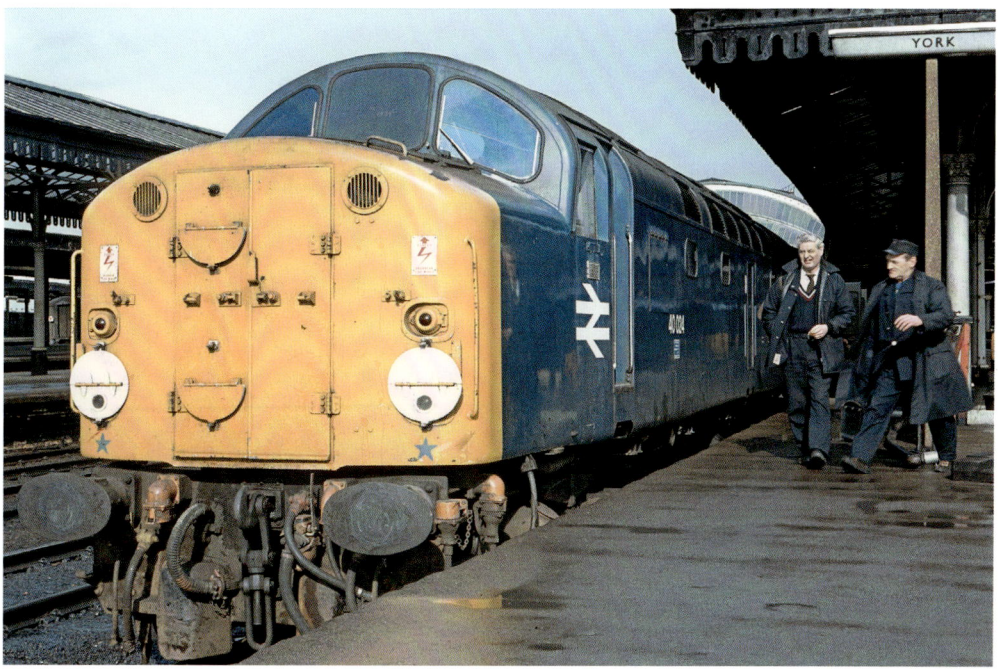

This pair seem to be racing each other for the chance to get into the driving seat of No. 40024 first on 14 March 1978. (Colin Whitbread)

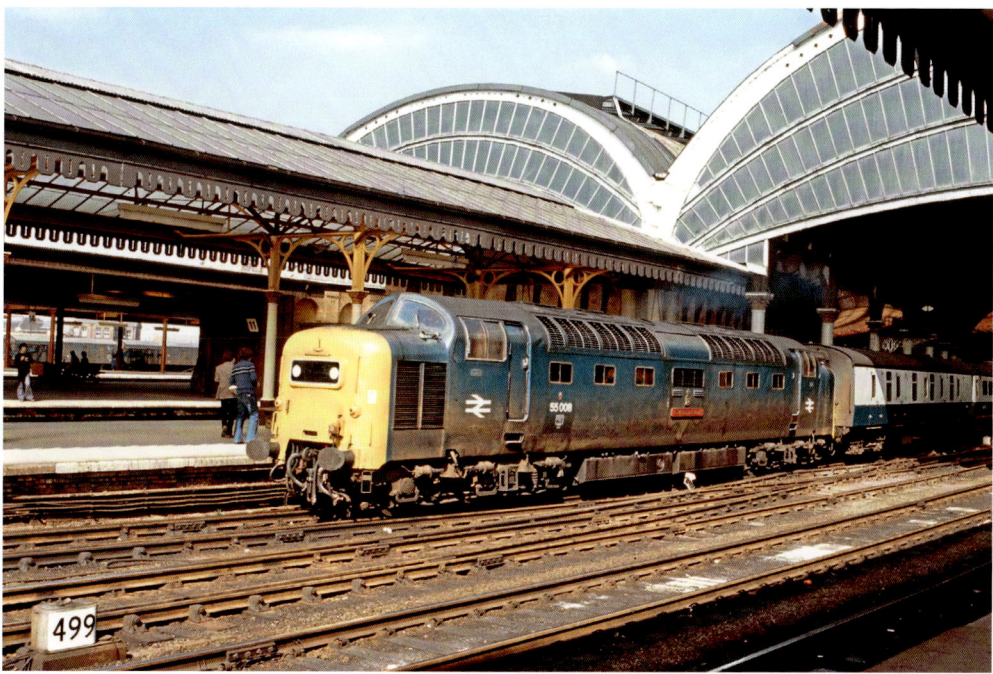

Standards of cleanliness of Deltics varied in this decade. However Gateshead kept alive their tradition of dirty top link locomotives from the sixties as seen by No. 55008 *The Green Howards* which would be allocated away from Gateshead to York in May 1979 for the last couple of years before withdrawal. (Dennis Feltham)

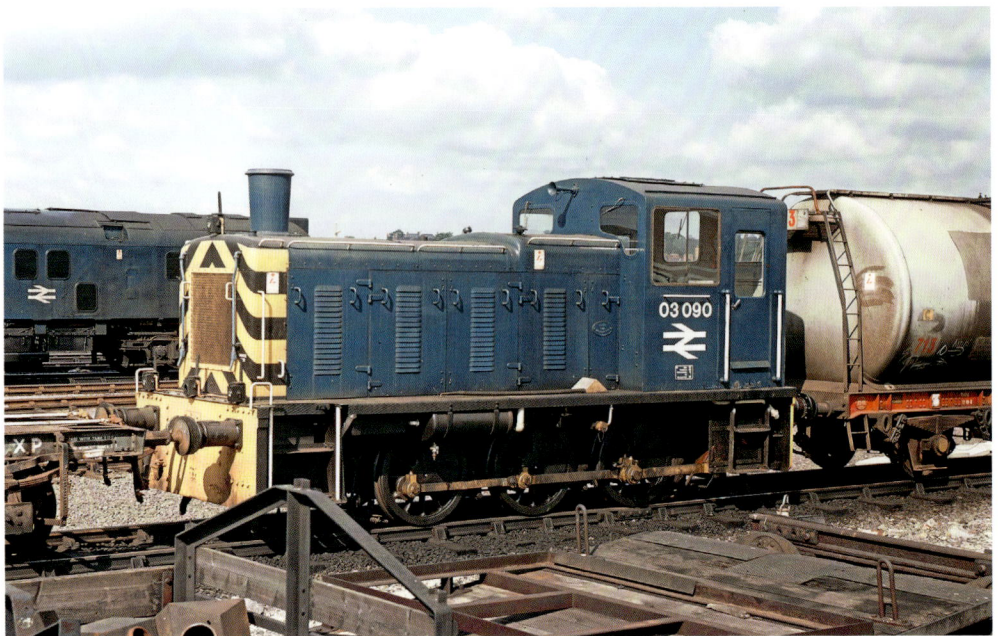

Still in everyday service when seen at the depot on Sunday 25 May 1975 was York-based Class 03 No. 03090. By 18 July 1976 this locomotive would be withdrawn and in October of the same year it was claimed by the National Railway Museum as their pilot and preservation was thus assured. (Roger Bradley)

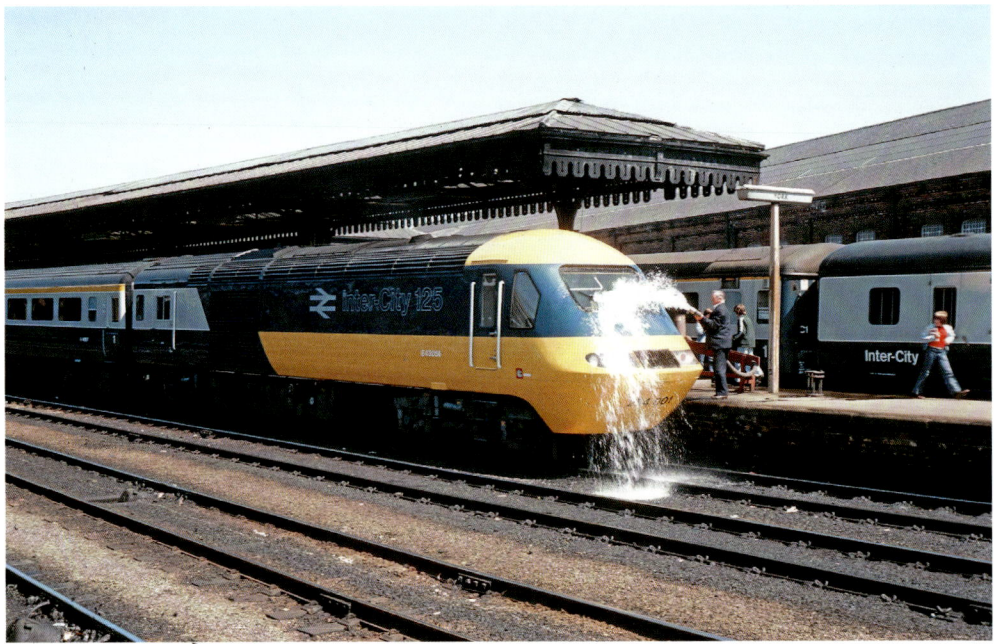

The driver on board No. 254001 was obviously very keen on a clean windscreen while making a call at York in June 1978. On the 14th of the month the Prime Minister, James Callaghan MP, threatened an early general election with the phrase 'Keep Britain Labour'. The press was against him with claims he was running scared, and thus it was that Margaret Thatcher had to wait until the following year. (David Williams)

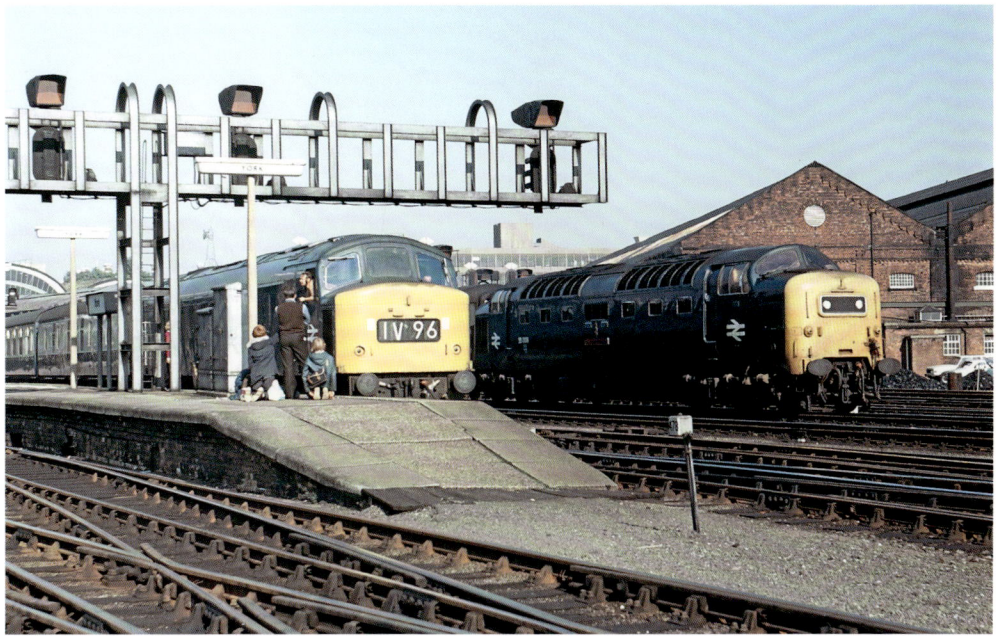

Spotters on the platform ends on Saturday 14 September 1974 to greet Nos 45016 and 55008 *The Green Howards*. The Peak was previously D16 when new and managed to gain a new TOPS number in line with its previous identity when renumbered in April that year. (Roger Bradley)

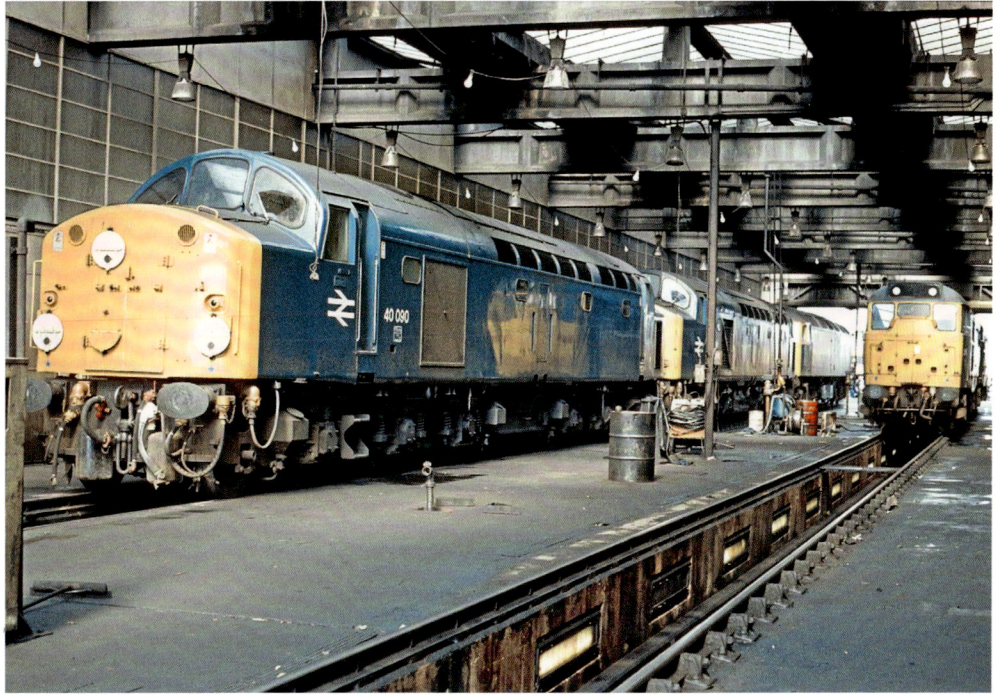

The diesel depot here was just five minutes' walk from the station and home to a Class 31 and 47 as well as a pair of Class 40s, with No. 40090 visiting from Springs Branch when seen in 1978. (Arthur Wilson)

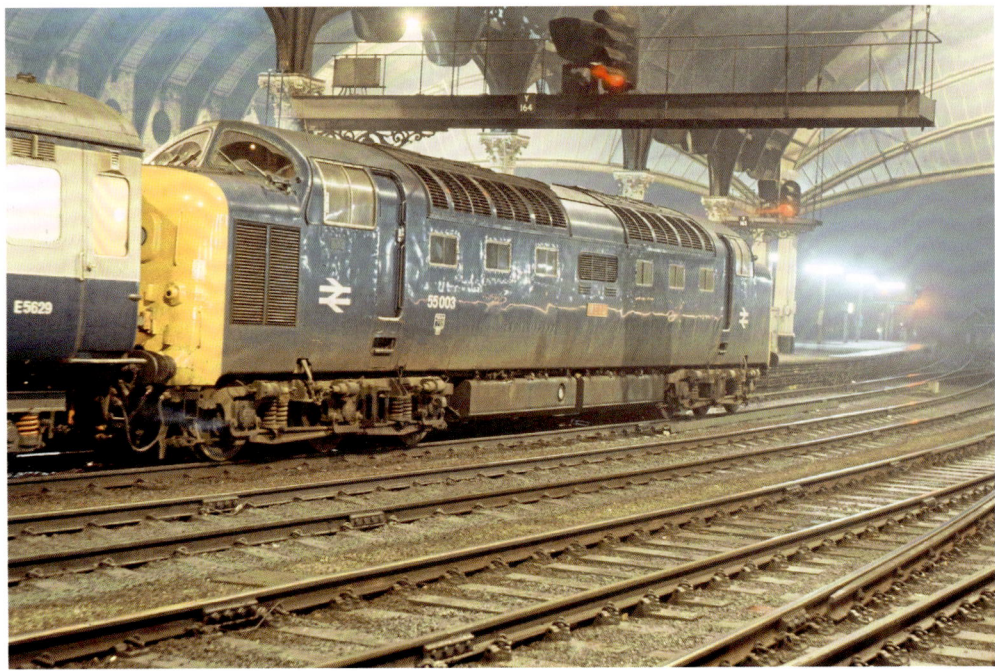

Ready to head off into the night on 10 December 1977 was No. 55003 *Meld*. Over in the United States, *Star Wars* had just been released, but we would have to wait until the 27th of the month for release of the George Lucas film into British cinemas. (Ian James)

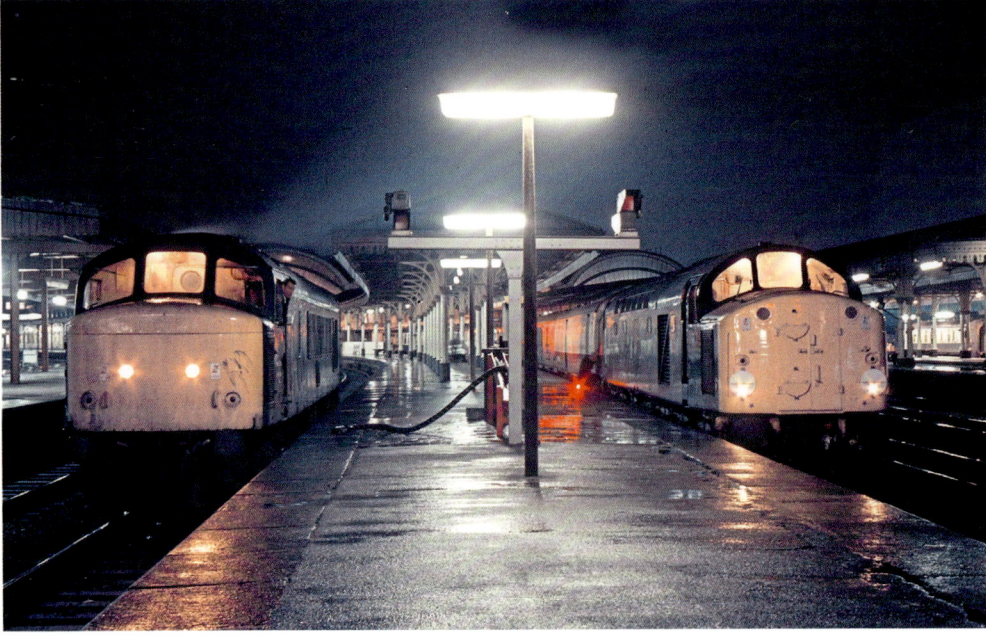

Two years later and Peak No. 46004 was about to take over the 19.35 Newcastle–Bristol from Class 40 No. 40081 on 19 December 1979. At the cinema it was Ridley Scott's *Alien* that had some too frightened to go out in the dark. (Colin Whitbread)

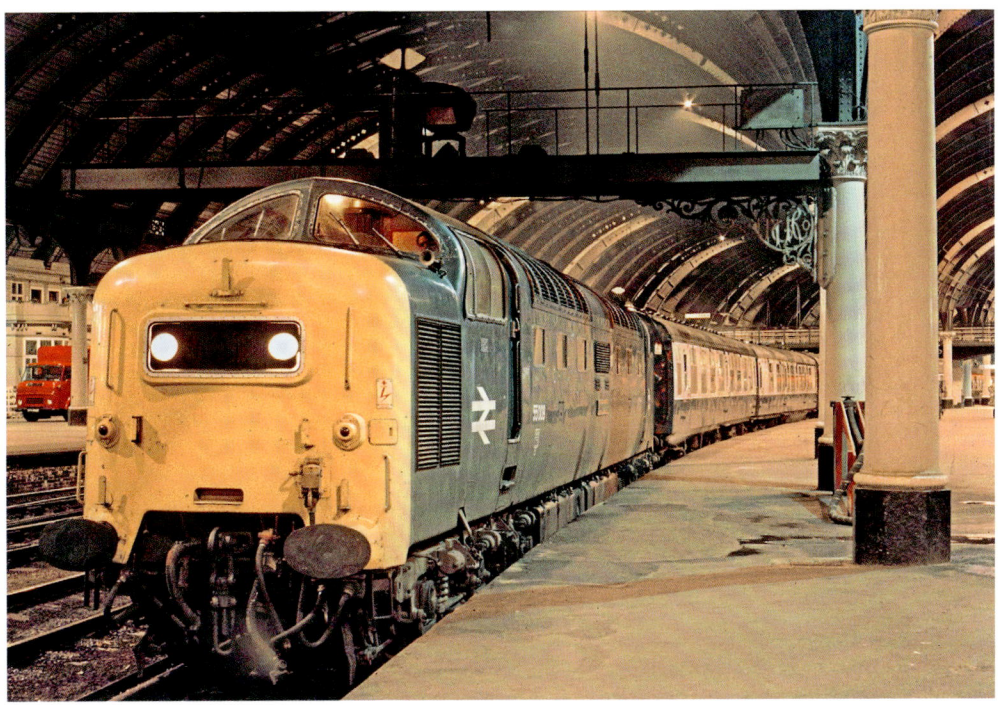

On an inclement Wednesday 23 November 1977, Deltic No. 55009 *Alycidon* has arrived with the 20.15 King's Cross–Edinburgh. (Colin Whitbread)

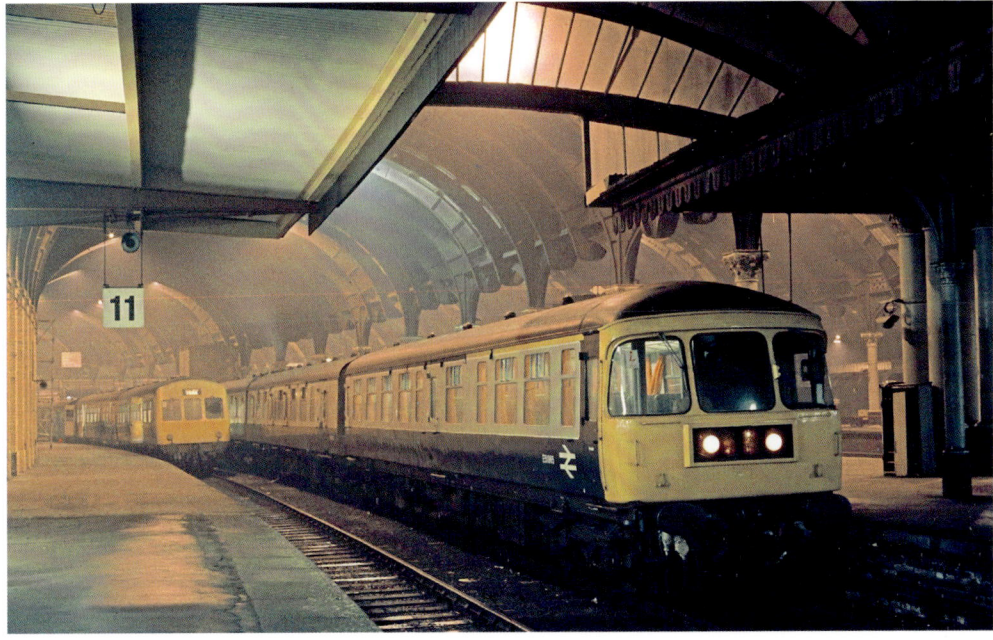

Contrasting styles of DMU on the evening of 15 January 1979, with the Metropolitan Cammell engaged in local stopping services, while one of the Trans Pennine sets has paused on its journey from Liverpool. (Colin Whitbread)

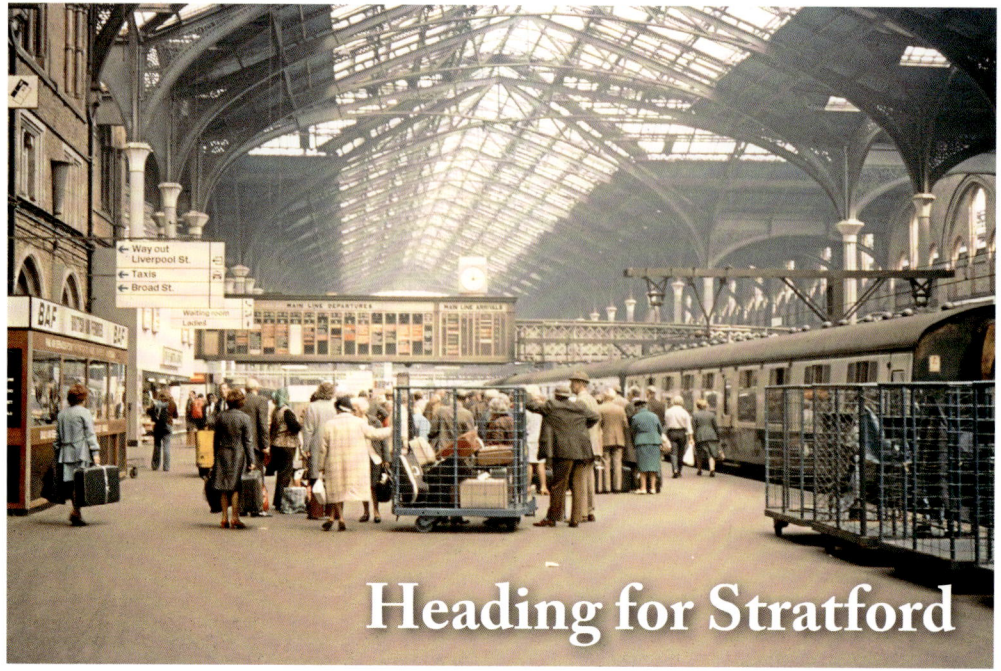

Heading for Stratford

The station at Liverpool Street had celebrated its centenary two years before when visited on 8 May 1976 by our cameraman. Many a visitor to Stratford may well have come here before catching one of the AM6, Shenfield sets to visit 30A, or SF as it became after 6 May 1973. (Frank Hornby)

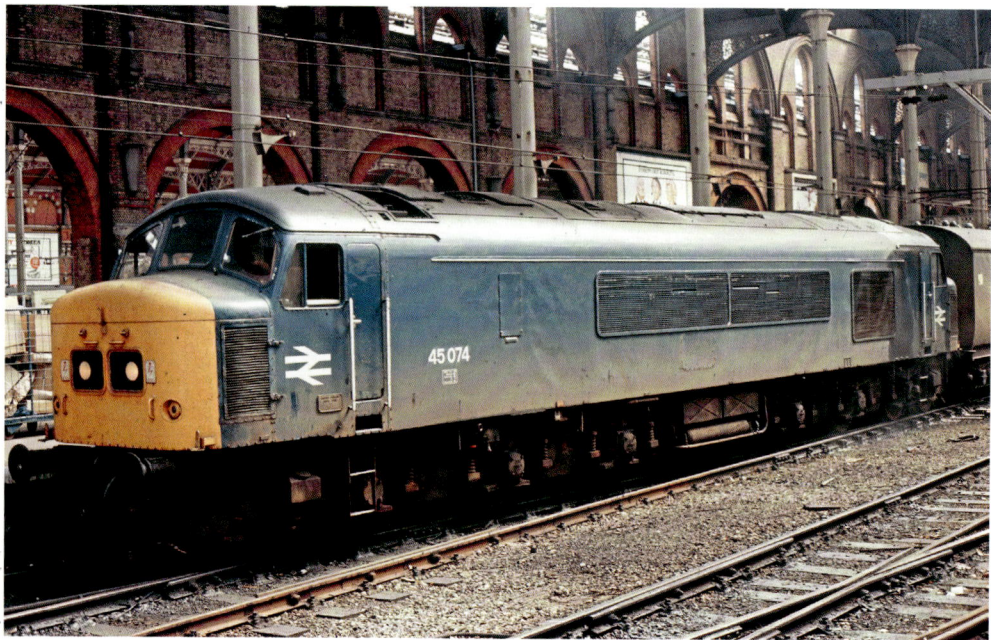

A stranger to Liverpool Street on 27 April 1979 was Peak No. 45074, which arrived at platform 10. Surviving the seventies but not the eighties, this engine met its demise in Vic Berry's famous yard at Leicester in October 1988. (Steve Barnes)

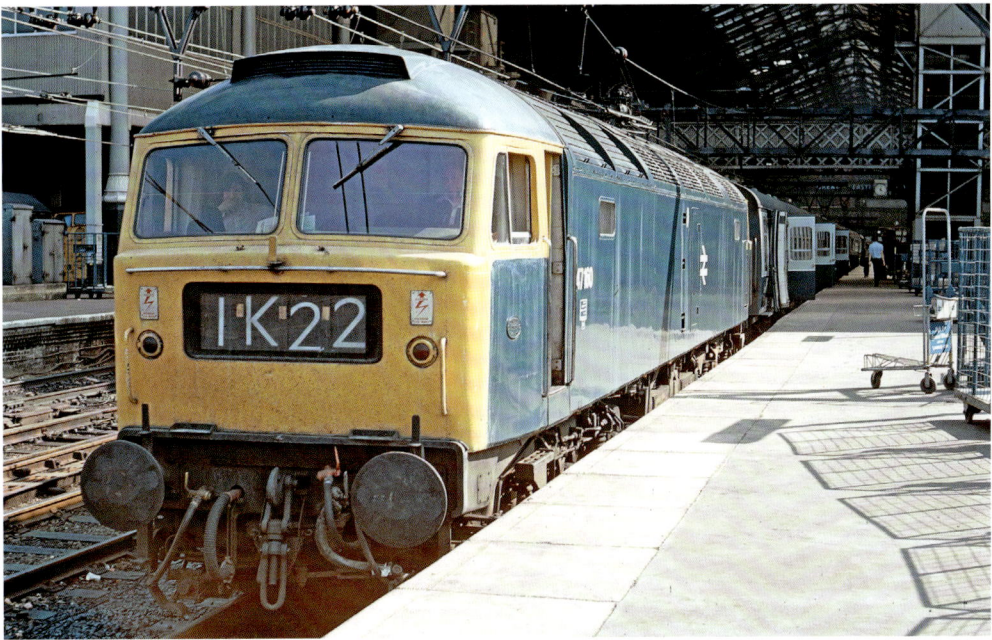

It is June 1975 and the BBC and Independent Radio News transmit the first live radio broadcast of the House of Commons proceedings to the British public, so we can all hear what goes on at last without visiting the public galleries. Outside in the sunshine was Class 47 No. 47160 which had arrived at Stratford that January from Immingham for services on the former Great Eastern routes. (Arthur Wilson)

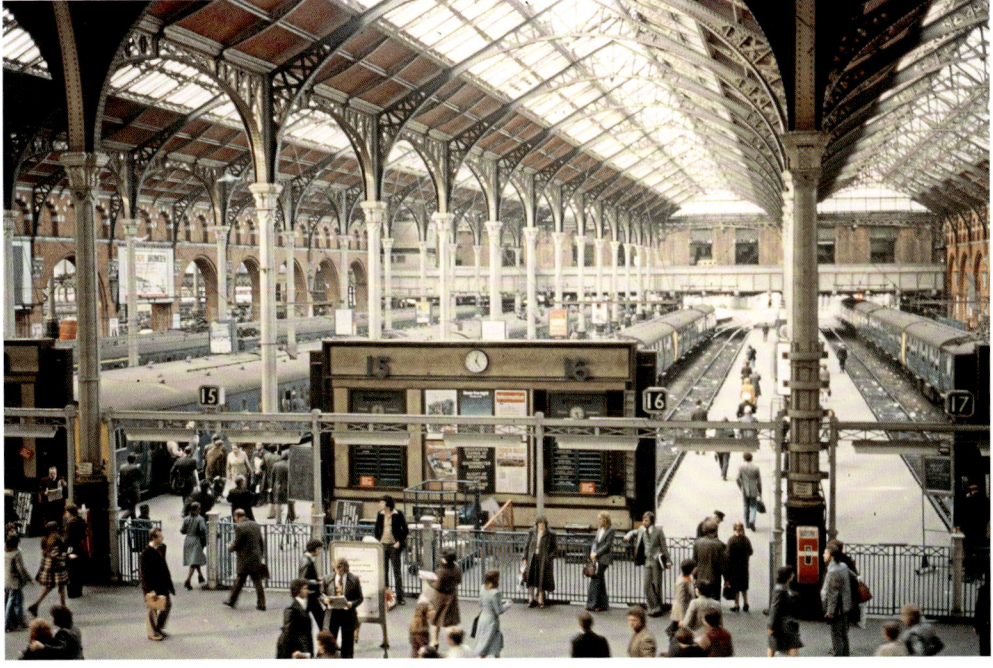

Time for a shot from the gallery by the Great Eastern Hotel before joining a train for Gidea Park to take us to Stratford on 8 May 1975. (Frank Hornby)

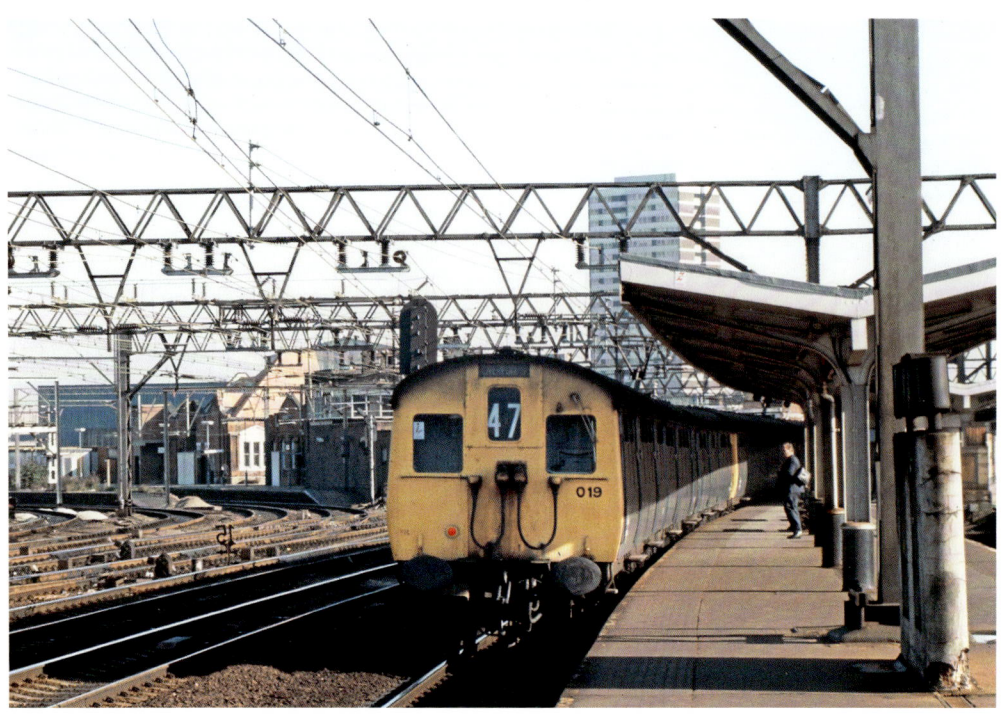

Alighting through the sliding doors of AM6 set at Stratford in October 1979 in hopeful expectation of being able to get around the depot without any problems or a permit! (Ian James)

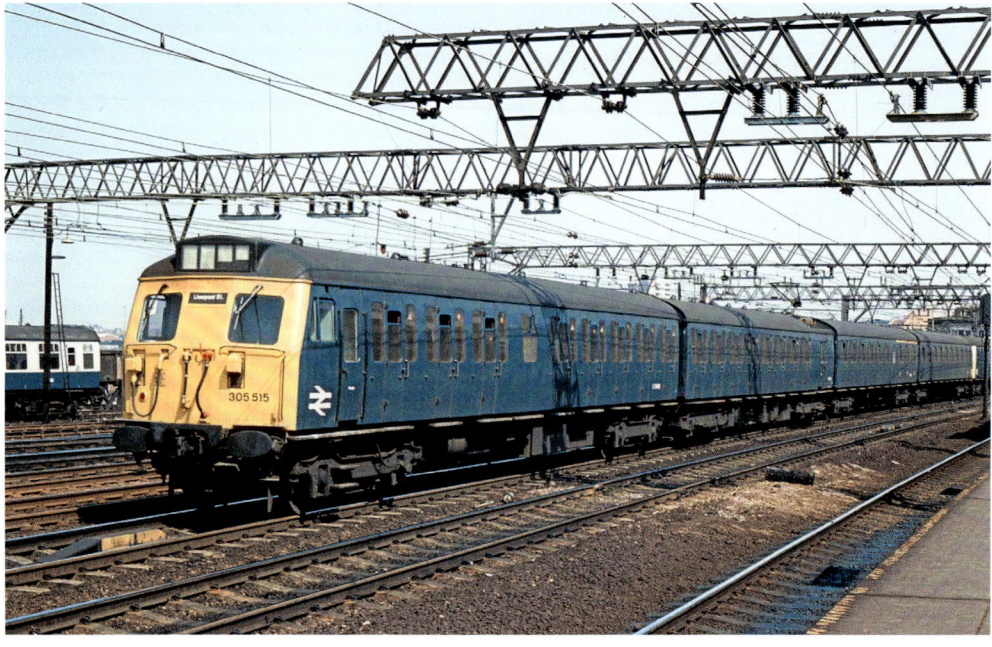

Many of us will have spent a while on the platforms here watching the procession of expresses and semi-fasts running by, punctuated by appearances of loco-hauled trains including a good number of freights coming around the mass of lines around Stratford. (Arthur Wilson)

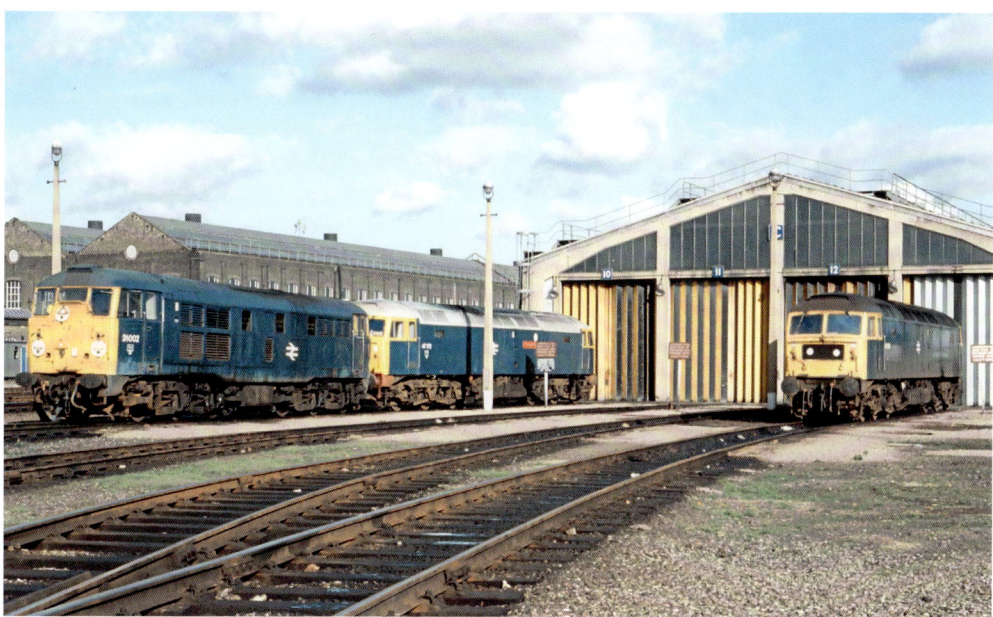

One of Stratford's trademark white roofs can be seen on No. 47172 *County of Hertfordshire* behind Toffee Apple Class 31 No. 31002, while No. 47370 awaits alongside on Monday 5 November 1979. Peaceful here in East London, but the day before, Islamists had stormed the US Embassy in Tehran, taking over ninety hostages. On 21 January 1981, on the same day as the inauguration of President Reagan, the crisis came to an end when fifty-two American hostages were freed after 444 days. (Colin Whitbread)

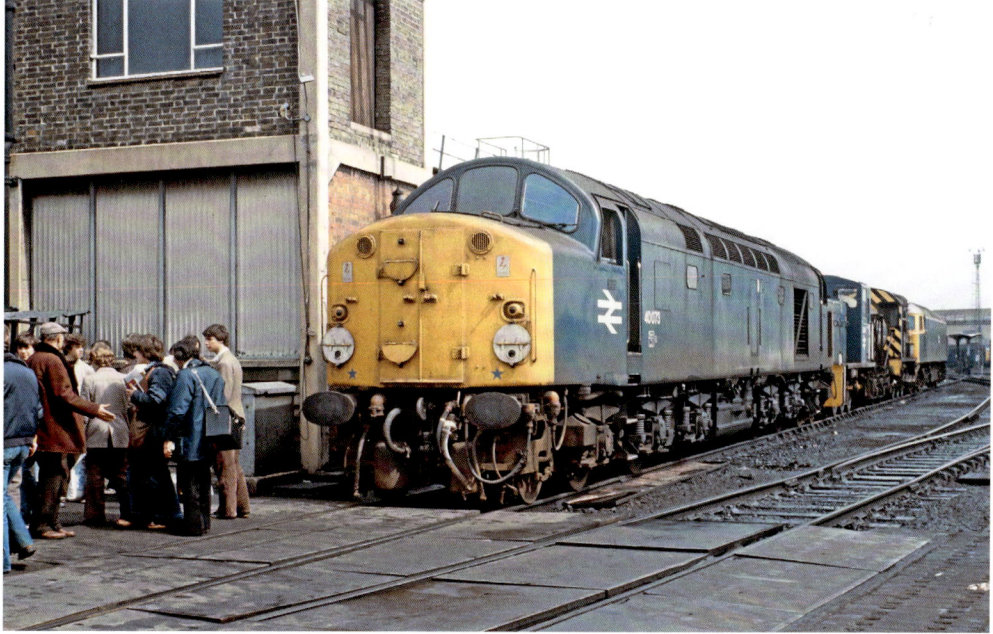

A visit to the depot and works a few months earlier with a permit saw this group making their way around this once large site, stopping to note Class 40 No. 40073 on 12 May 1979. Based at Thornaby at the time, this Class 40 would later lose its discs before being withdrawn from Longsight in June 1983. (Steven Feltham)

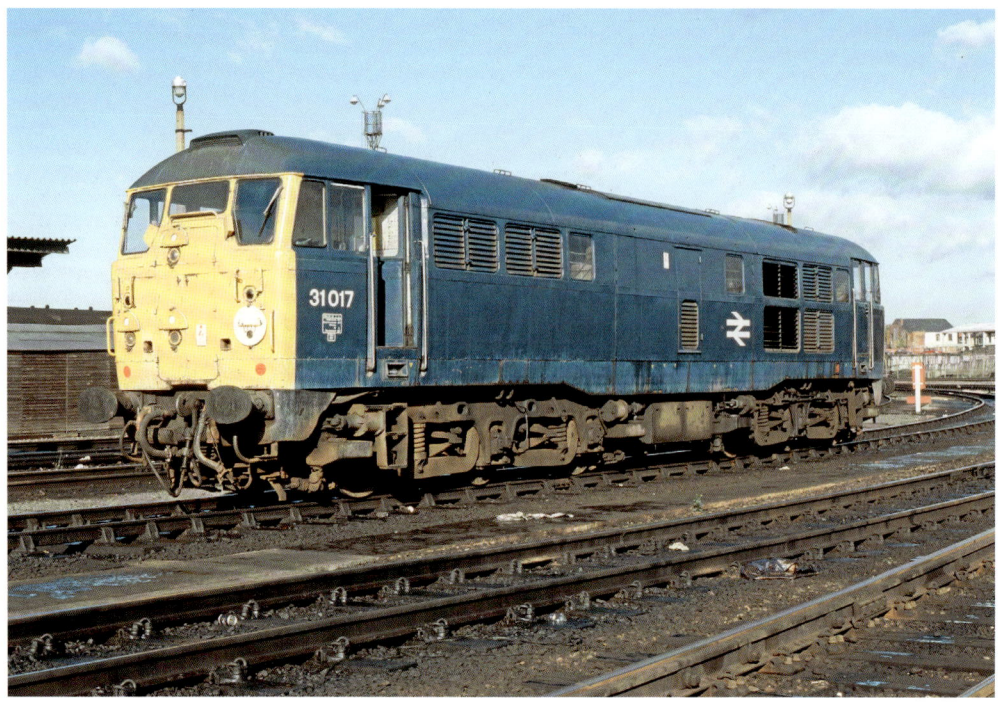

Back to that visit on Bonfire Night 1979 to find another of the last few surviving Toffee Apple Class 31s, No. 31017. This one would only last a few more months in traffic. (Colin Whitbread)

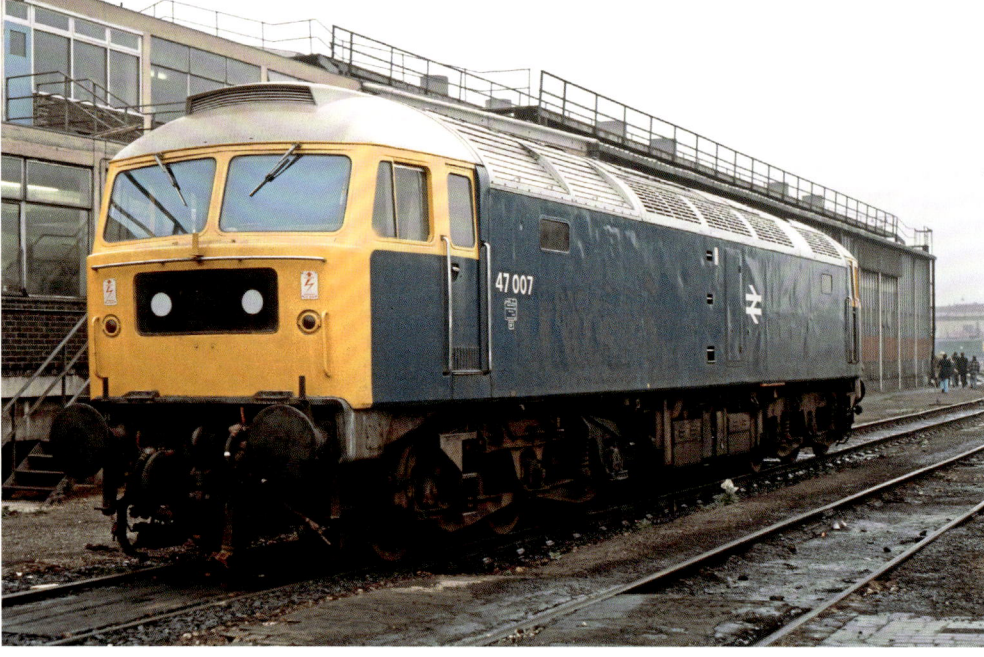

The advance party of spotters in this society visit on 3 December 1978 are well ahead of our photographer, who has stopped to record another of Stratford's customised Class 47s, No. 47007. (Aldo Delicata)

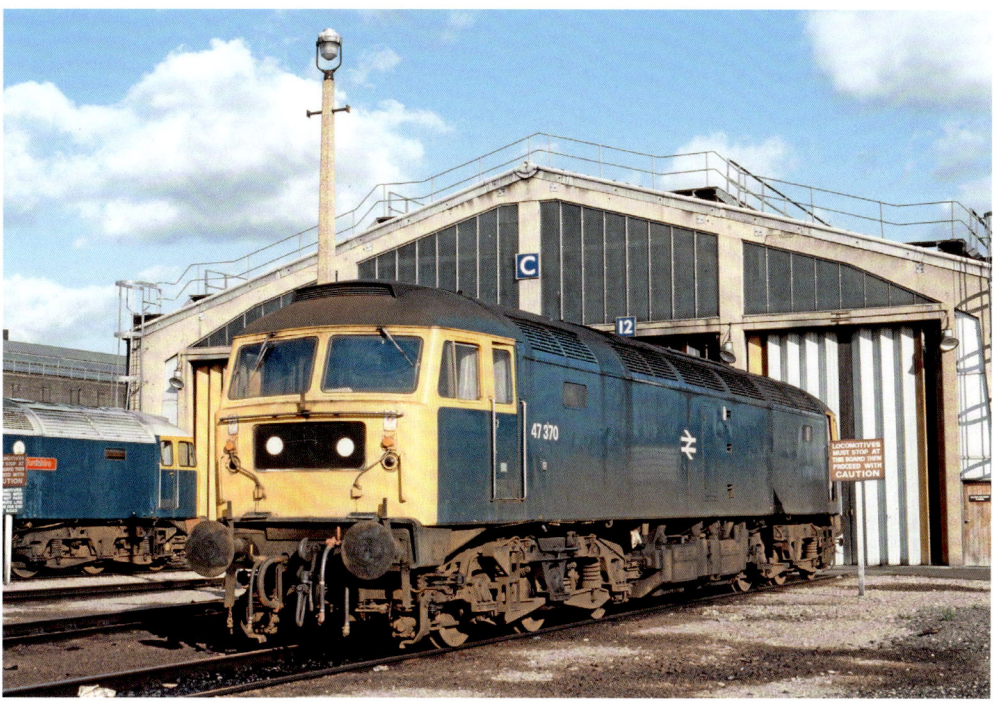

A close-up of No. 47370 from Immingham fitted with additional jumper cables outside C shed again in November 1979. (Colin Whitbread)

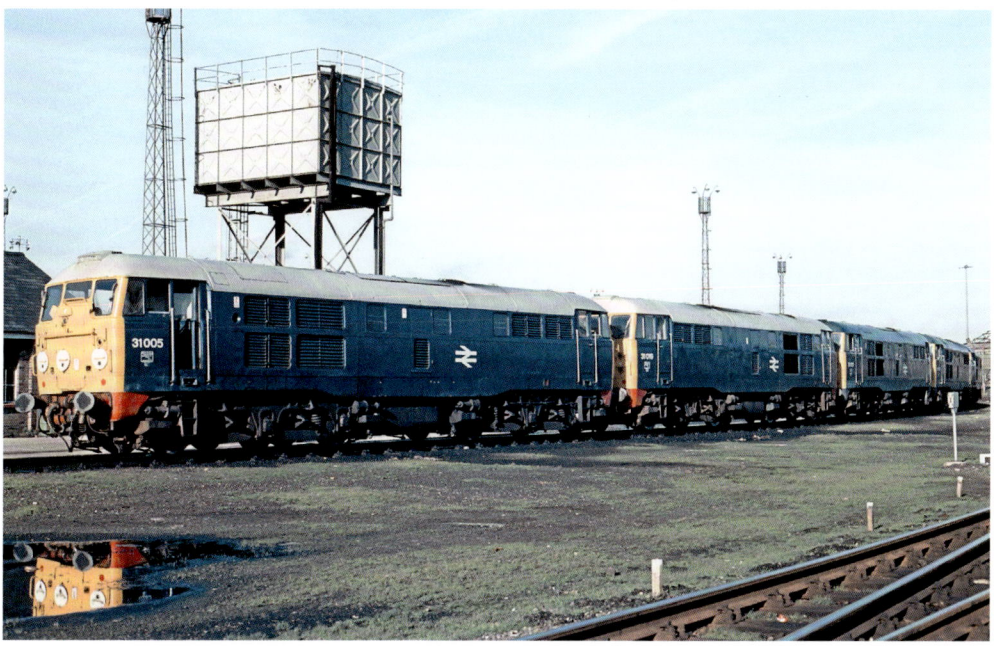

Seen in a companion volume on the Western Region were Class 31s No. 31005 and 31019, which had been smartened up for The Toffee Apple Farewell tour. The pair were again back on shed at Stratford in November 1979 after their adventures to Bristol the month before. (Arthur Wilson)

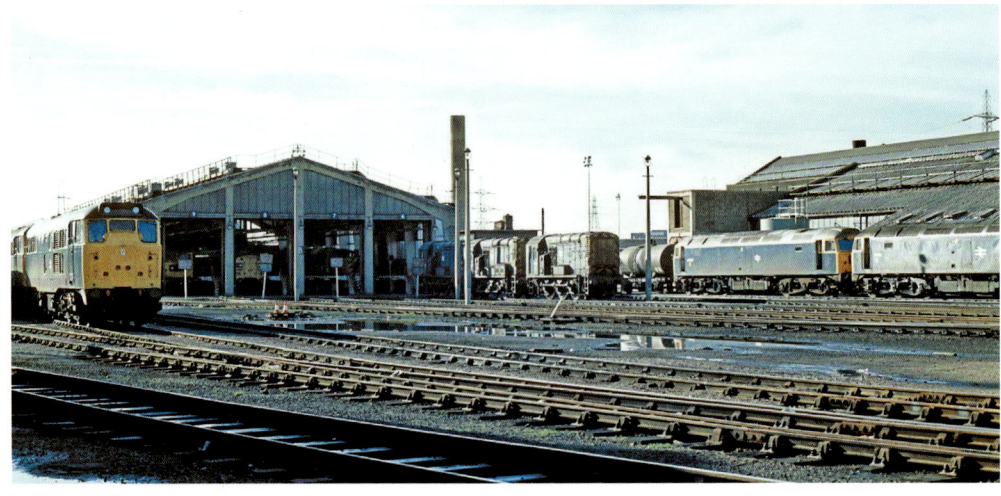

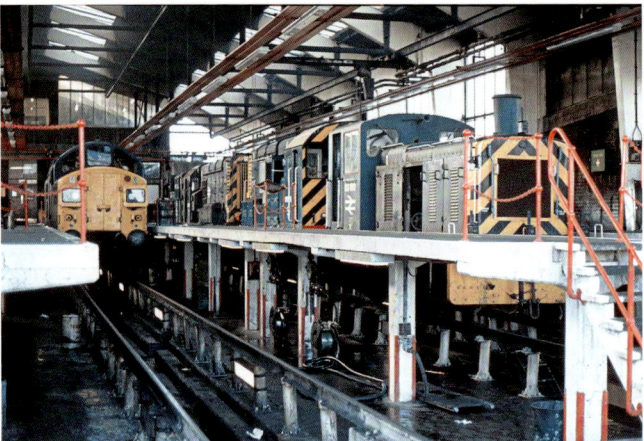

Above: Large puddles in the oil-soaked ash and gravel ballast outside Stratford B Shed on that same visit in 1979. (Arthur Wilson)

Left: Tucked away inside on an earlier trip in 1976 were Classes 03, 08 and one of the home shed's many Class 37s. (Arthur Wilson)

Below: Back through the pedestrian tunnel to the main-line and underground station on 14 July 1979 in time to find a pair of Class 31s led by No. 31192 on a container train. (Steve Barnes)

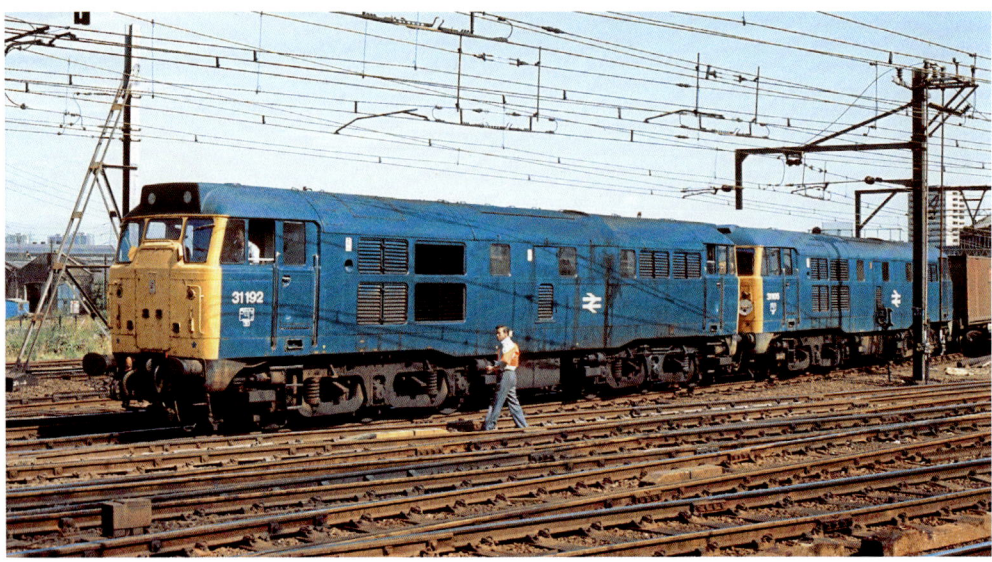

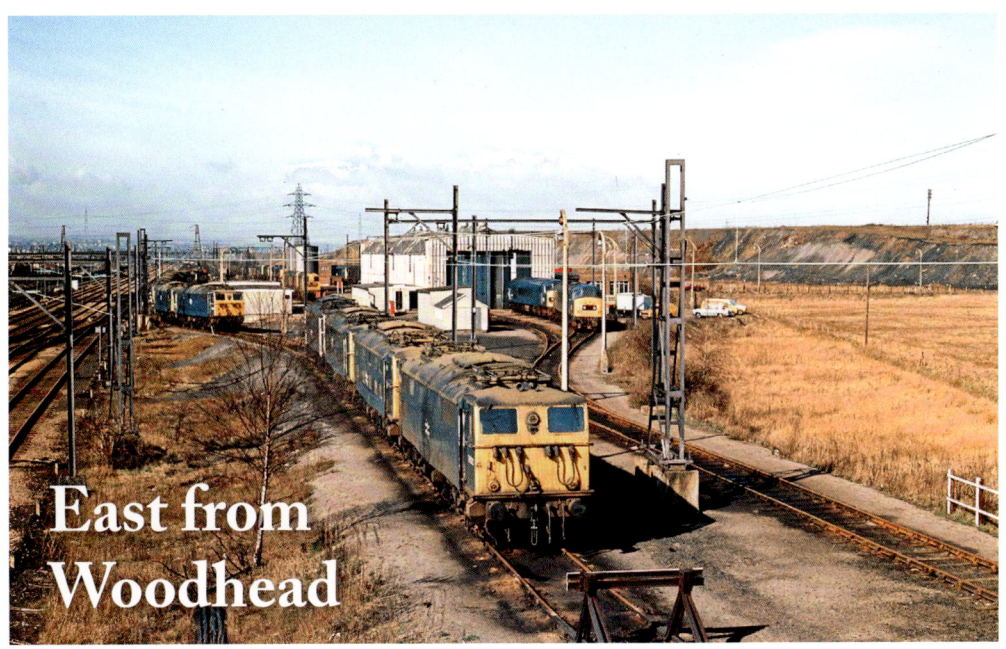

East from Woodhead

All cleared away today, but to greet any visitors to Wath back in the seventies would be the long lines of Class 76 electrics, as here in 1975 with a supporting cast of Peaks and Class 20s. Anyone fancy a quick trip around with a notebook and camera? (Arthur Wilson)

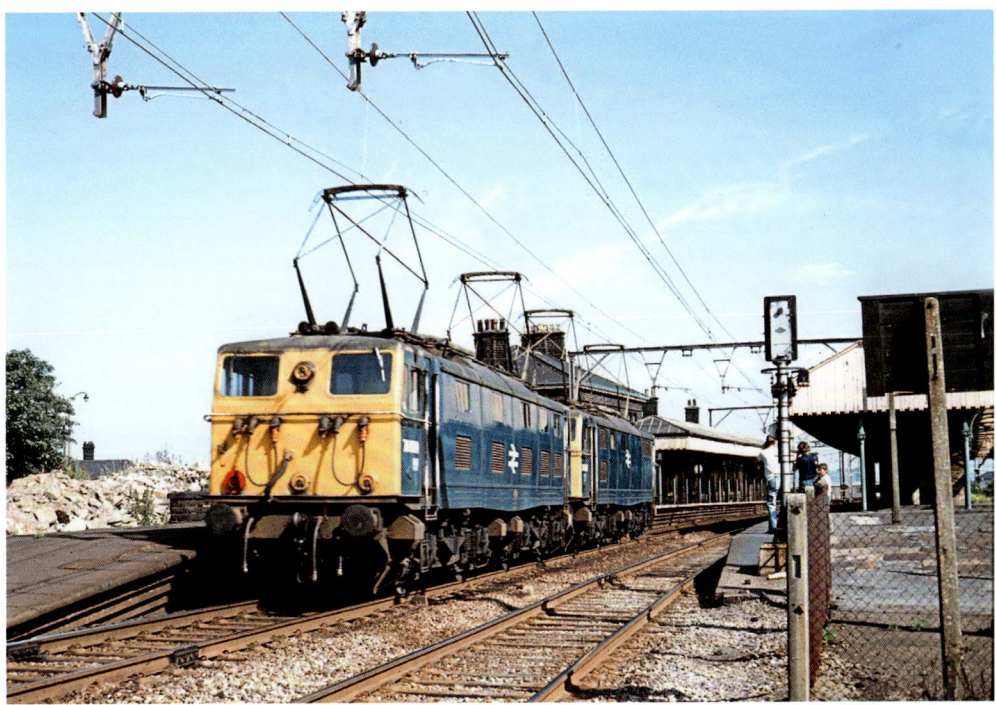

A couple of lads are on the platforms at Penistone on 1 August 1977 to witness a Class 76 light-engine pairing of Nos 76026 and 76009 between turns. (Strathwood Library Collection)

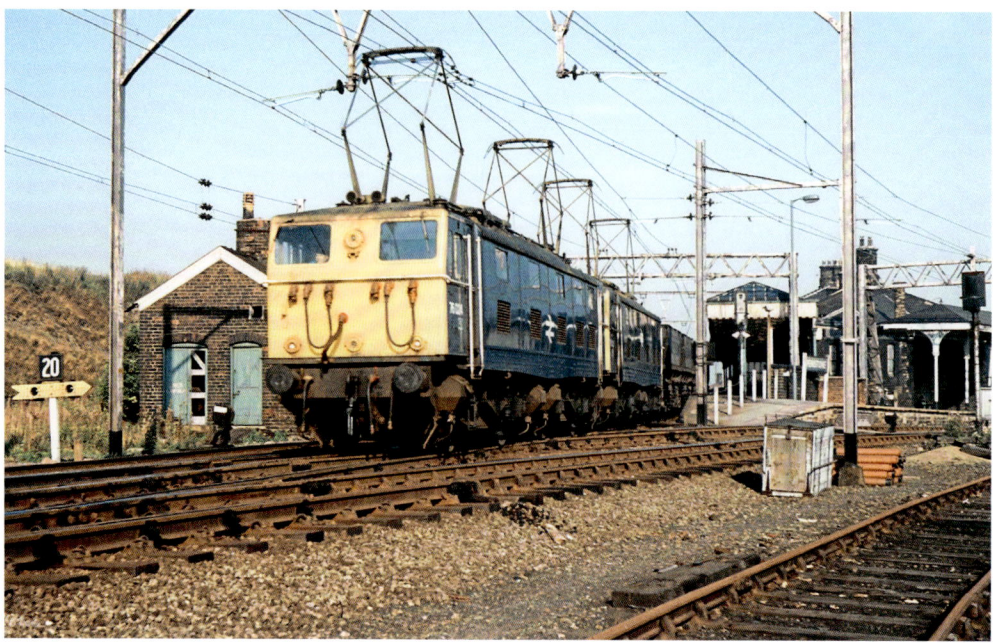

Class 76 No. 76026 is paired this time with No. 76024 once more at Penistone on 30 August 1979. On the radio at the time The Boomtown Rats had declared 'I Don't Like Mondays' and spent almost all of the month at number one as a result of their popularity. (Sid Steadman)

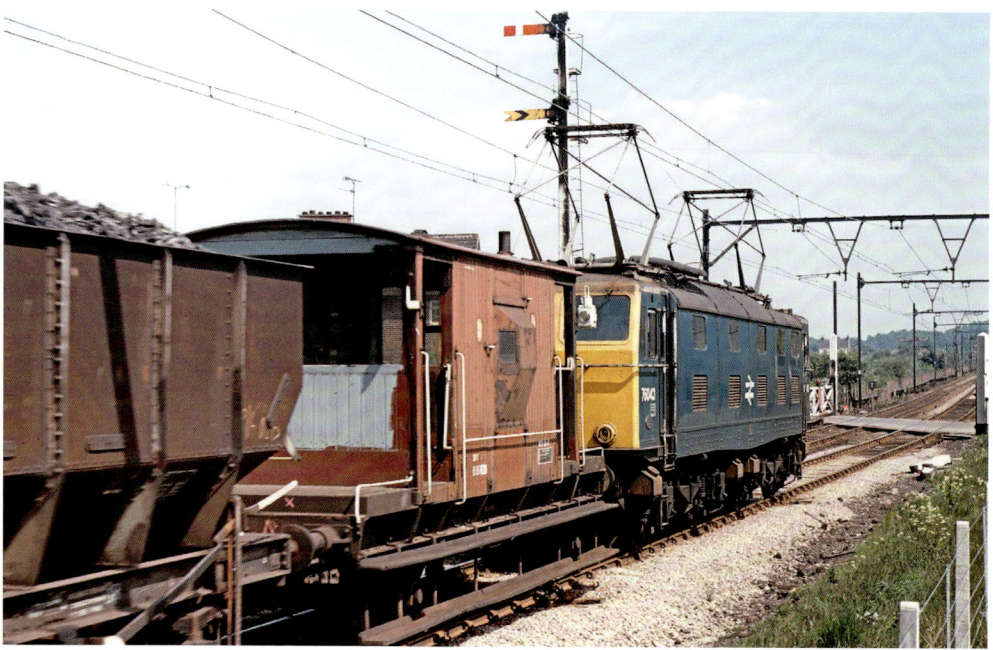

Traction motors working hard and engaged in banking duties; we find Class 76 No. 76043 on the steep climb at Worsborough on Wednesday 28 May 1975. We were all buying into eight-track cartridges as they were being sold to us as the way we would all listen to music in our cars and homes in the future. Like the eight-track, the Woodhead route has passed into oblivion. (Roger Bradley)

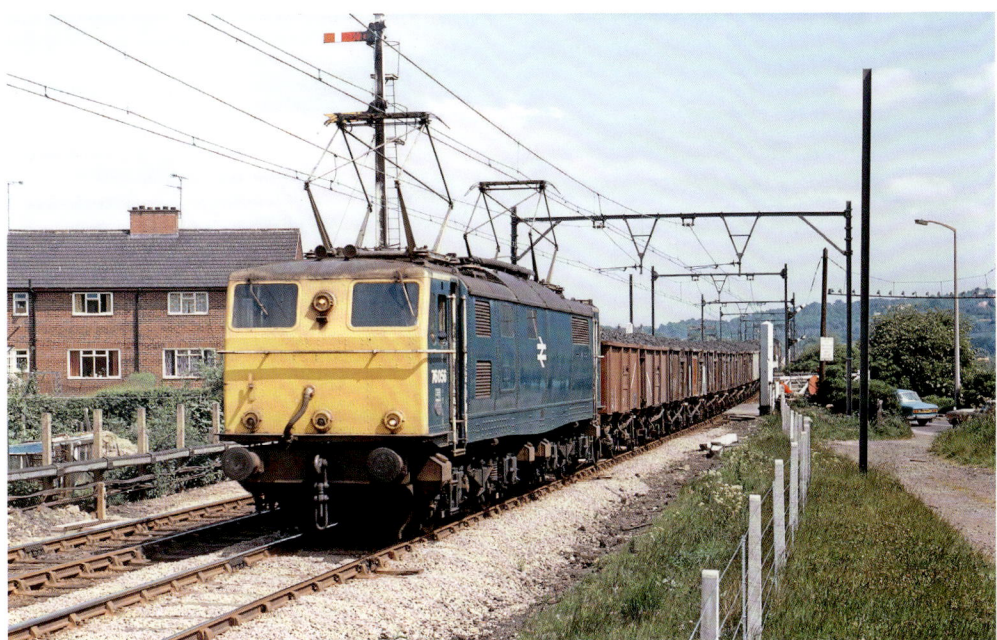

Staying alongside the signal box protecting the crossing at Worsboro on 28 May 1975, we find Class No. 76056, which had once been named *Triton*, the son of Poseidon, who in Greek mythology was a merman sea god and messenger of the deep with the lower body of a dolphin. (Roger Bradley)

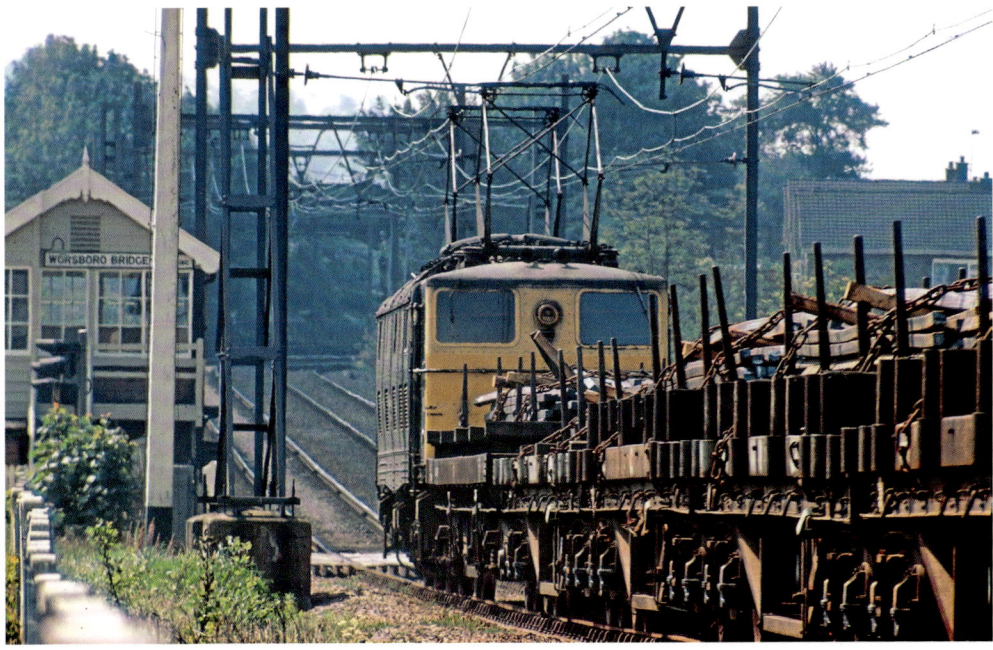

The effect of the telephoto lens brings home the nature of Worsboro incline with another Class 76, No. 76003, and a rake of bolsters full of steel components. Tragically the headlines of the newspapers this same sunny day were describing the Dibble's Bridge coach crash near Grassington, North Yorkshire which had resulted in thirty-two deaths (the highest ever toll in a United Kingdom road accident). (Roger Bradley)

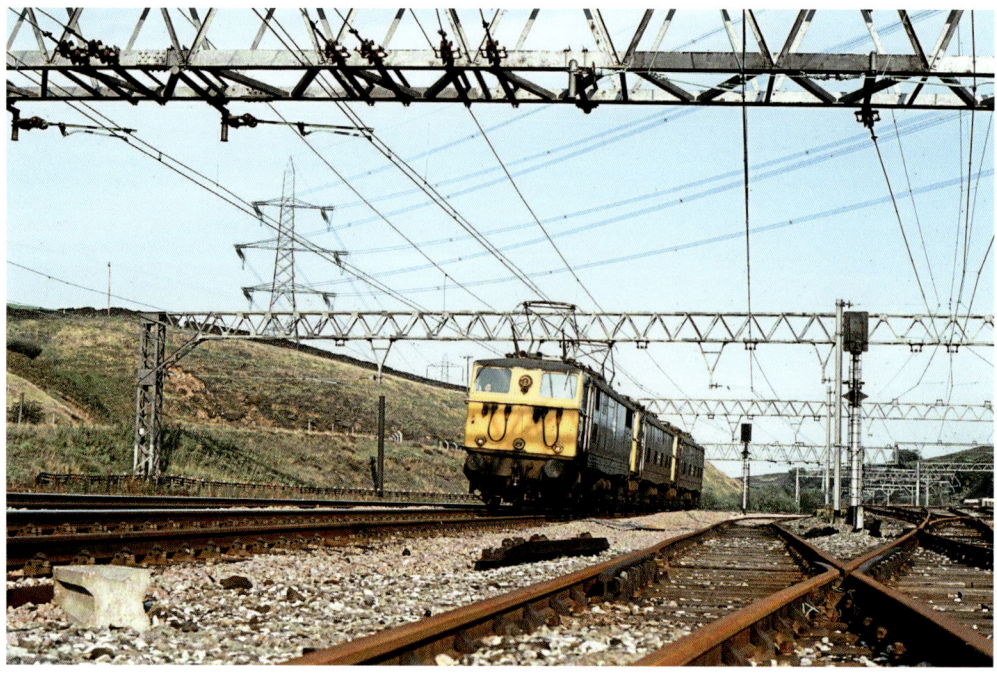

The refuge sidings at Dunford Bridge show little signs of recent activity as a rake of Class 76s Nos 76034, 76009 and 76030 make for Guide Bridge on 13 September 1977. (Nick Gledhill)

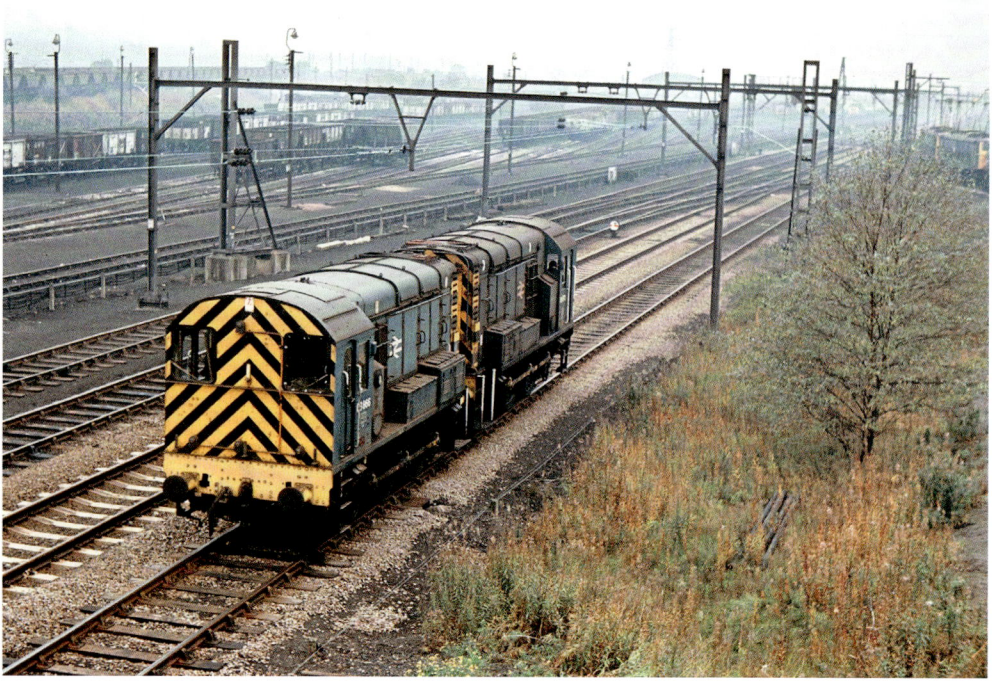

A much slower light-engine working would be with Class 08 shunters Nos 08870 and 08866 at Wath, working wrong road to go onto the shed on 21 October 1978. (Greg Wyatt)

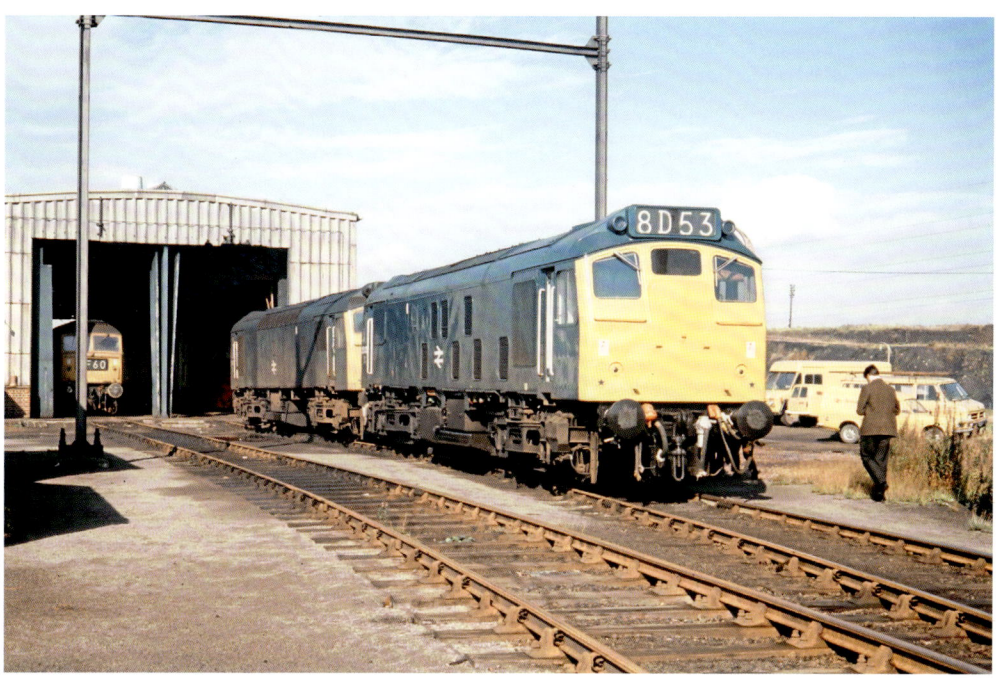

A small party are making their way around Wath on 28 September 1974, noting Class 25s Nos 25035 and 25101 outside in the sun. Both were allocated to nearby Tinsley at the time. (Frank Hornby)

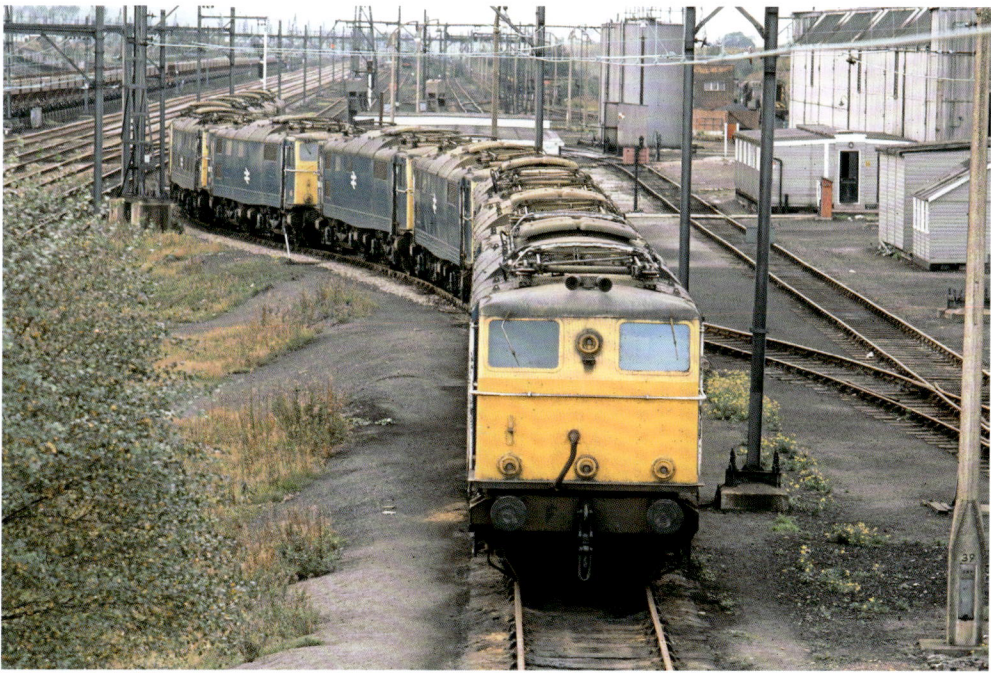

Taken from the road bridge by the shed entrance with a powerful telephoto lens, we find 23 per cent of the active Class 76s on Saturday 30 September 1978, they were Nos 76051, 76009, 76016, 76026, 76014, 76054, 76010, 76023, 76041, 76013, and 76021, all ready for the resumption of freight traffic on Monday. (Aldo Delicata)

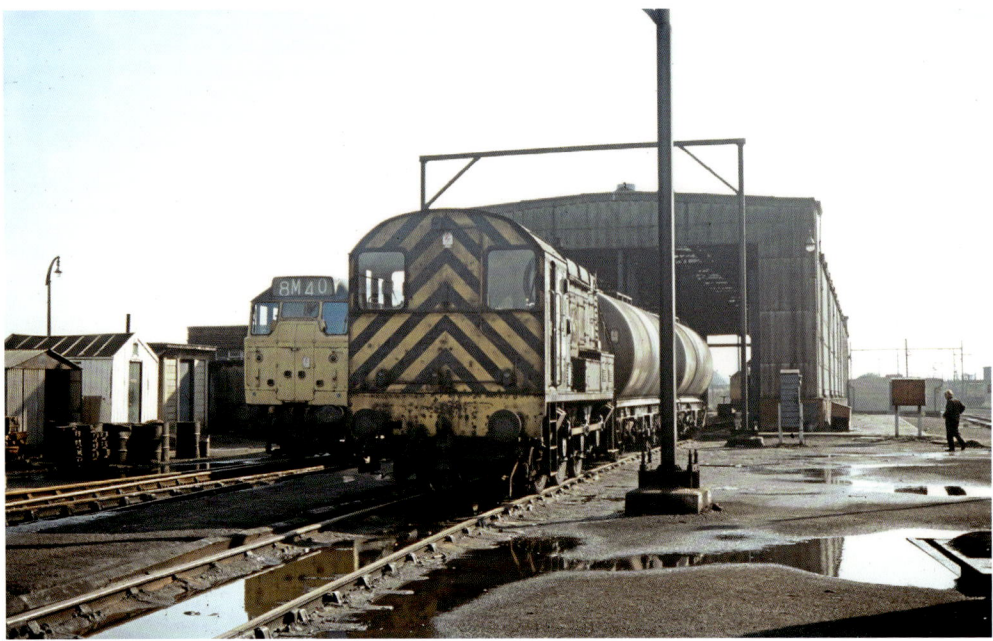

This Class 08 shunter has brought fresh fuel supplies for the diesel fleet to be serviced at Wath on 28 September 1974. Musically, Carl Douglas was convinced everyone was 'Kung Fu Fighting', and doing well with it too, with three weeks at number one. (Frank Hornby)

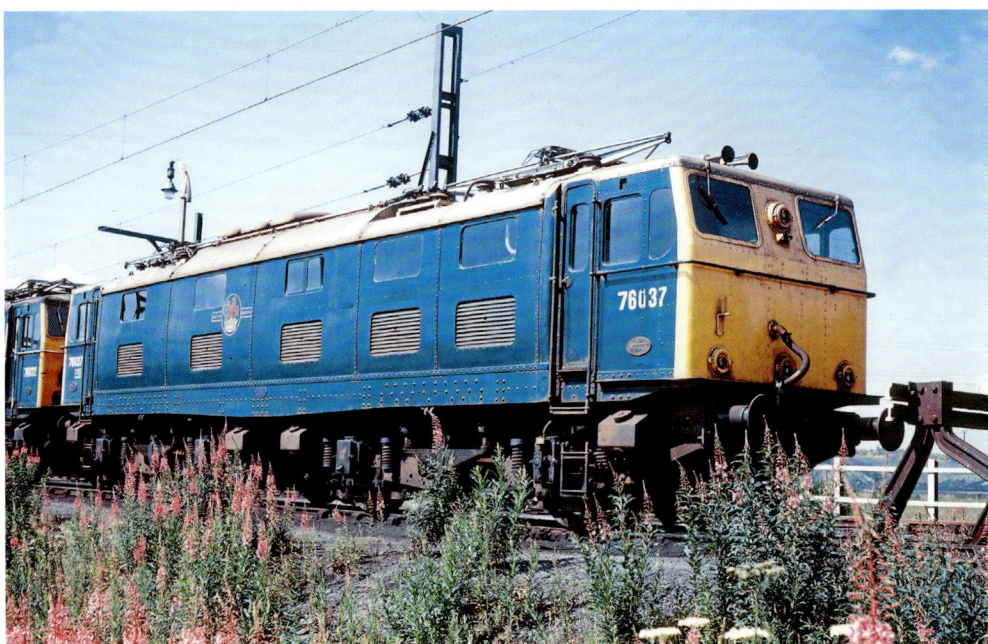

Among the Rosebay Willow herb alongside the shed entrance at Wath on 16 July 1972 was Class 76 No. 76037, which was one of the very earliest engines to be renumbered in the TOPS scheme on 23 March 1972. Surprising, perhaps, as it had been withdrawn in October 1971 along with a few classmates. It went on to manage another nine years' service after this photograph. (Sylvester Booth/Strathwood Library Collection)

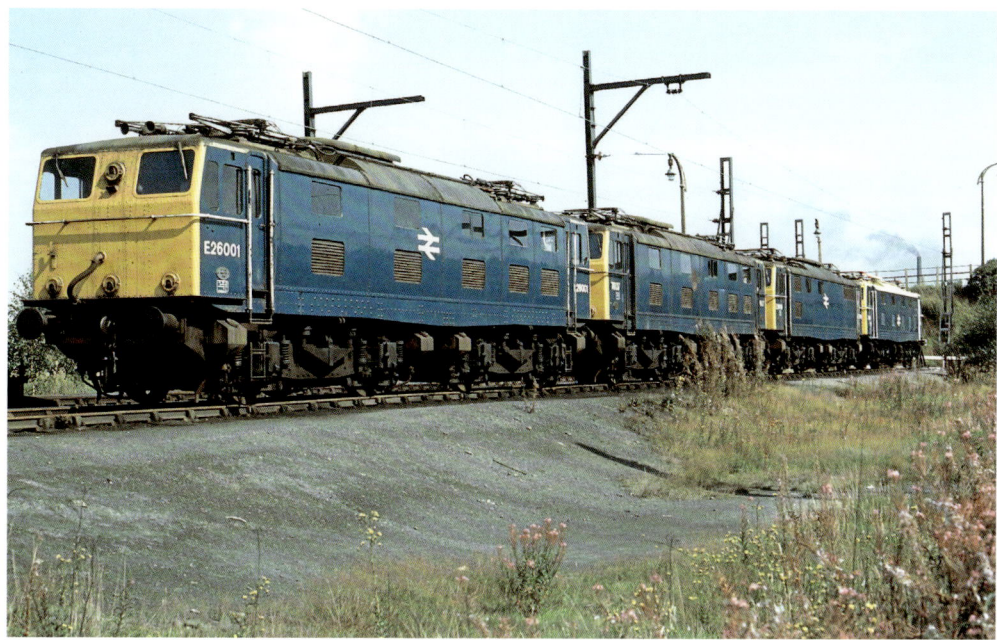

Still wearing the E prefix among others already renumbered was E26001 in June 1973. The month started badly at the Paris Air Show on the 3rd when a Tupolev Tu-144 or, if you prefer, Concordski, tragically crashed dramatically in front of the television cameras, with the loss of fifteen lives. (Ian King)

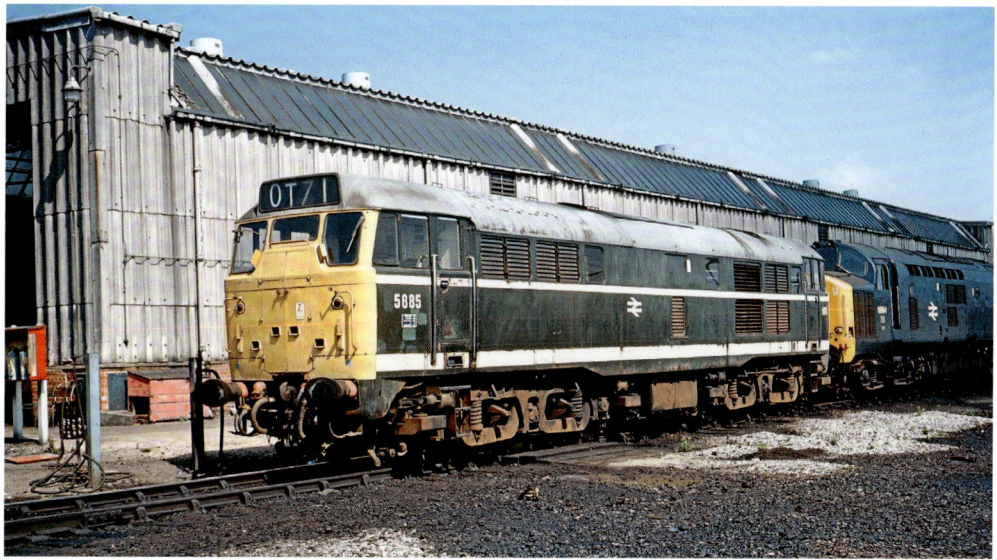

Keeping company at Wath with a Class 37 was Class 31 No. 5685 on 16 July 1972. Popular on our televisions at the time was *Columbo*, whereby Peter Falk played America's most unlikely police detective, who turned up on the scene and always managed to solve the crime by piecing together even the most minute fragments of evidence. Famous killers were played by Leonard Nimoy, Patrick McGoohan, William Shatner, Dick Van Dyke, and Janet Lee (the only person who ever got away with it). Suspects were lulled into a false sense of security by his tramp's raincoat, battered old car and well-chewed cigar. No-one believed this scruffy cop could nail them. (Sylvester Booth/Strathwood Library Collection)

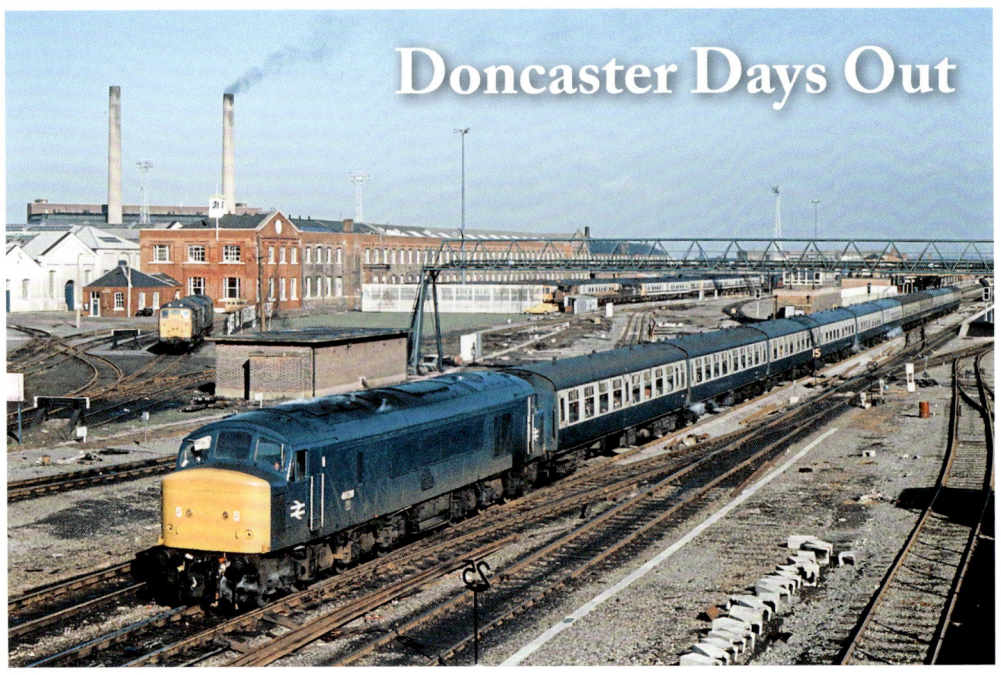

Doncaster Days Out

The steam heating seems to be working on board the train as Peak No. 46028 heads south past the works. (Arthur Wilson)

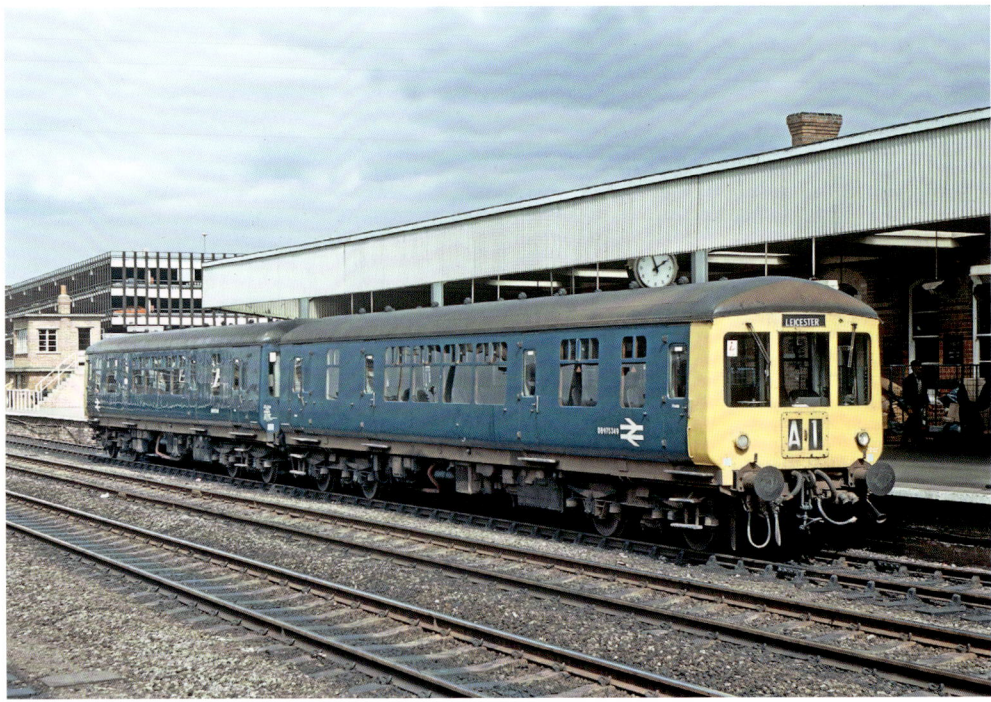

Now renumbered into departmental service are Gloucester RCW-built DB597349 and DB597348 labelled for Leicester around lunchtime on Saturday 24 August 1974. (Roger Bradley)

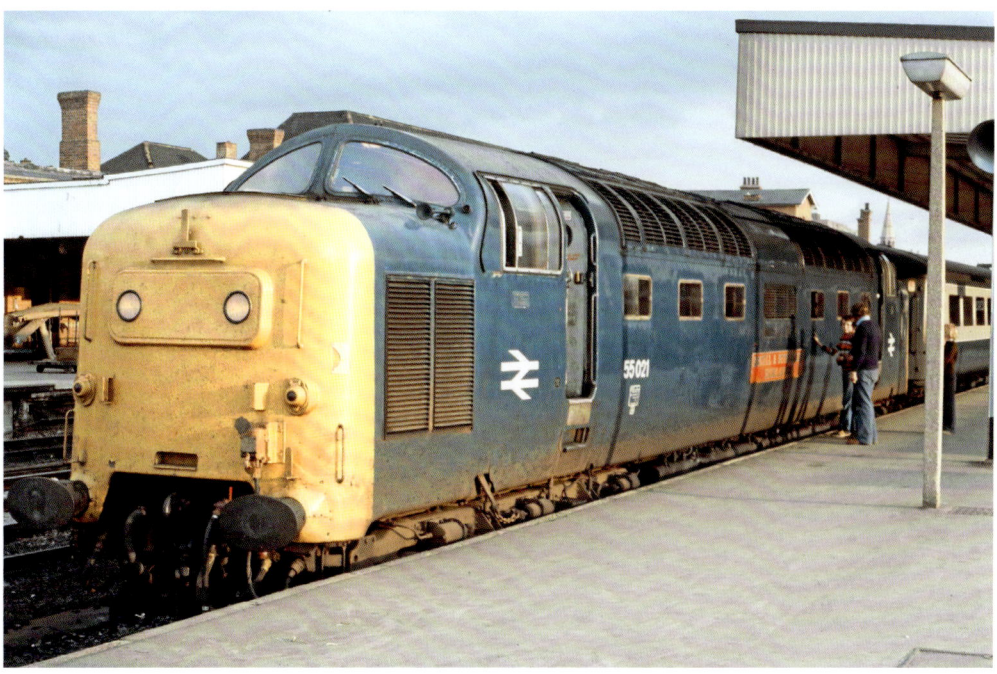

A chance for a closer look at Deltic No. 55021 *Argyll and Sutherland Highlander*, which has pulled up while, working the 17.05 King's Cross service for Hull on 22 September 1979. (Len Ball)

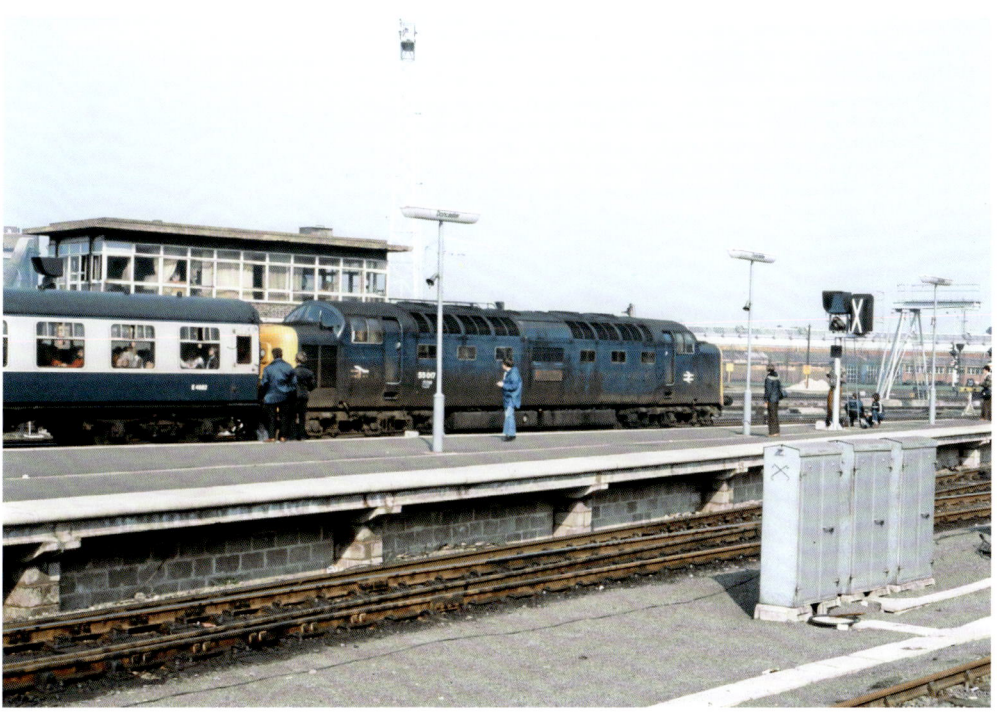

Any Deltic departure would catch the attention of spotters and No. 55017 *The Durham Light Infantry*, with a King's Cross to York job, would be no exception as here on 14 April 1979. (Len Ball)

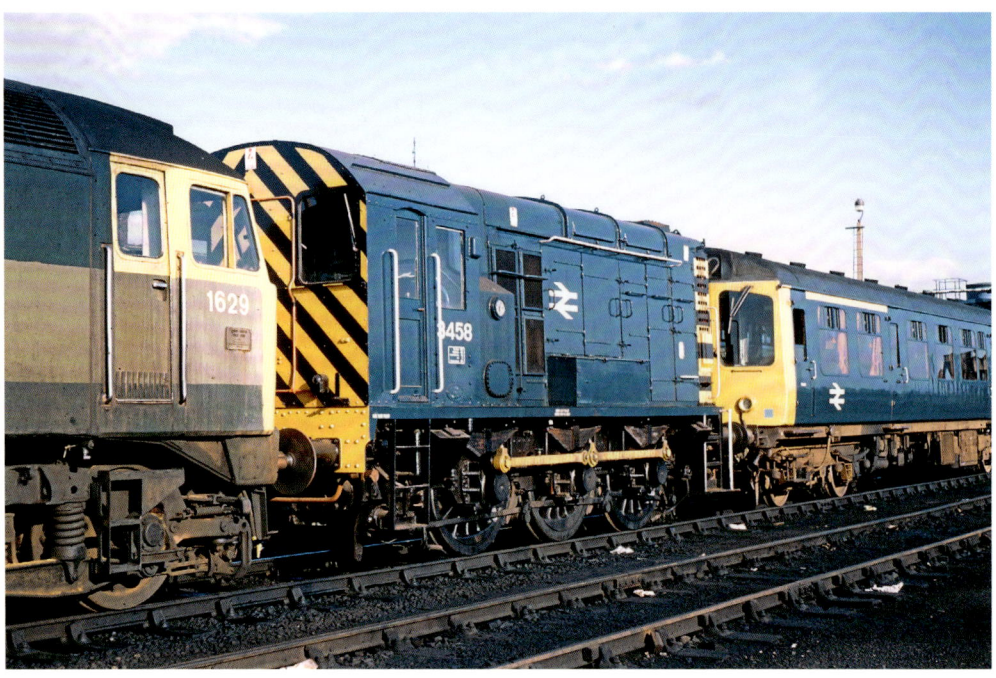

The day after the US pulled its last ground troops out of Vietnam, our visitor to Doncaster found recently ex-works No. 3458 on the depot on 13 August 1972. (Sylvester Booth/Strathwood Library Collection)

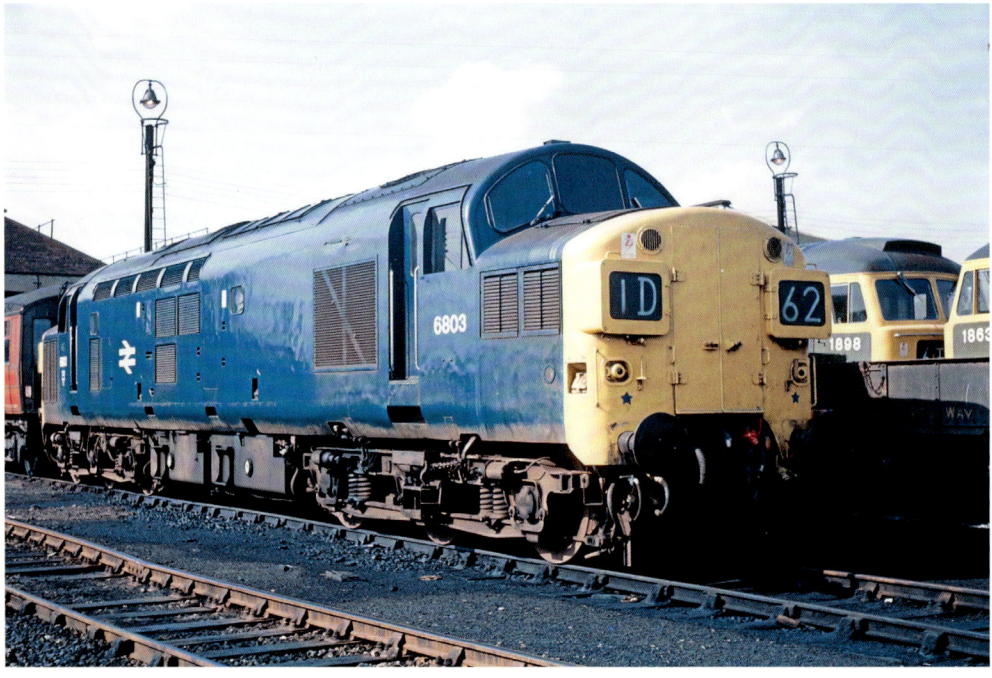

Also there on the same day were a number of Class 47s and Class 37 No. 6803 from 41A Tinsley. This engine was nine years old, having gone new to Tinsley in January 1963. (Sylvester Booth/Strathwood Library Collection)

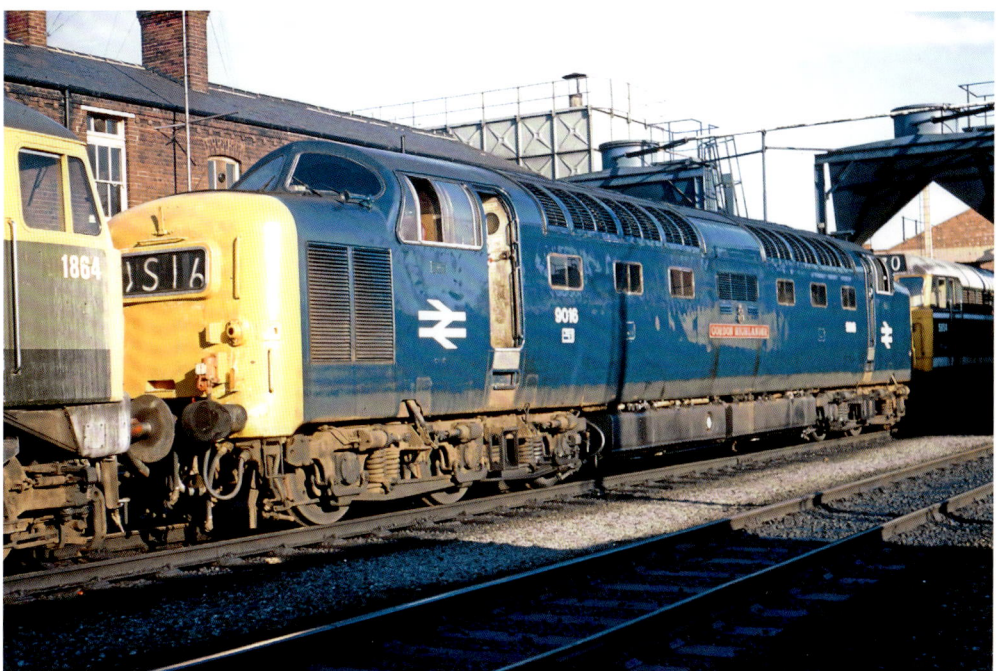

Edinburgh Haymarket-allocated Deltic No. 9016 *Gordon Highlander* could also be found stopped on shed at Doncaster in August 1972. This same month, the second of the pioneer High Speed Train Class 252 prototype power cars No. 41001 was introduced, and the writing was on the wall for the Deltic fleet from then on. (Sylvester Booth/Strathwood Library Collection)

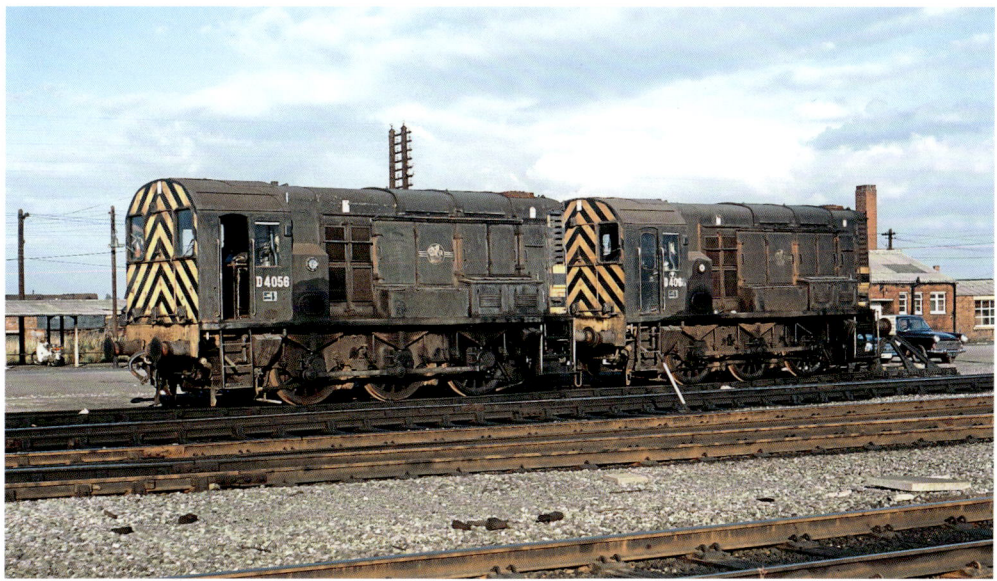

Withdrawn in June 1972 when just over ten years old were D4056 and D4068 seen in the sun on 36A Doncaster in August 1972. Both would find further employment in the north-east with the National Coal Board at Ashington initially, before various moves to Northumberland and County Durham collieries prior to their closure. (Sylvester Booth/Strathwood Library Collection)

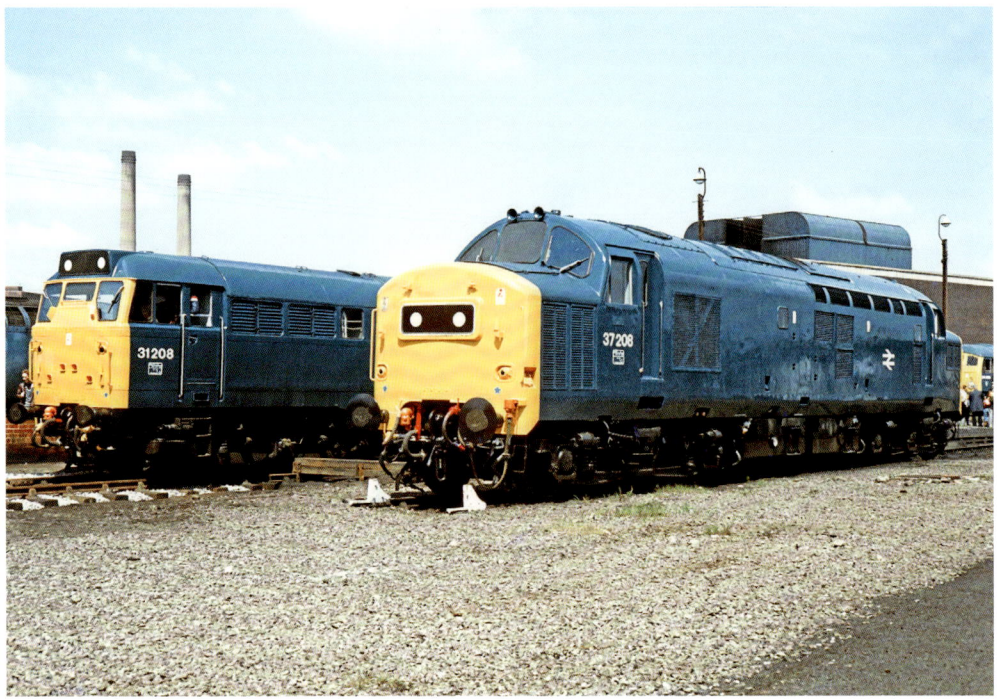

Spick and span ex-works and ready for display for the Open Day at Doncaster Works on 17 June 1978 are Class 31 No. 31208 and Class 37 No. 37208. (N. P. Cannon)

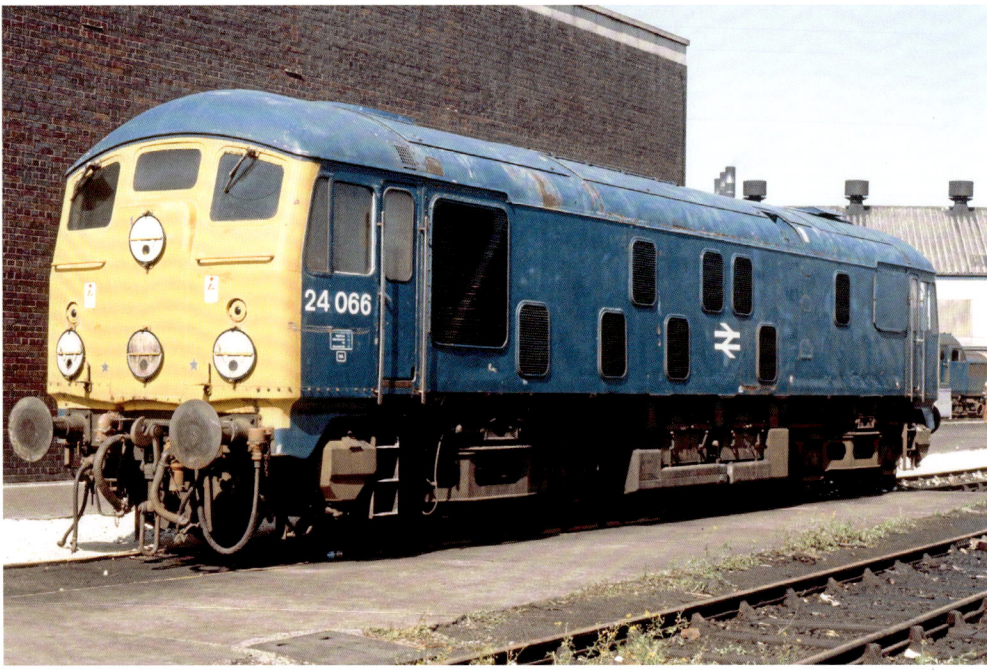

Almost certainly less respectable was withdrawn Class 24 No. 24066 after almost three years stored out of use at Carlisle. It would be cut up in the works yard a few weeks after the open weekend in June 1978. (Aldo Delicata)

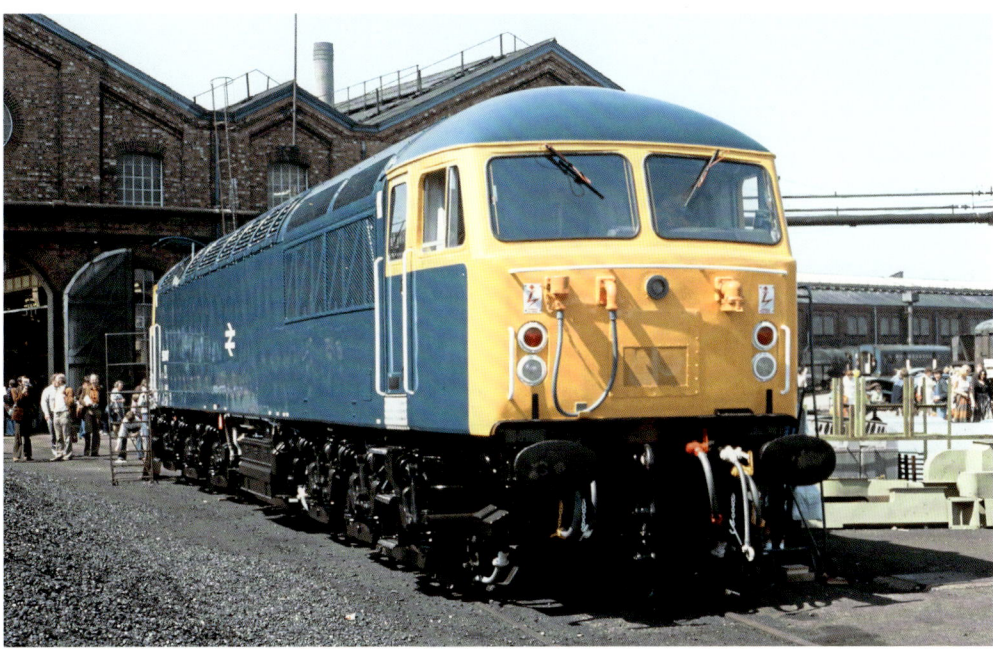

Brand new and displayed outside to the visiting public on 18 June 1978 was Class 56 No. 56047, which would enter traffic at Toton the following month. In the cinemas that summer was *The Boys from Brazil*, starring Gregory Peck as Dr Josef Mengele, with a supporting cast of Sir Lawrence Olivier and James Mason. Also on the cast list was Prunella Scales, working on the big screen between the two series of *Fawlty Towers*. (Aldo Delicata)

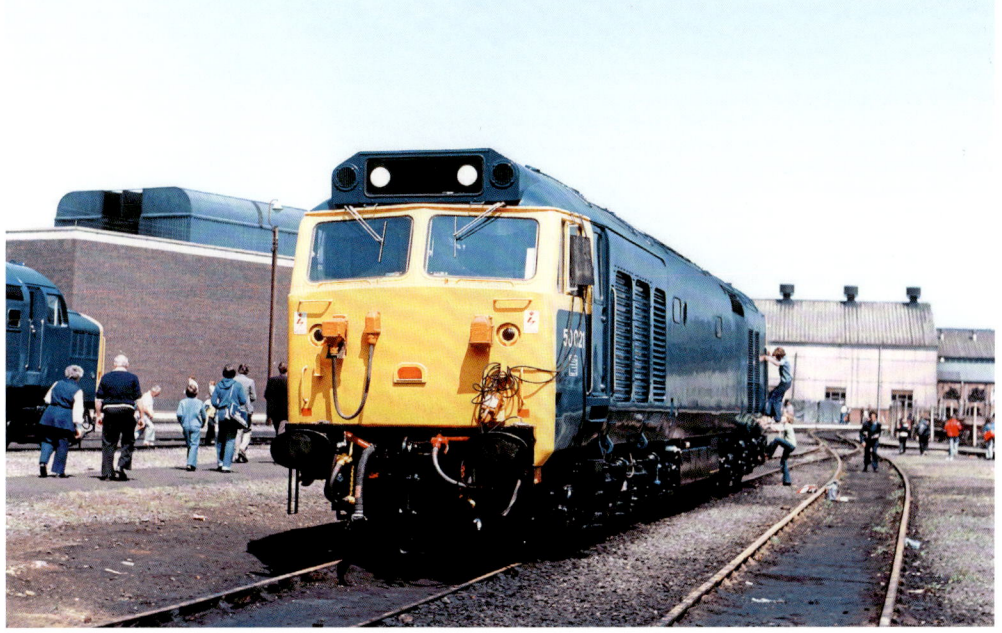

Just a few weeks before picking up the name *Rodney* was this visitor from the Western Region for works attention, Class 50 No. 500210, also on public display during this pleasant June weekend for the open days in 1978. (Strathwood Library Collection)

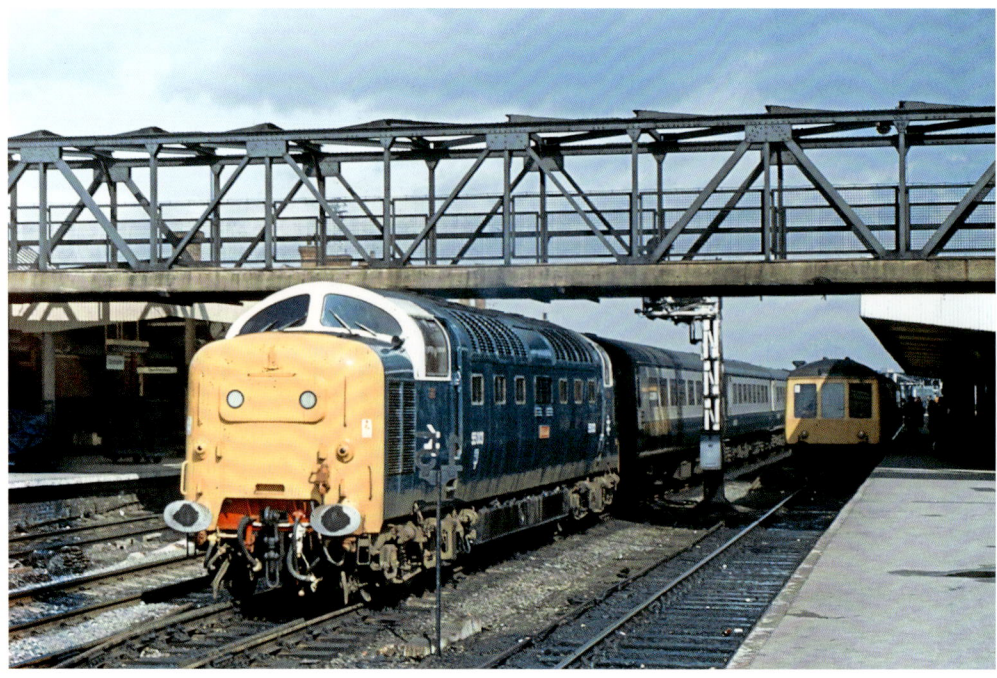

Having seen the attentions of Finsbury Park's painters, Deltic No. 55003 *Meld* comes through on the fast on 13 April 1979. Prime Minister James Callaghan MP was keeping his fingers crossed whilst on the hustings, but in three weeks' time Mrs Thatcher would move into Number 10. (Adrian Griffith)

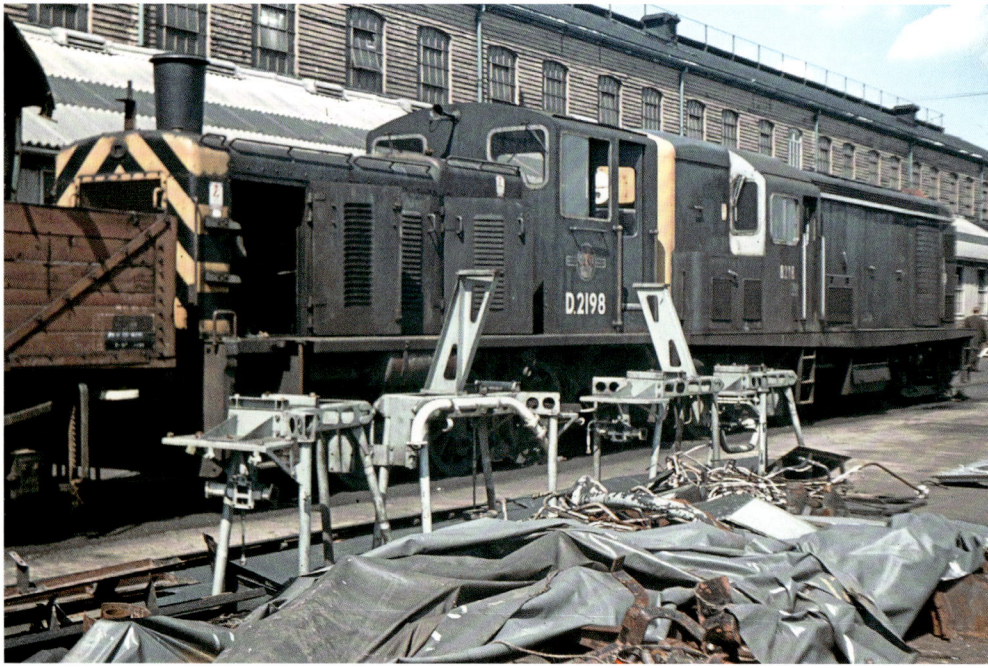

Also cast aside a few years before were Class 03 D2198 and Class 15 D8218, with a combined service life of just twenty years, alongside Doncaster Works in June 1971. (Neil Snuggs)

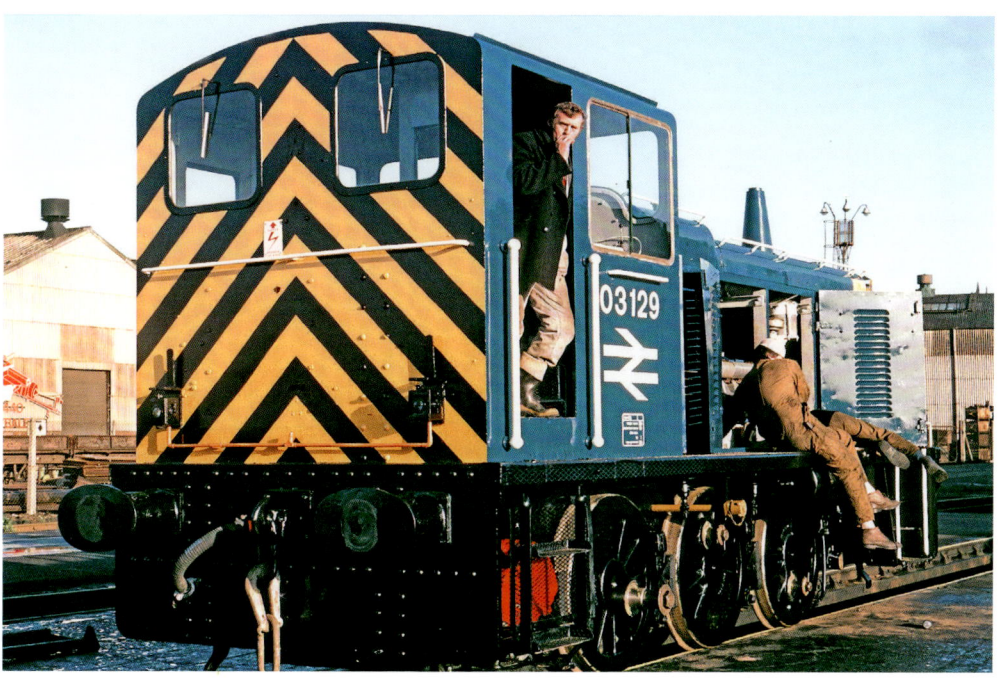

More fortunate was Class 03 No. 03129, being prepared for a return to traffic outside the works in December 1979. (Sylvester Booth/Strathwood Library Collection)

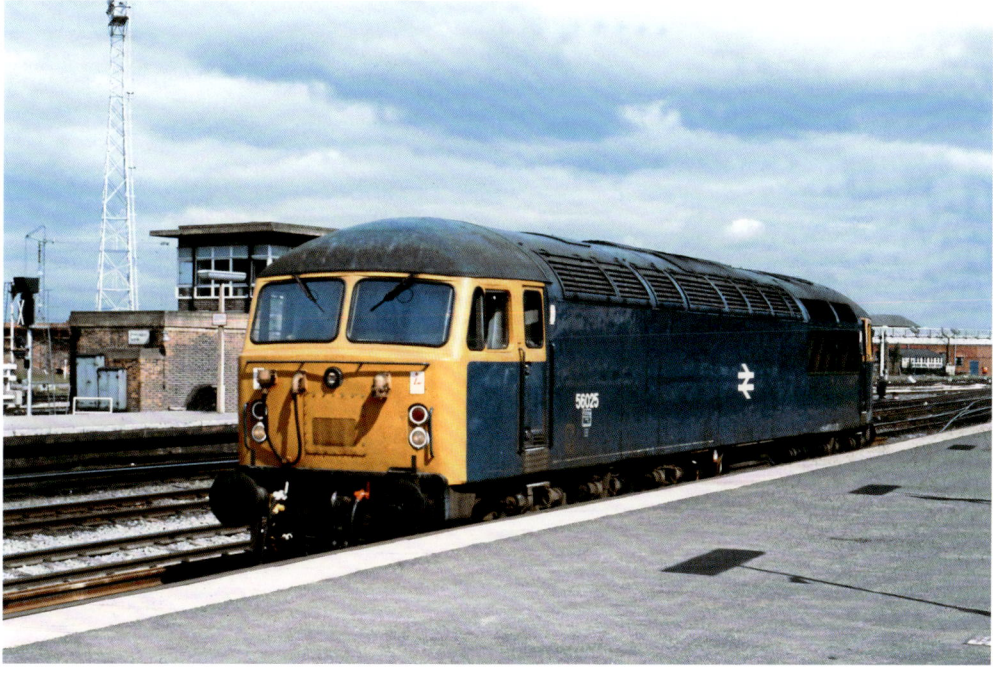

This Romanian import landed at Harwich on 22 April 1977 and entered active service from Tinsley from 5 July that year. By the time of this shot of Class 56 No. 56025 running light on 30 June 1979, deliveries of the class had progressed as far as No. 56060. (Len Ball)

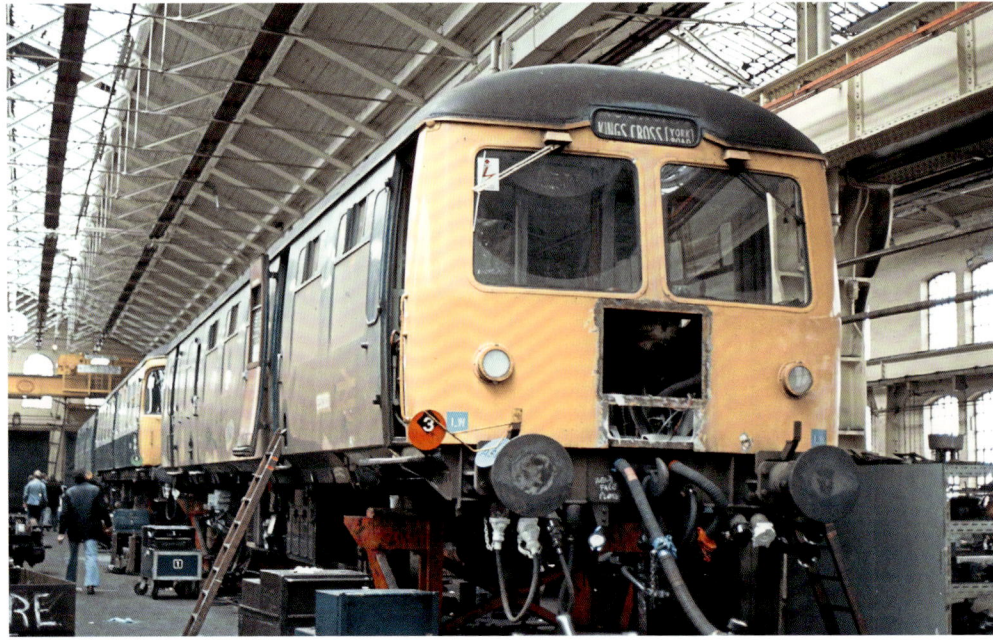

Repairs for future service are underway inside the DMU shop on 2 April 1978, with a Cravens car up on the jacks in front of a Trans Pennine car and what looks like a Metropolitan Cammell car behind that. All the seats would come out for refurbishing and to allow access to all of the wiring during these repairs. Not that this party seem to be taking that much notice. (Arthur Wilson)

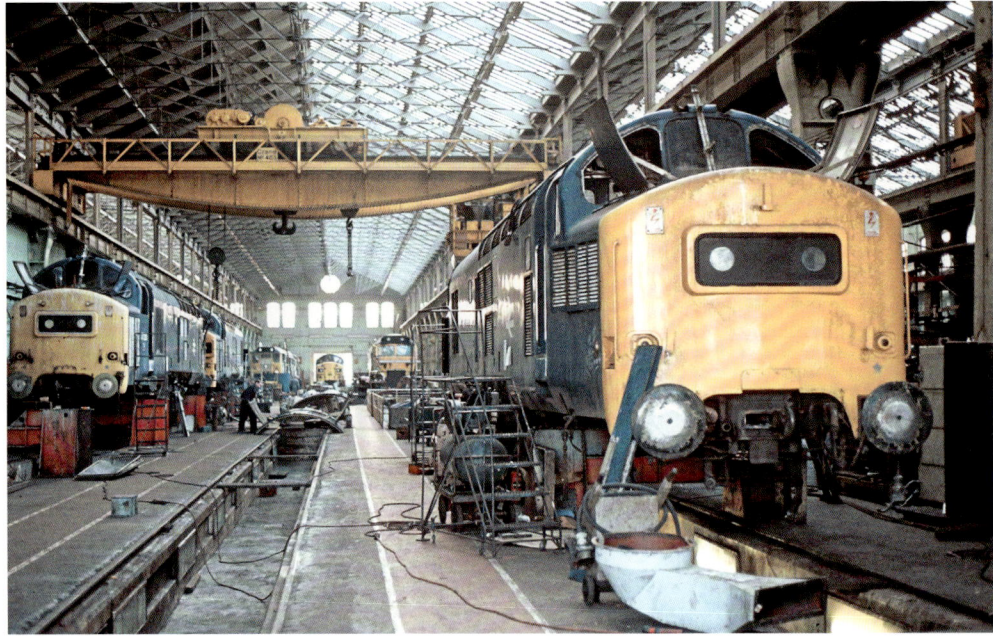

Class 37s Nos 37265, 37220 and 37111 dominate the main erecting shops with a Class 31 and 50 in the distance on 5 November 1978. More unrest in Iran as after days of rioting the prime minister resigns, and calls for the Shah to go get louder. (Arthur Wilson)

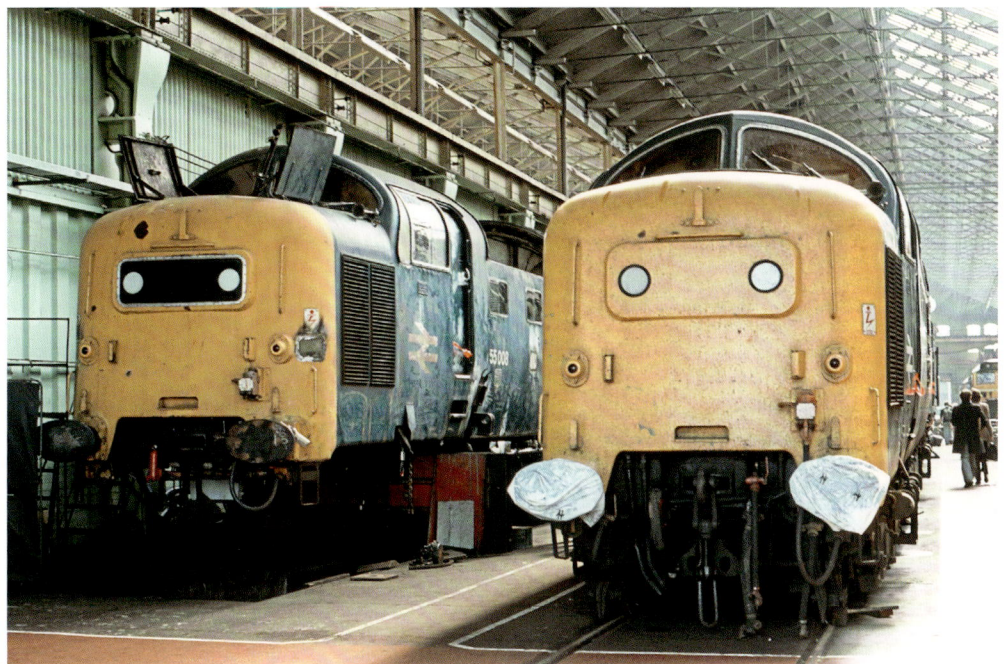

Another society visit to the works a month or two earlier on 18 June found a pair of Deltics in the shops, with No. 55008 *The Green Howards* identifiable. 18 June 1978. (Strathwood Library Collection)

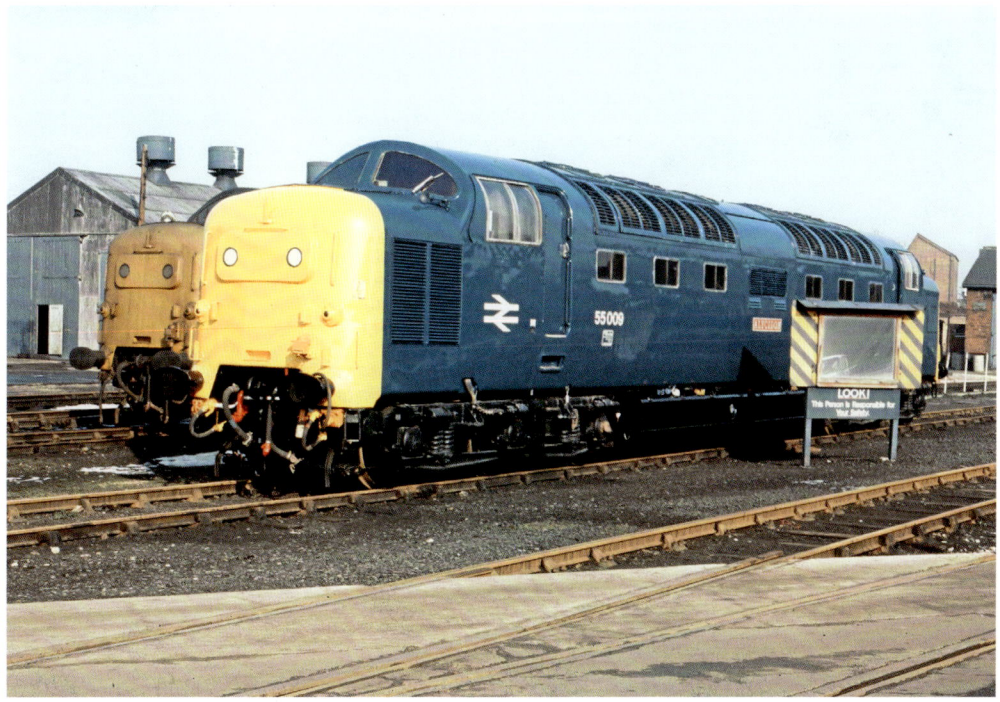

What spotter with a camera could resist a shot of ex-works Deltic No. 55009 *Alycidon* ready for a return to traffic at The Plant on 22 February 1979. (Len Ball)

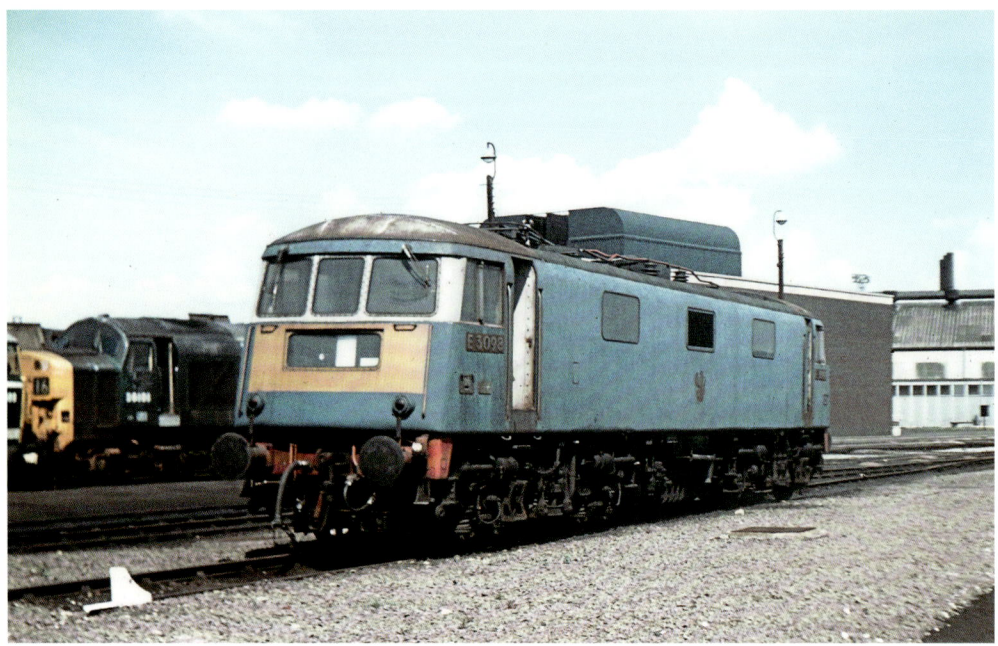

After three years in store, first at Allerton, then at the closed steam depot at Bury, Class 83 E3098 arrived at the works in the summer of 1971 for refurbishment and a re-entry to traffic. Further broken service with periods in storage would befall this engine again until finally being put down for good at Vic Berry's in Leicester in October 1984. (Neil Snuggs)

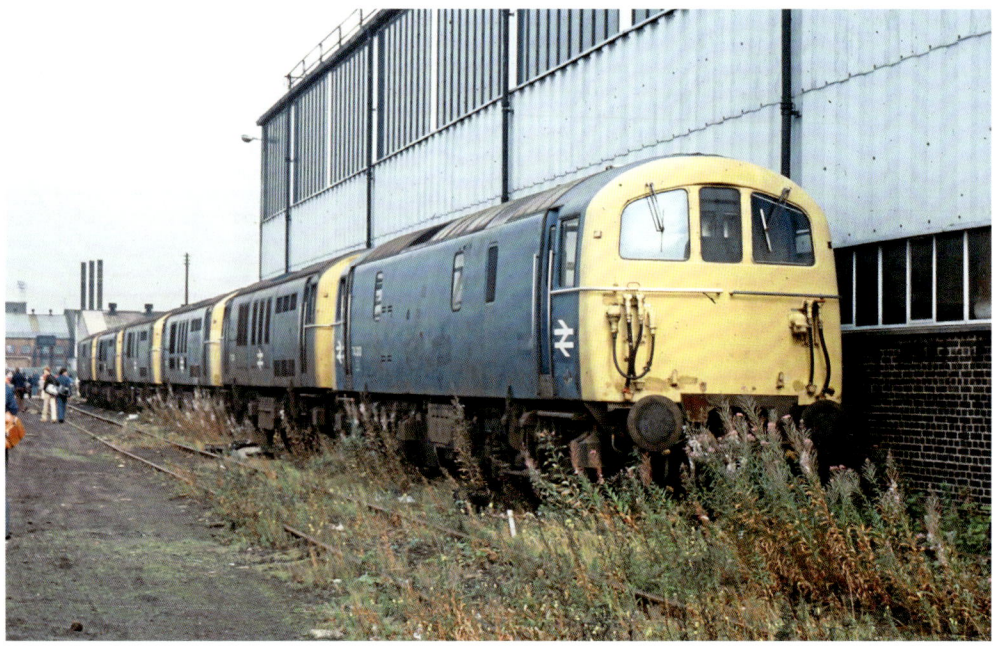

Another collection of visiting electrics from outside the Eastern Region has arrived on the works, this time for cutting up. They are: Nos 74010, 71004, 71009, 71011, 71013 and 71014 seen here on 19 August 1978. (Strathwood Library Collection)

ECML Southern Stretches

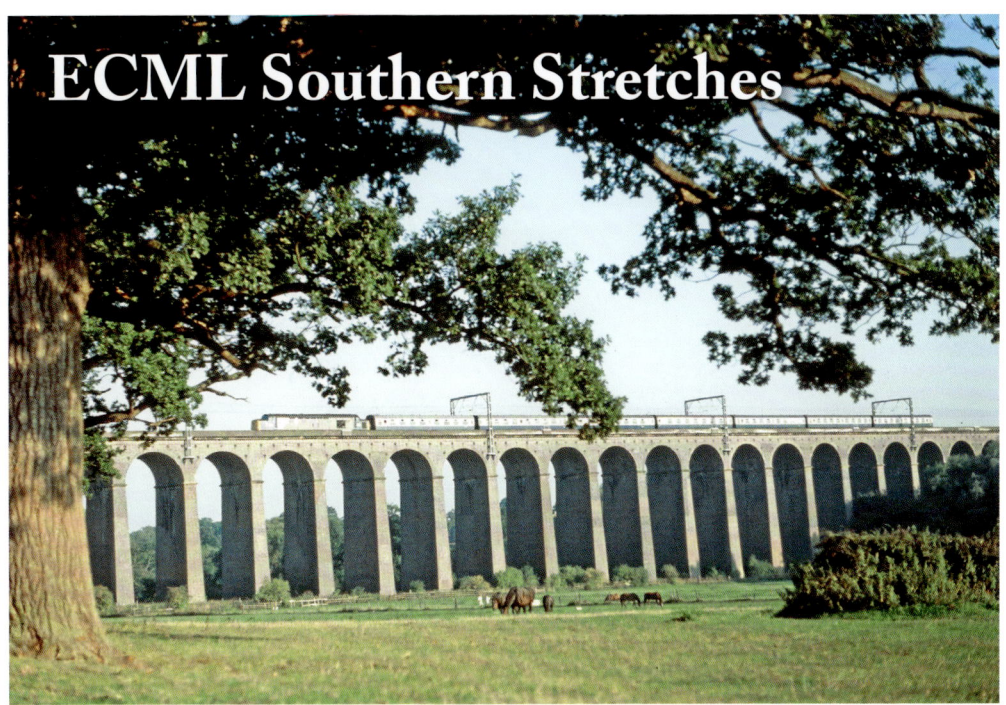

The afternoon sun catches the 17.12 King's Cross–Grantham with Class 40 No. 40083 in charge at Welwyn North on 5 September 1979. (Colin Whitbread)

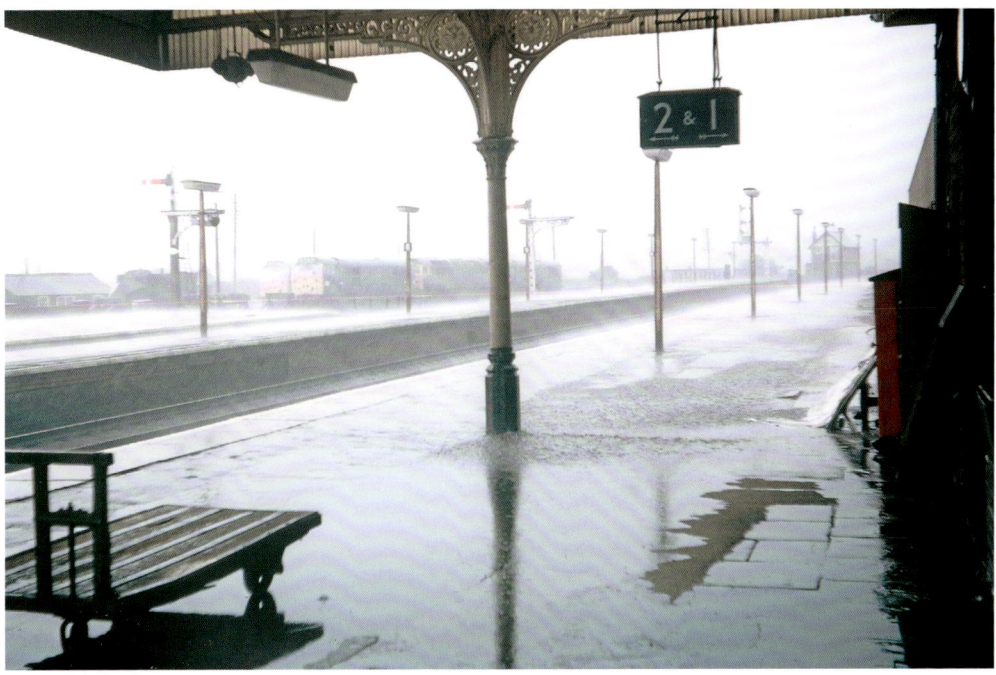

Far less inviting weather was to be found on 27 June 1970 while our cameraman sheltered at Grantham. (Michael Beaton)

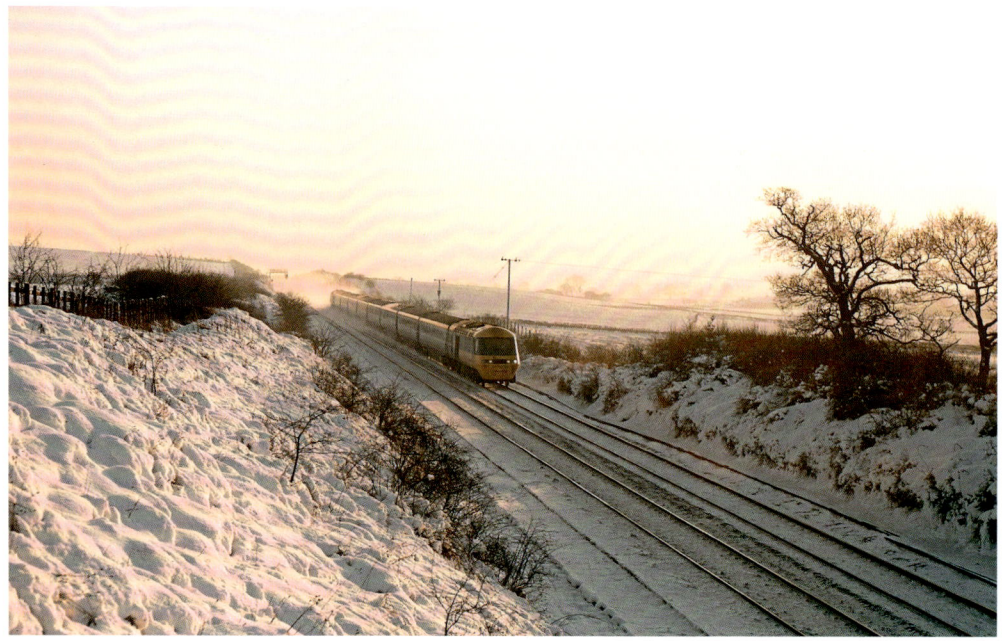

A wintry start to the new year at Gamston on 2 January 1979 for our frozen cameraman hoping for shots of Deltics. A few days later and record sales would send The Village People to number one with 'YMCA'. (Ian Harrison)

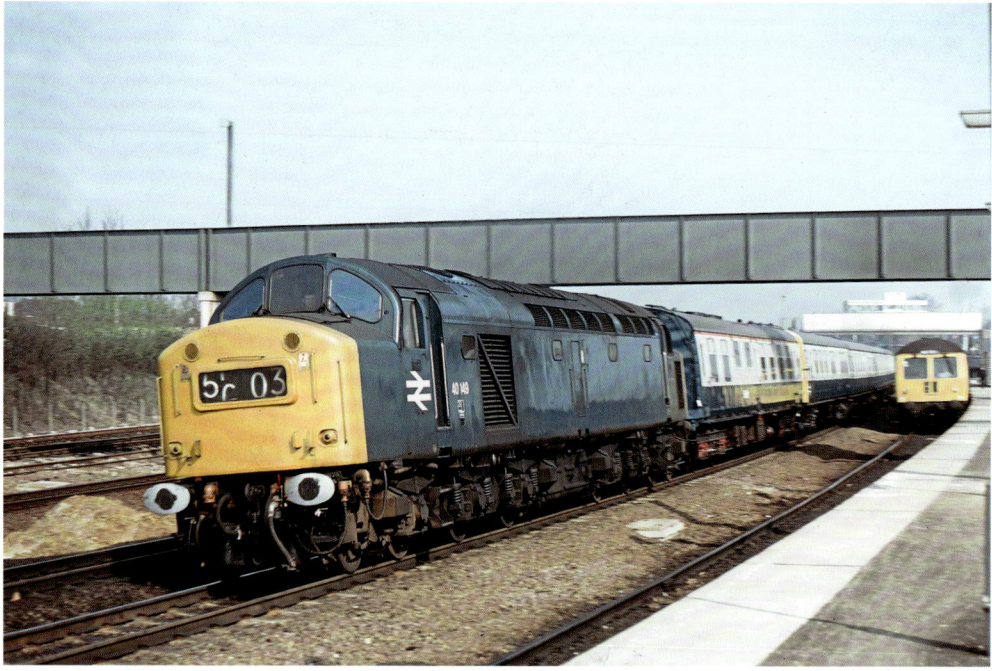

Bringing fresh deliveries to the Southern Region of new 4-CIGs is Class No. 40149, speeding its load through from York in April 1974. The following month the prototype HST set No. 252001 was to complete its first 100,000 miles of test-running. Not only Deltics should watch out I fear! (Strathwood Library collection)

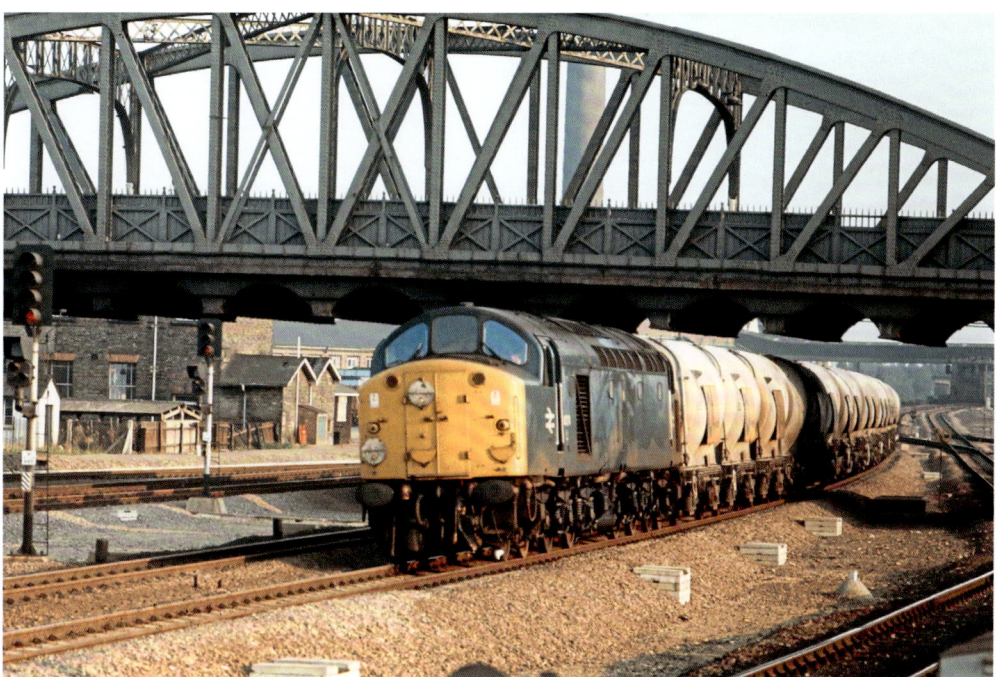

One of the cars of choice for top sales reps up and down the country in September 1974 was the British Leyland-built Triumph Dolomite Sprint. We find Class 40 No. 40074 hard at work with a cement train at Peterborough on the 20th of the month. Twenty years later, all the Forties would be gone and the car of desire for sales reps would be made in Germany by BMW or Audi. (Ian James)

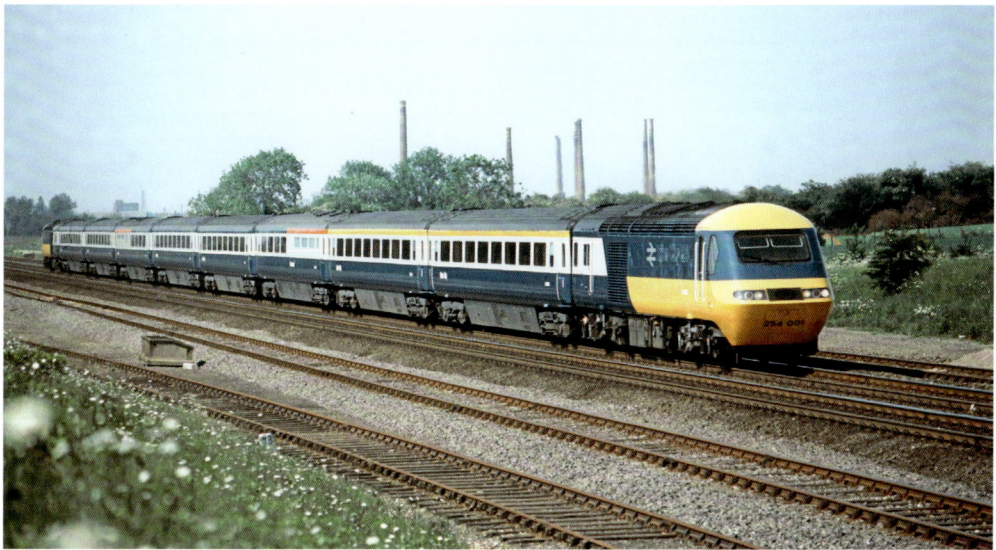

Passing one of the many brickworks once around Peterborough on 3 June 1978, our cameraman has recorded this view of the first of the Class 254 HST sets, No. 254001, on an Up train. Later in the month a somewhat slim line and un-beefy Ian Botham becomes the first man in the history of cricket to score a century and take eight wickets in one innings of a Test match. The Pakistani Captain Wasim Bari said of the twenty-two-year-old that he was just unplayable. (Aldo Delicata)

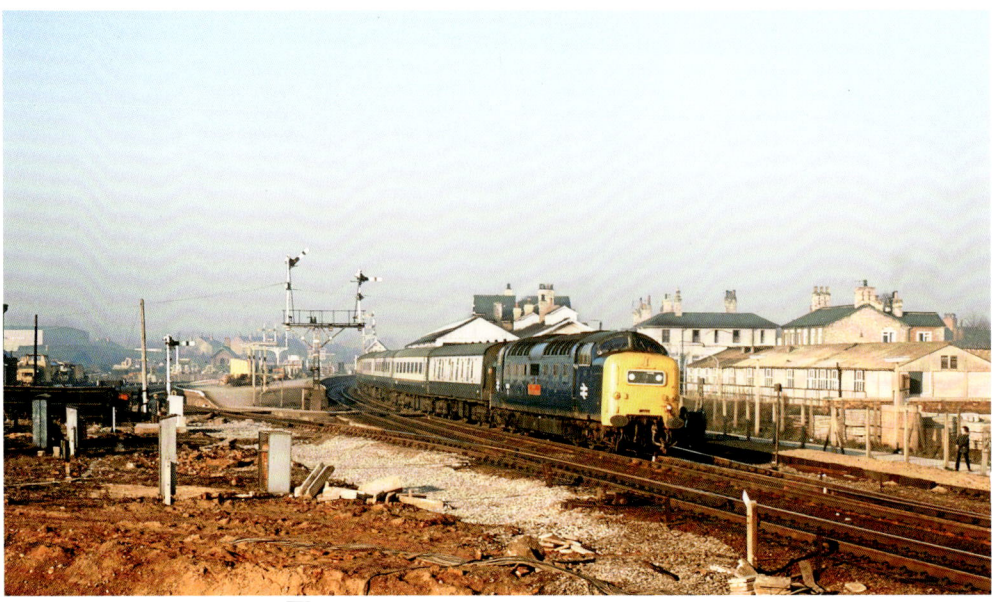

Sweeping through Retford and the track works in connection with the old crossover two days after Christmas in 1975 was Deltic No. 55006 *The Fife and Forfar Yeomanry*. The British tabloids were having a field day with headlines over the raging Cod War, when an Icelandic gunboat opened fire on unarmed British fishery support vessels in the North Atlantic Sea on 11 Decmber. This was to be the third such conflict over cod with Iceland. This time it was triggered by Iceland extending its control over fishing rights from 50 to 200 nautical miles from its coast, which affected Britain from November of that year. Cod-fishing was a major part of Britain's economy in Humberside, Fleetwood, Aberdeen and North Shields and the proposed reduction would cost an estimated 9,000 jobs. This would of course also have an effect on the railway, with a loss of fish traffic. (Ian Harrison)

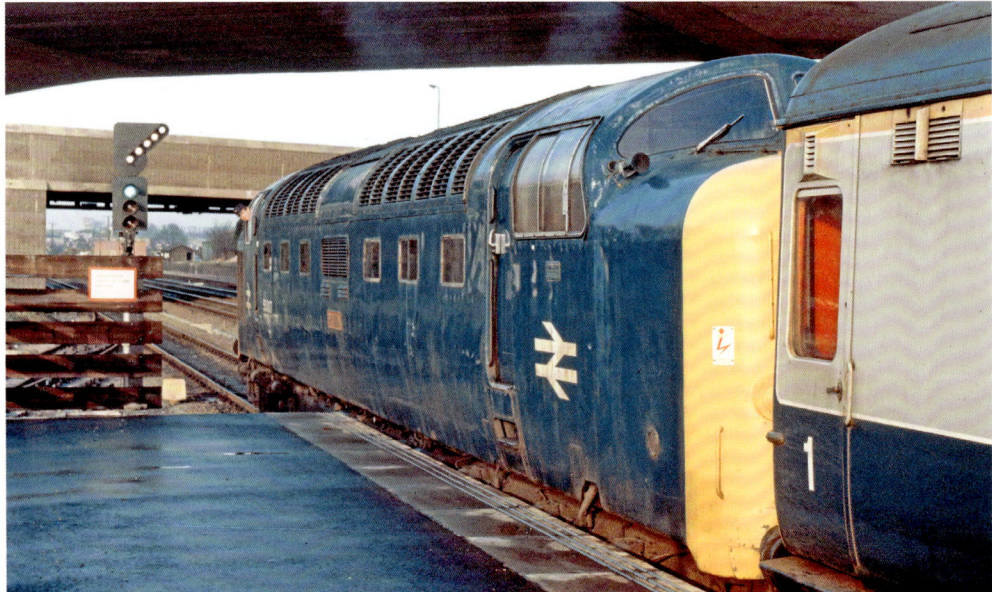

With a familiar show of smoke from the Napier engines, the driver of Deltic No. 55007 *Pinza* opens up his steed at Huntingdon after a stop on 31 January 1978. (Ian James)

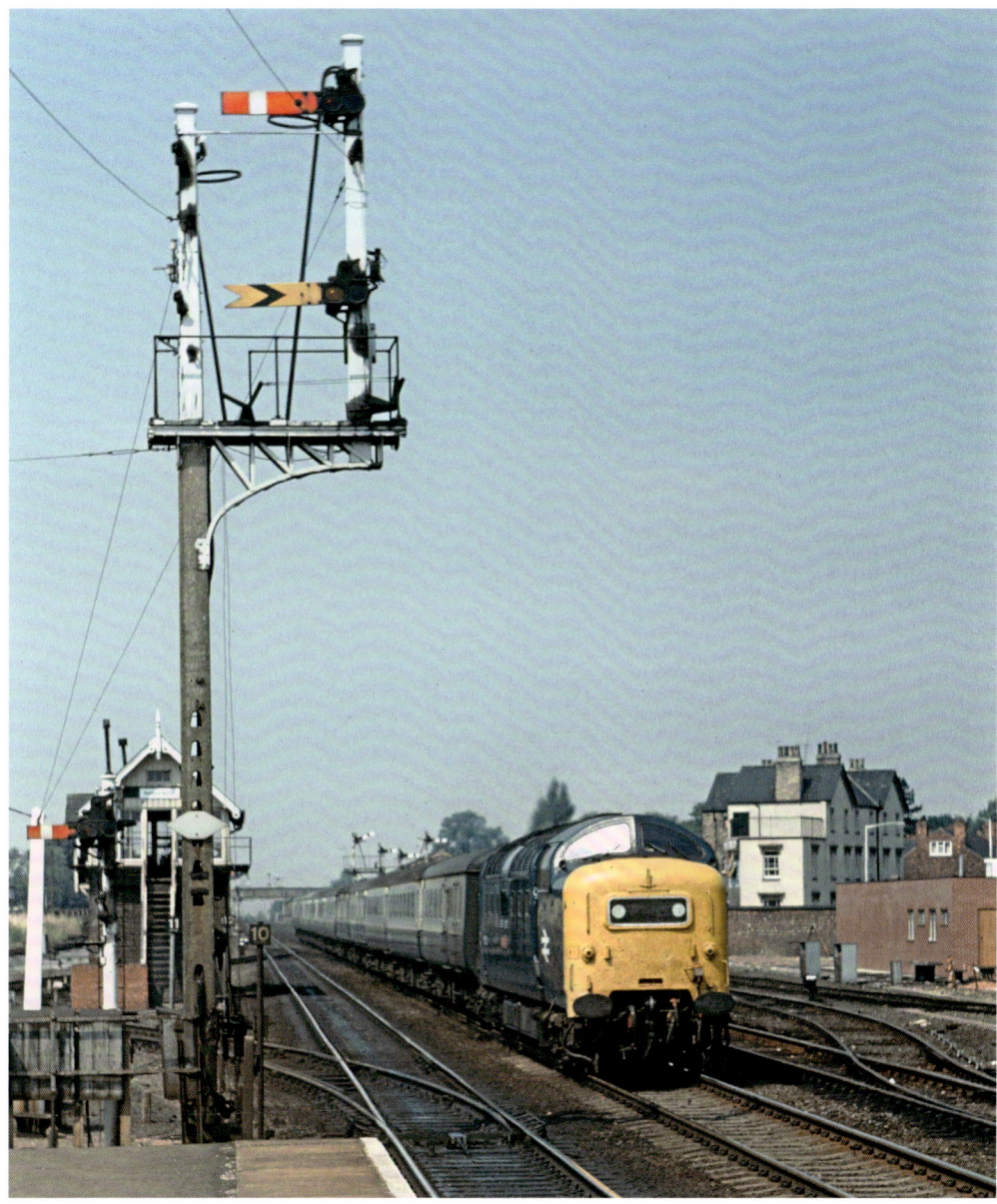

Running fast under semaphores at Retford on 2 August 1975 is Deltic No. 55012 *Crepello*, with an Anglo-Scottish express. Also crossing from north of the border at the time were The Bay City Rollers with their sixth hit single 'Give A Little Love'. (Ian Harrison)

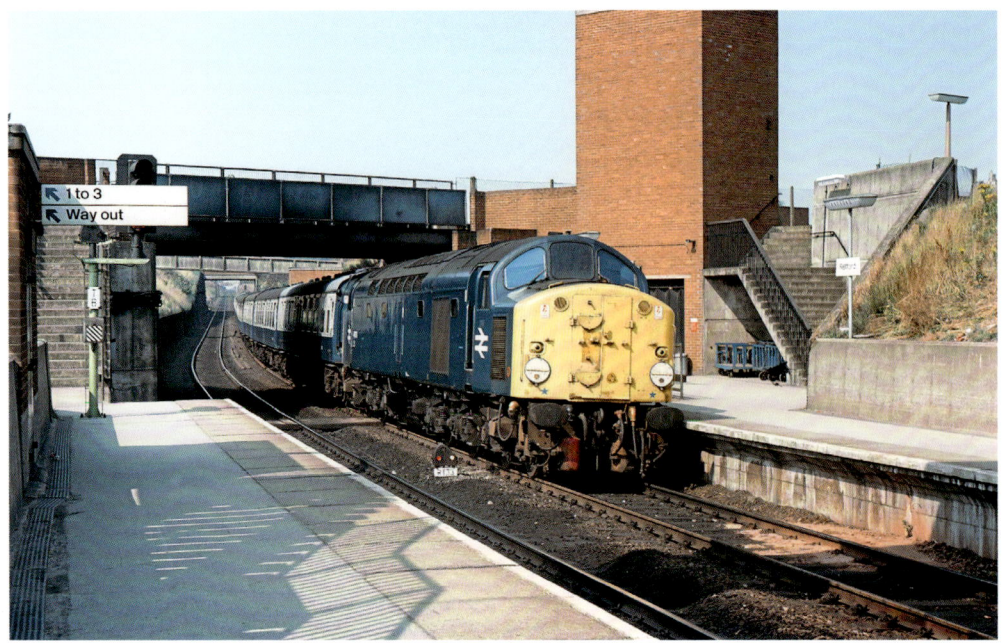

Running into Retford low level station from Manchester with a service for Skegness, no doubt full of holiday-makers, also in August 1975. The brick structure in the background is a lift for luggage and mail trolleys to gain access to the ECML station. (Ian Harrison)

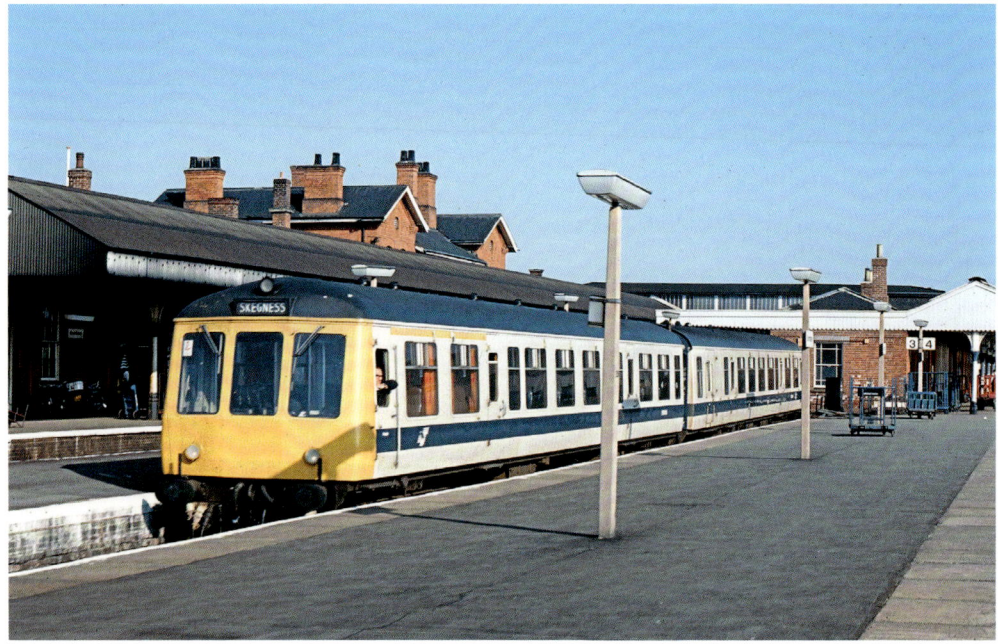

A refurbished Derby-built two-car unit will also head for Skegness, this time from Grantham on 27 May 1978. A new television programme for motoring enthusiasts and car owners had just arrived on our television screens, hosted by Angela Rippon. It was a more matter of fact affair, aimed at a wide audience. This was some time before the appearance of Jeremy Clarkson, after all. (Stuart Broughton)

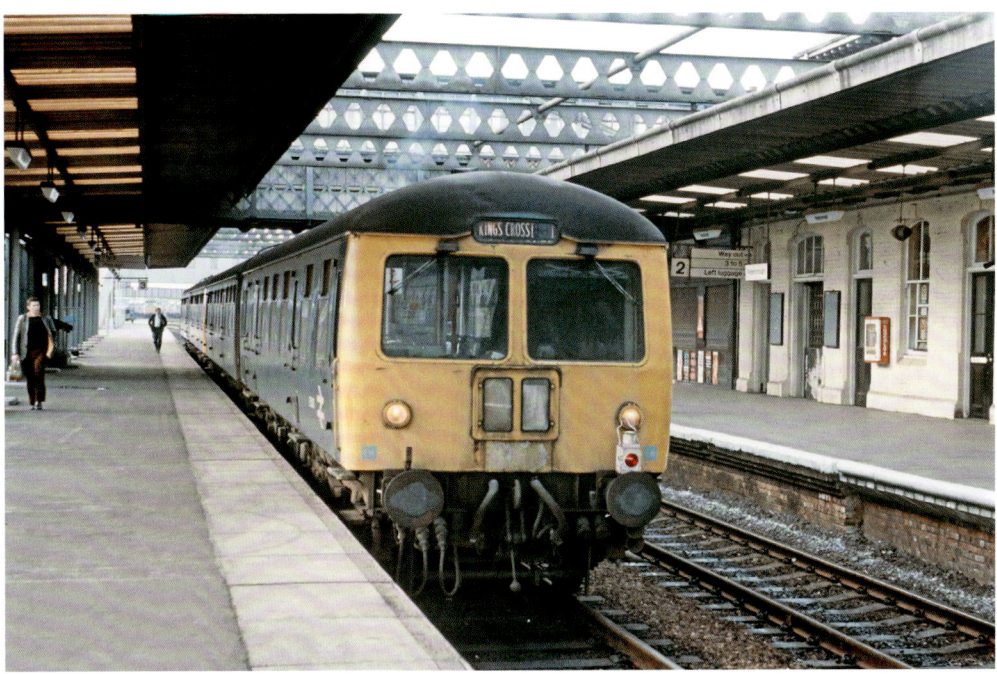

A fairly quiet moment at Peterborough, aside from the steady throb of the engines of a pair of Cravens DMU sets forming the 19.33 to King's Cross at Peterborough on 2 May 1976. (John Dawson)

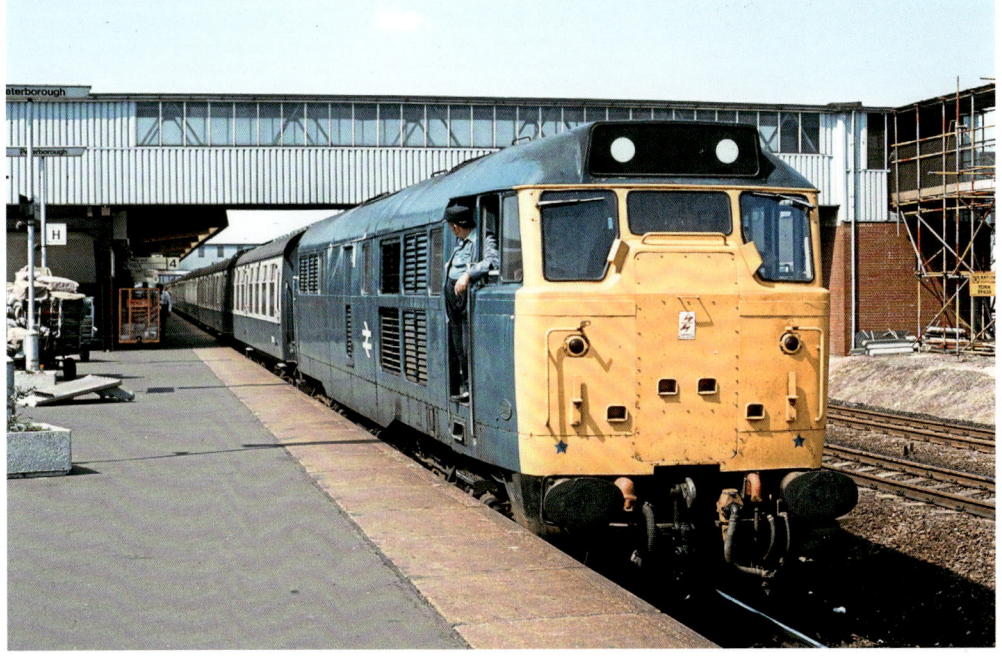

Class 31 No. 31169 at Peterborough with the 14.55 to March on 5 May 1977. As can be seen to the right, the station was still being rebuilt as part of eliminating the one-time speed restriction and bottle-neck here. (Arthur Wilson)

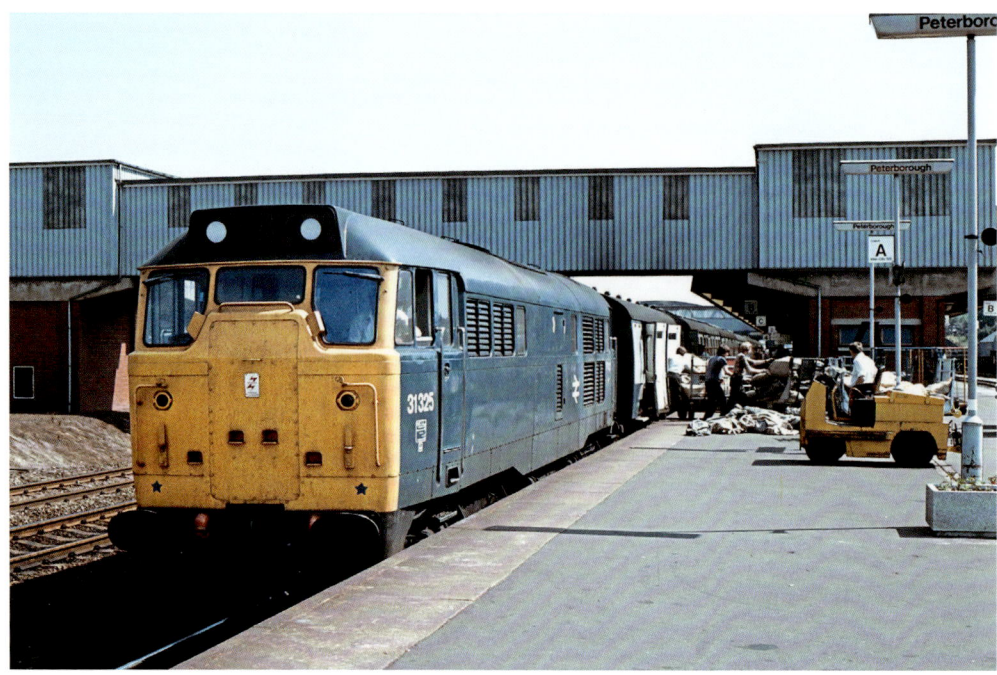

One of March's allocation of Class 31s No. 31325 is also seen the same summer at Peterborough, while staff deal with a large amount of mail traffic on the platform. (Arthur Wilson)

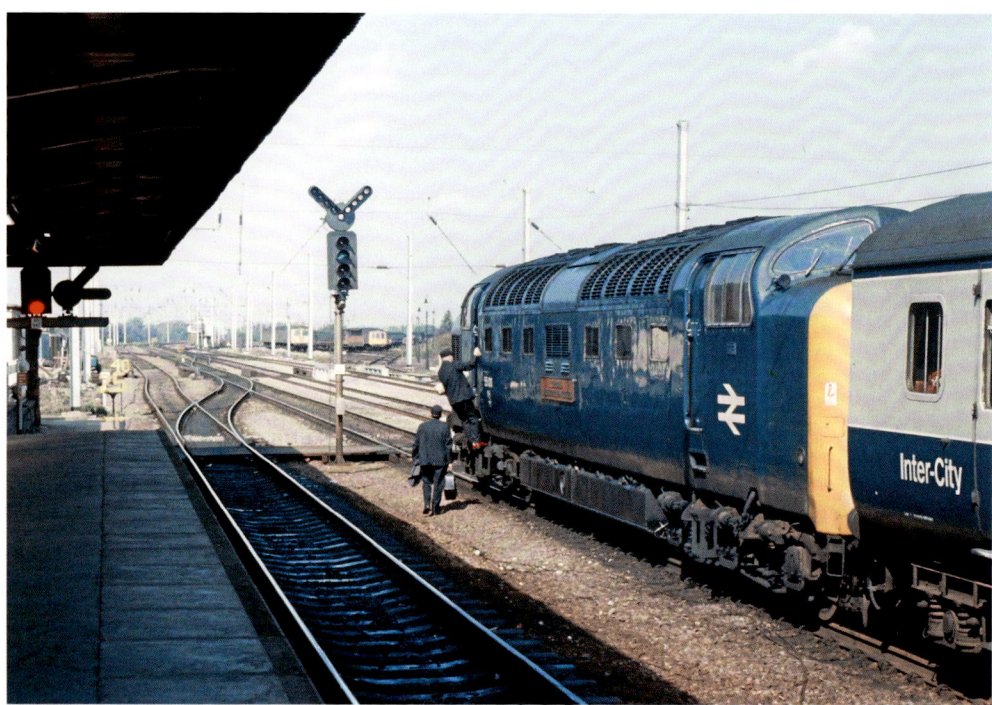

The 12.00 King's Cross–Edinburgh has been stopped at Hitchin to pick up additional crew for No. 55011 *The Royal Northumberland Fusiliers* on 19 September 1976. (John Dawson)

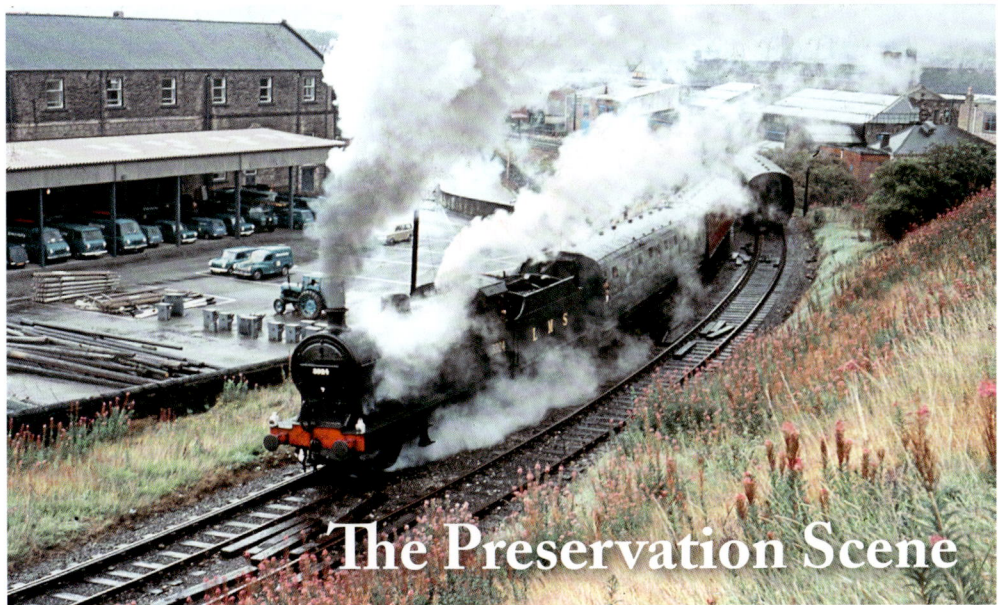

The Preservation Scene

The sanders are working well on wet and greasy rails climbing through the curve away from Keighley on board Fowler Class 4F 3924 in the early seventies. In 1968 this locomotive was the first engine to depart from Barry Scrapyard for preservation. Note the light commercial vehicles of the day in the gas company's yard. (Trans Pennine Publishing)

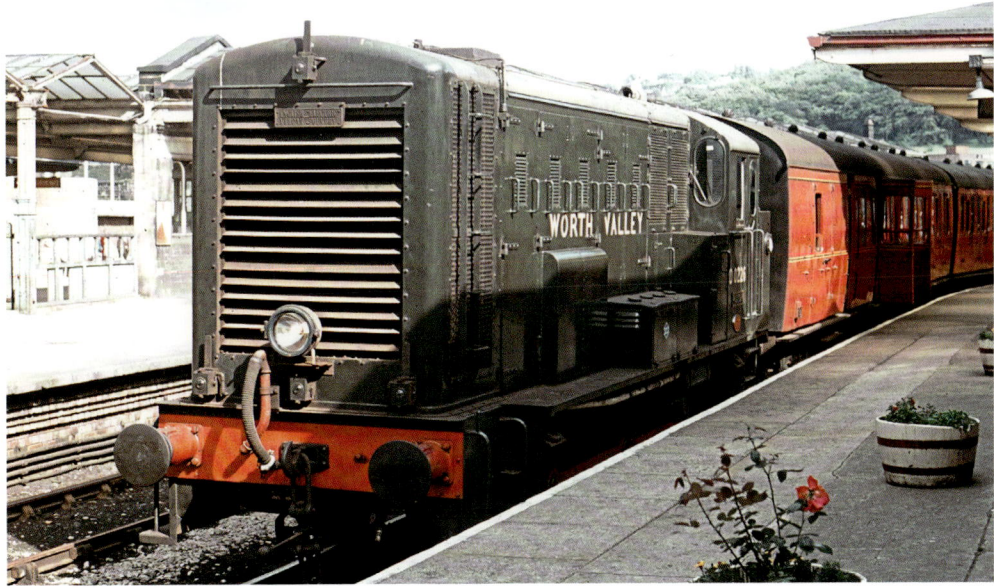

Perhaps a remarkable survivor into preservation was the English Electric prototype D0226, one of a pair given a couple of years of trials on British Railways based at Stratford in the late 1950s. This one returned to its makers for storage before being passed to the infant Keighley & Worth Valley Railway in 1966. We find it having a day out engaged in passenger services for the railway on 14 July 1974 at Keighley. (Nick Gledhill)

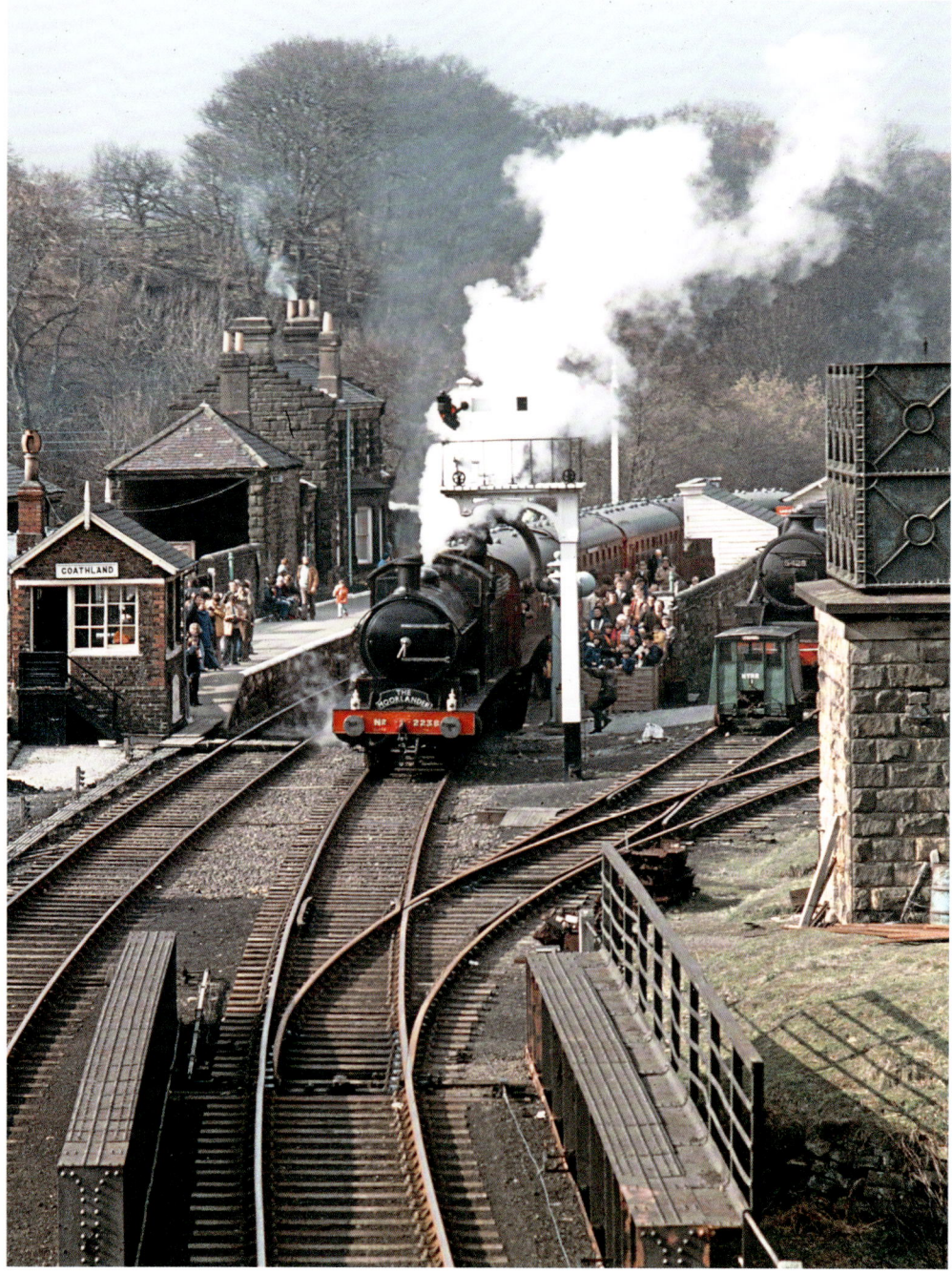

A good crowd on the platforms at Goathland to witness Raven-designed Class Q6 No. 63395 taking water. This engine came to the North Yorkshire Moors Railway after periods of storage at various locations in the north-east, including Thornaby depot. (Strathwood Library Collection)

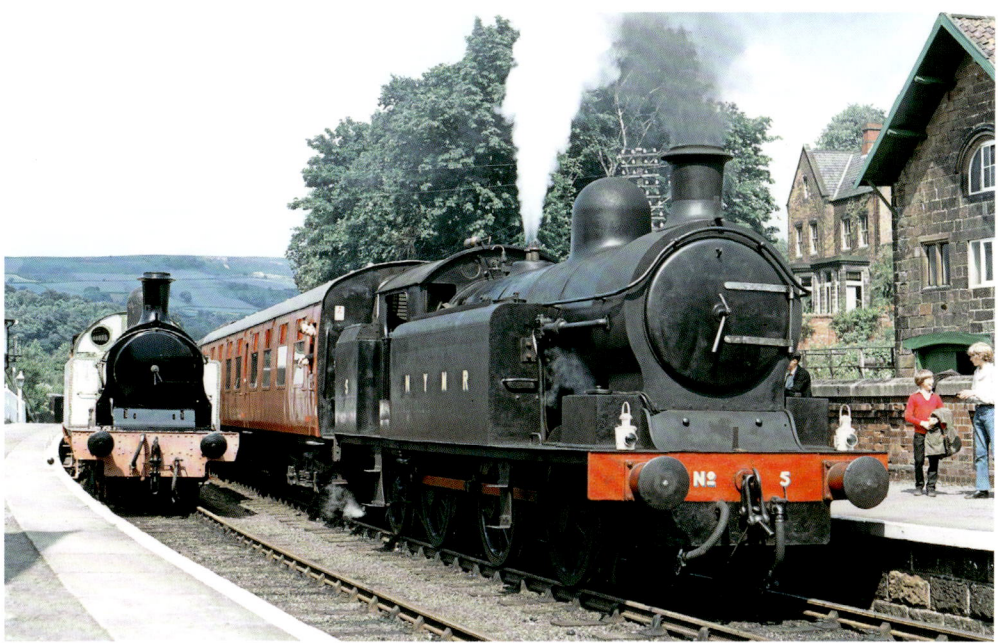

One of the early bases for preservationists in the north-east was at the National Coal Board's workshops at Philadelphia, near Washington, where this pair of Lambton tanks originally worked before arrival at the North Yorkshire Moors Railway, where we find them at Grosmont on 2 August 1971. (Aldo Delicata)

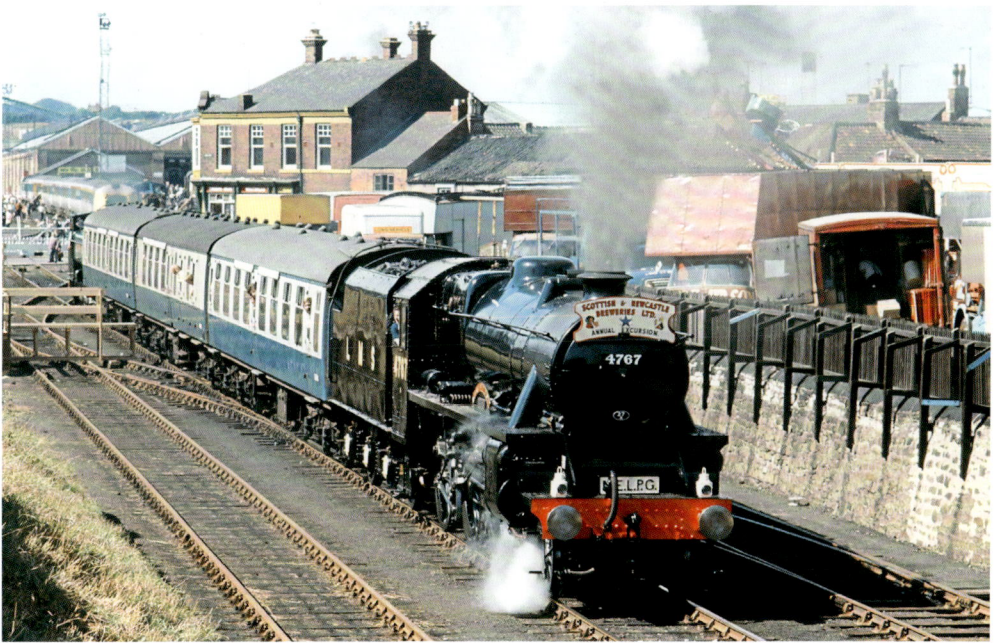

Celebrating the 150th anniversary of the birth of railways in 1975 a cavalcade was arranged for the public at Shildon, based on what was then one of the largest railway-wagon works in the whole of Europe. Various shuttles were run for the benefit of visitors, including this top-and-tail pairing of Black Five No. 4767 and Pannier Tank No. 7752 at the rear on 26 August 1975. (Aldo Delicata)

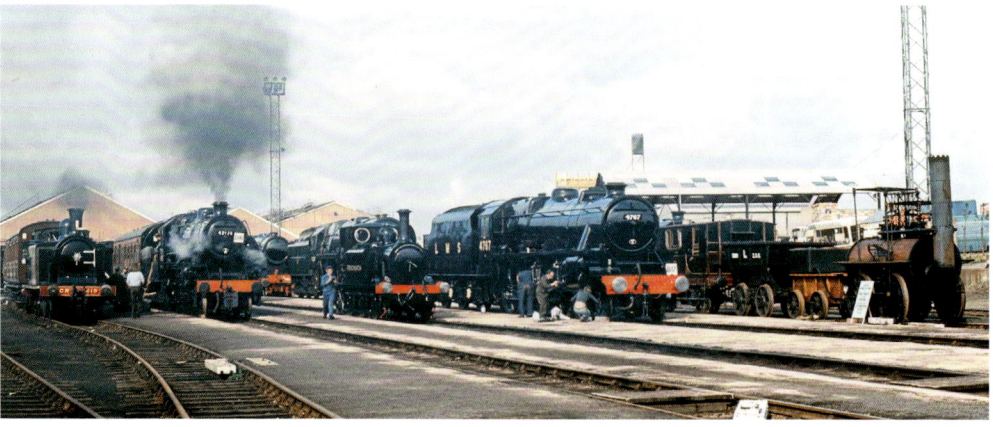

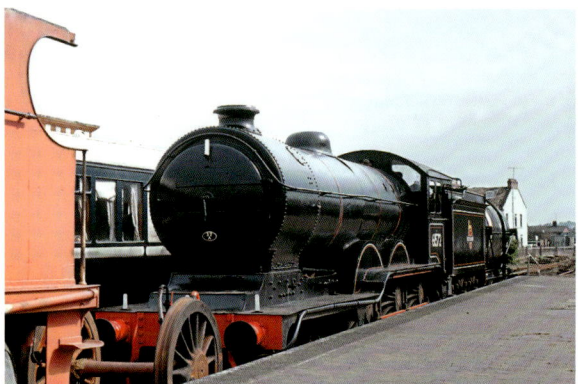

Above: Earlier the same day part of the line-up was caught on camera in the works yard, including the *Locomotion* replica. (Aldo Delicata)

Left: The sole surviving Holden Class B12 was to be found at Sheringham on 31 March 1975 although it would be a number of years before it was back in regular use. (Strathwood Library Collection)

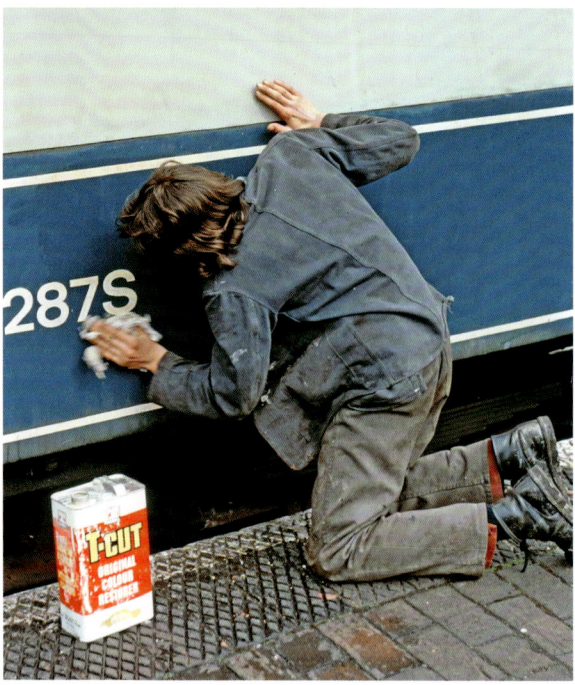

One hard-working volunteer gets stuck into restoring the paintwork on one of the ex-Brighton Belle Pullman cars the same day. The final run of this prestigious train had been on 30 April 1972, after which the sets were split up with the carriages going to various locations for storage and or further use. (Strathwood Library Collection)

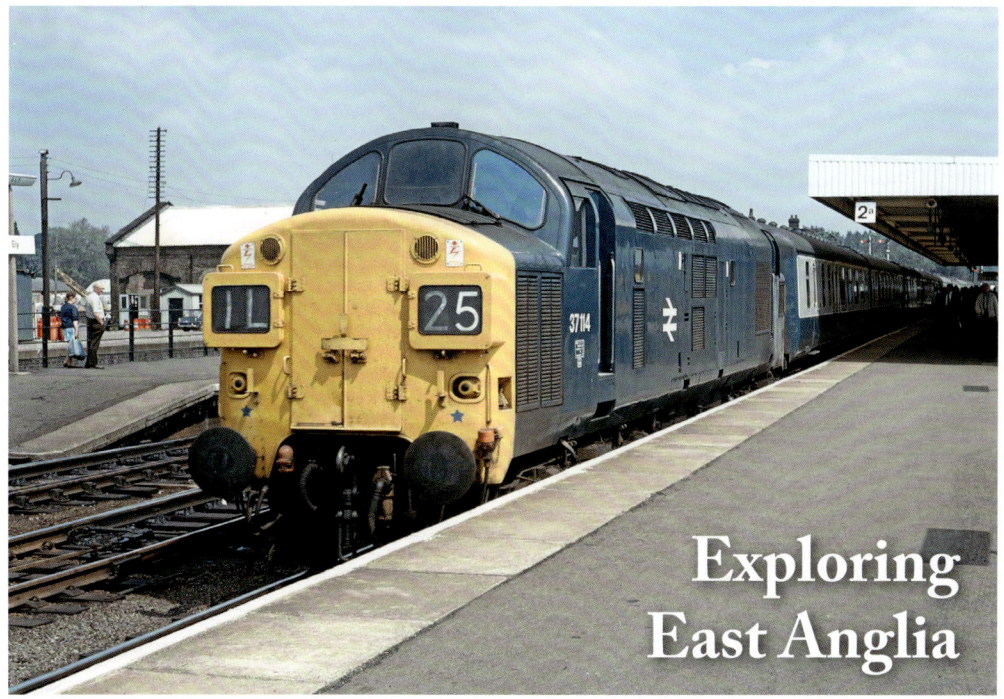

Exploring East Anglia

During the warm and pleasant early summer of 1975, Class 37 No. 37114 was caught on camera at Ely with the head-codes still in use. (Arthur Wilson)

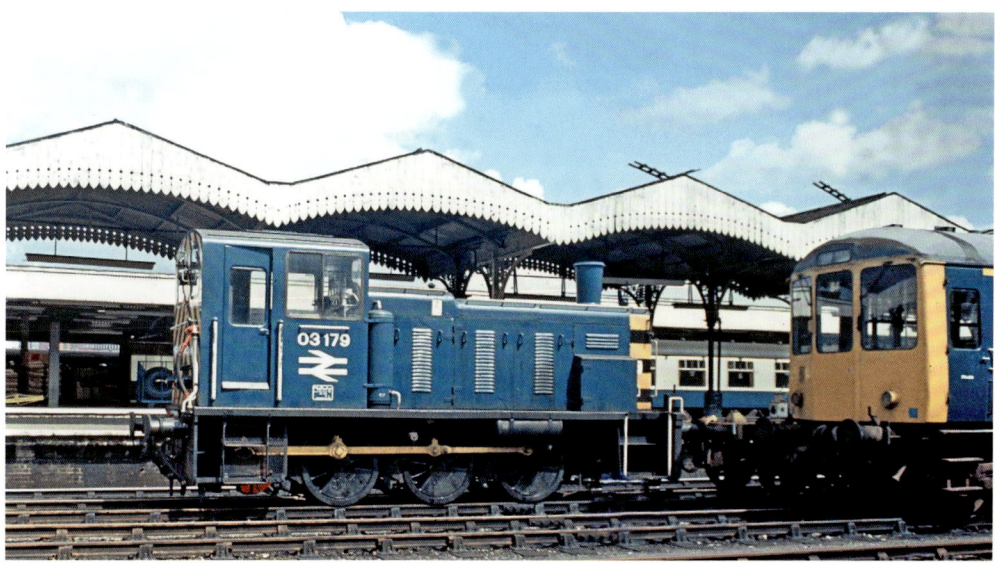

The former steam shed at Ipswich had closed officially on 5 May 1968, although it continued to be used as a stabling point. The first few years of the seventies saw it being used as a dumping ground for withdrawn British Thomson Houston-built Class 15s in great numbers as well as withdrawn DMUs, until scrapyard facilities could be found for them. Meanwhile, the small stabling point and refuelling area opposite the town's station could always be relied upon to have a few locomotives for the spotter, such as this Class 03 No. 03179 outbased from Colchester, for pilot work at the station or in the docks. (Barry Keighley)

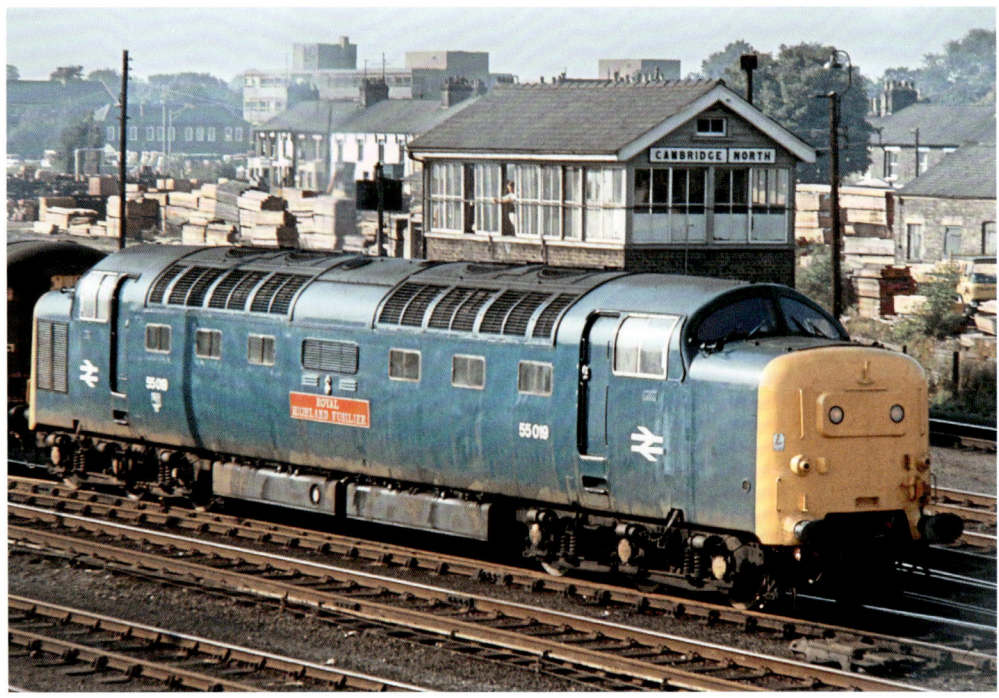

Diverted through Cambridge on 8 October 1978 was Deltic No. 55019 *Royal Highland Fusilier*. (John Harrup)

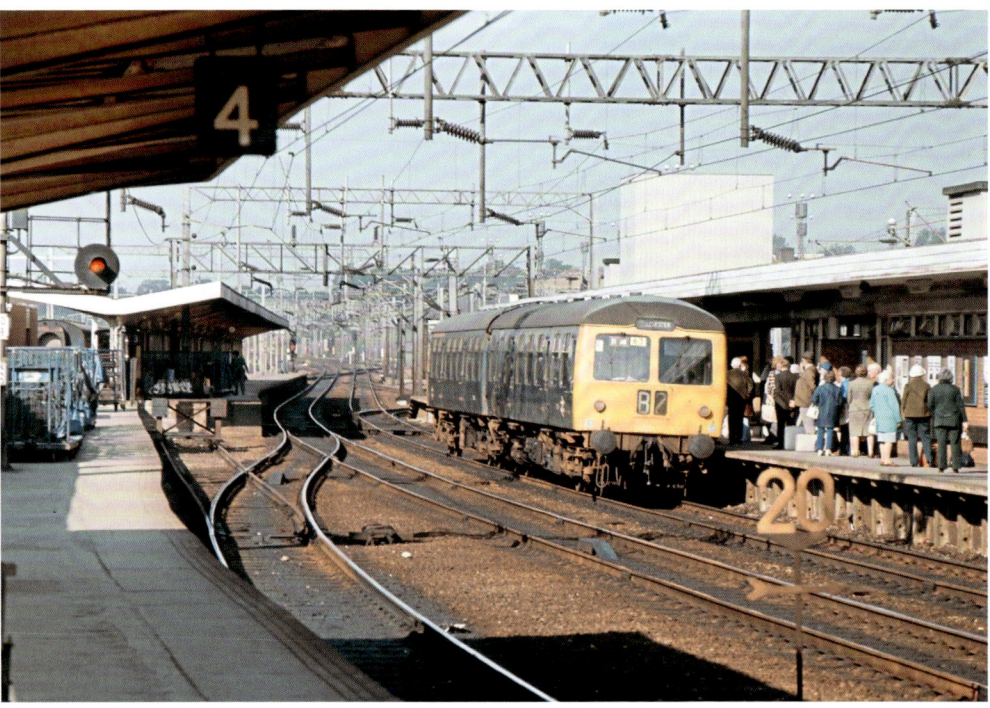

It would appear there are plenty of passengers for this two-car Cravens DMU at Colchester on 19 September 1974. (Ian James)

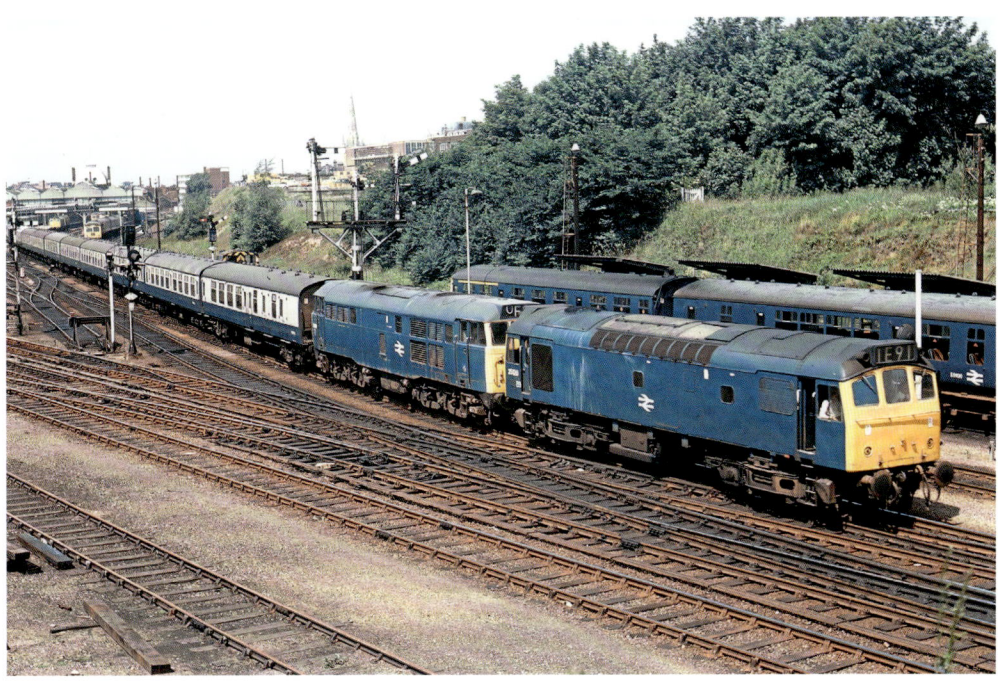

An interesting pairing for a holiday train at Norwich with Class 25 No. 25120 piloting an unknown Class 31 during June 1975. (Arthur Wilson)

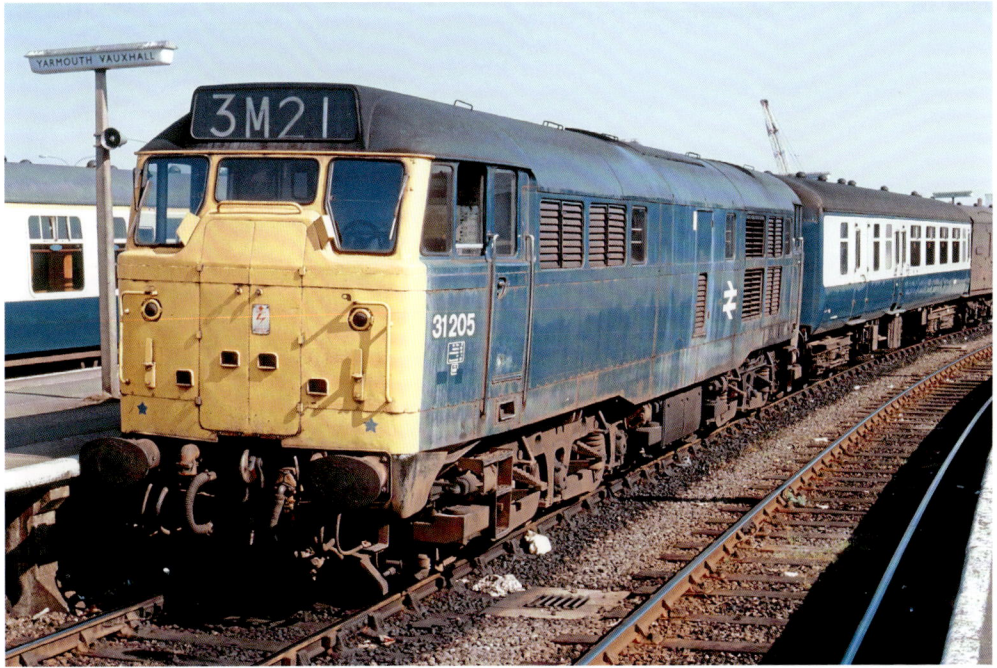

A somewhat scruffy Class 31 No. 31205 finds some useful work in the sun at Yarmouth Vauxhall the same month. This famous seaside resort once boasted two other stations, at Yarmouth South Town and Yarmouth Beach, with the former closing in 1970 and the other in 1959. (Arthur Wilson)

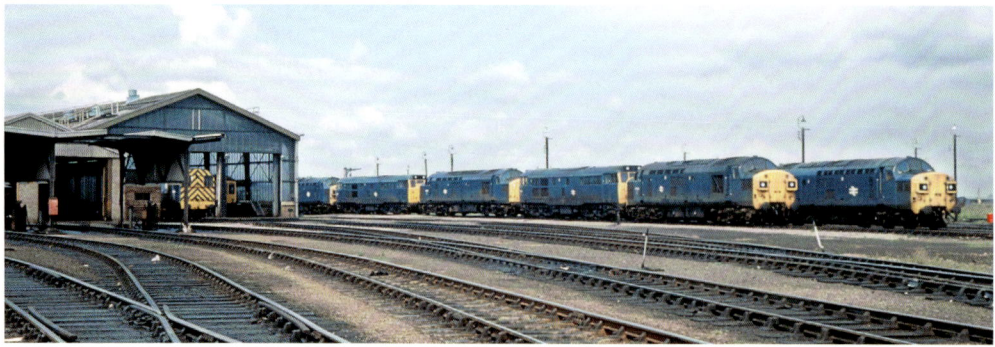

Class 37s and 31s abound as ever in the seventies at March in this 1978 view, with a Class 08 and a DMU cowering inside the shed. (Win Wall/Strathwood Library Collection)

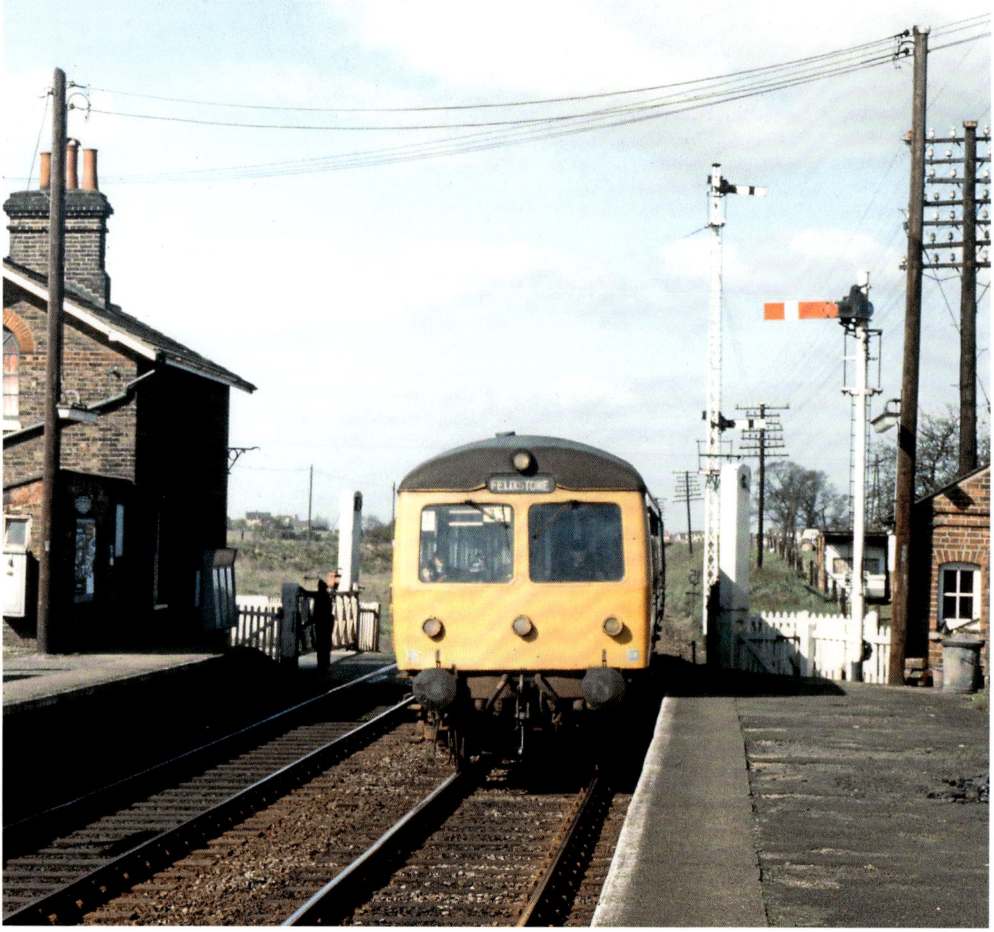

So many of the gated level crossings in East Anglia relied upon direct opening and closing by station or signal box staff, rather than remote mechanical means. The gates will be swiftly opened to road traffic once again after the passage of this Cravens DMU at Westerfield on 16 April 1974. For those not familiar with this sleepy location, it is the first station out from Ipswich on the Lowestoft line, just before the Felixstowe branch turns back south. (John Dawson)

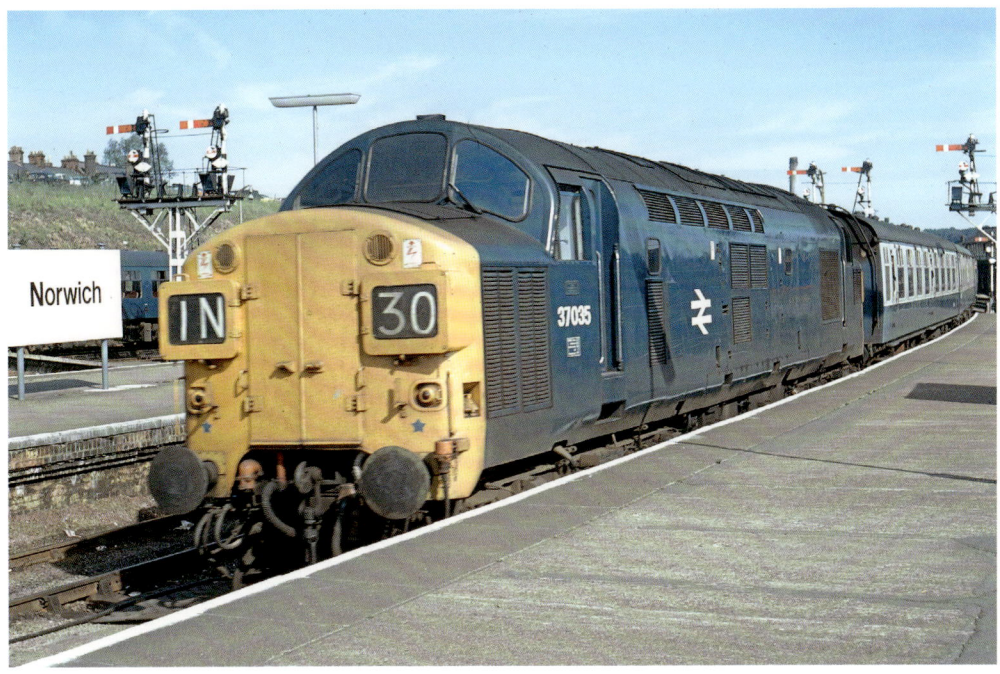

Long before the trend of plating over head-codes and gangway doors, which Class 37 No. 37035 would eventually submit to, this locomotive was photographed arriving at Norwich in June 1975. (Arthur Wilson)

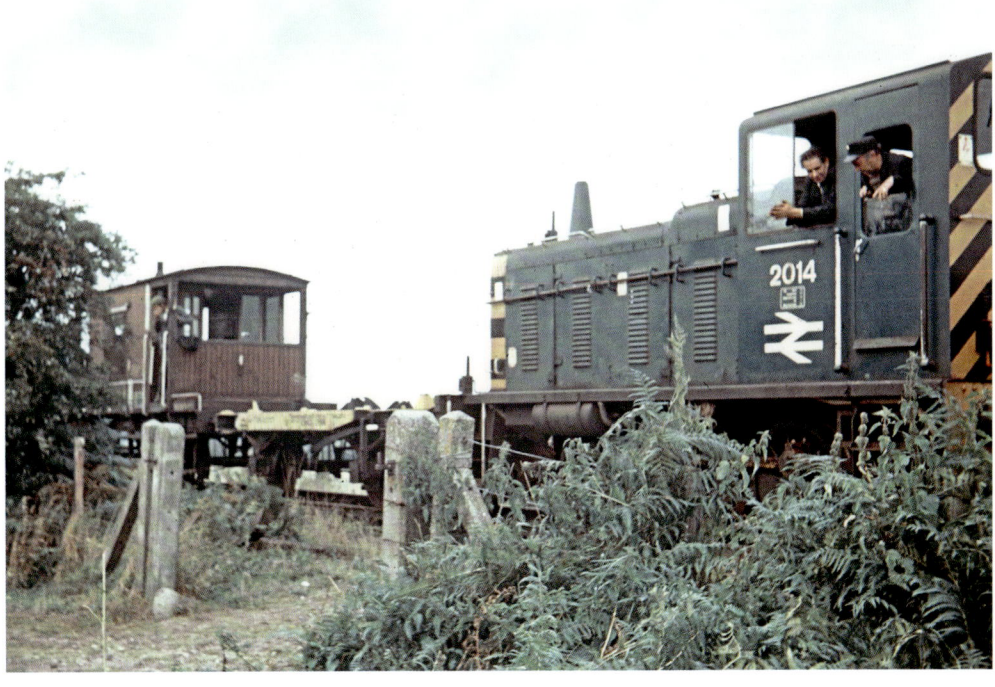

The train crew on board Class 03 No. 2014 appear very relaxed about their working of a track-lifting train at Hellesdon on the old M&GNR route from Norwich City, which last saw passenger services in 1959. (Ken Nash)

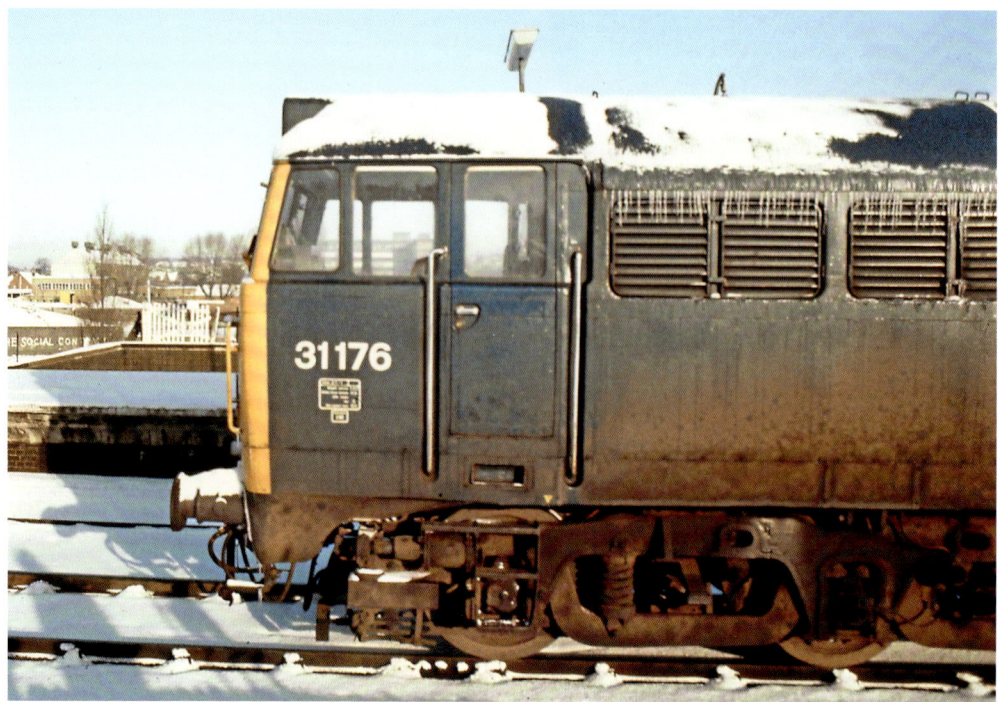

The snow and sun on New Year's Day 1979 tempted our cameraman out from the warm, to record what must have been a limited timetable of services at Ipswich, where Class 31 No. 31176 carries icicles along its flanks. (Martyn Hunt)

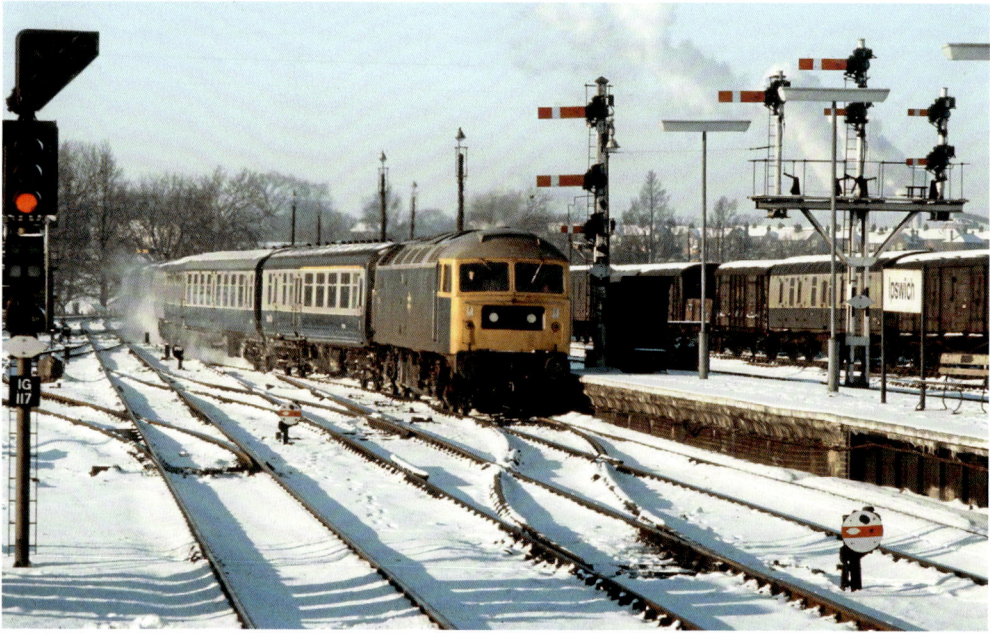

We are rewarded with this view of Class 47 No. 47118 arriving with an Up passenger the same morning. (Martyn Hunt)

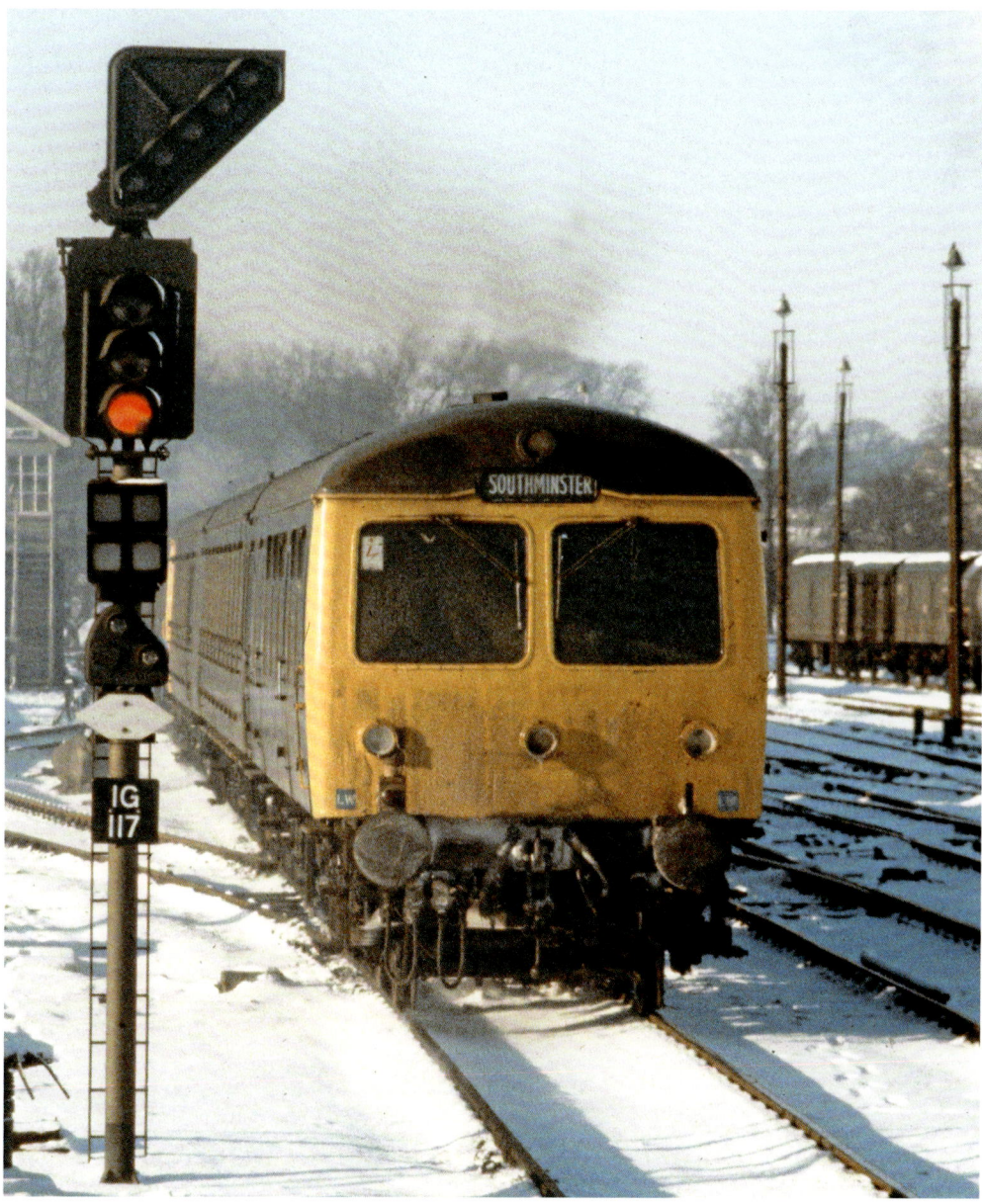

A Cravens car leads this set, labelled for Southminster, at Ipswich 1 January 1979. Packing people into the cinemas that winter was *Superman*, with a star-studded cast that brought Christopher Reeve to the attention of the British public for the first time. (Martyn Hunt)

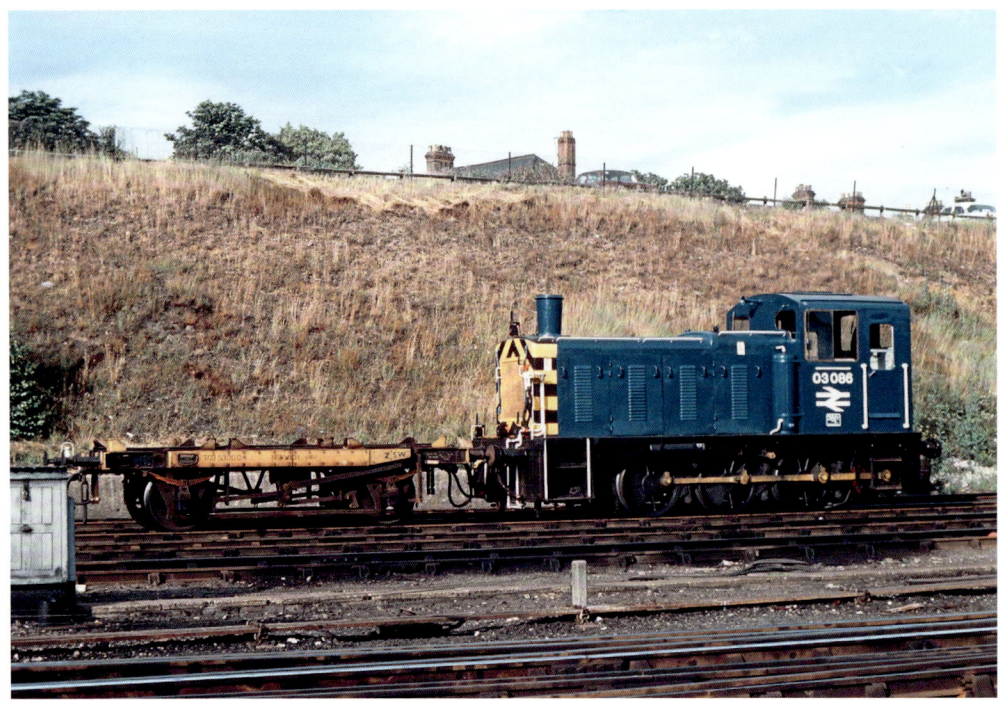

Coupled to the almost-regulation match truck to help trip track circuits, Class 03 No. 03086 cannot be long out of works when found at Norwich Thorpe on 23 July 1977. (Frank Hornby)

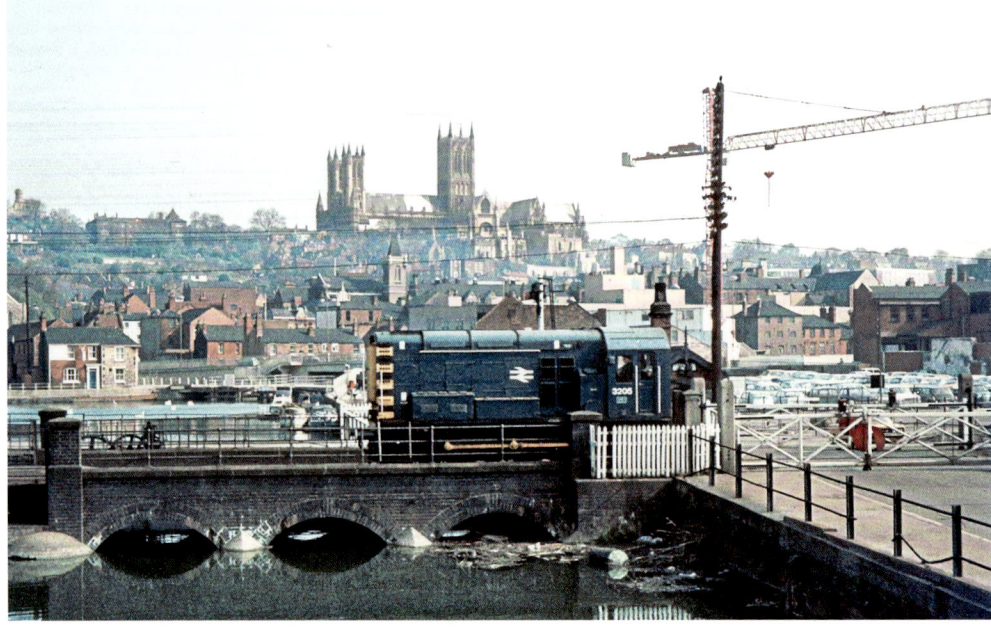

Progress for any movement of trains through Lincoln was always punctuated by negotiating a series of level crossings around the city, where we find Class 08 No. 3205 making a light-engine movement on 25 April 1973. (Strathwood Library Collection)

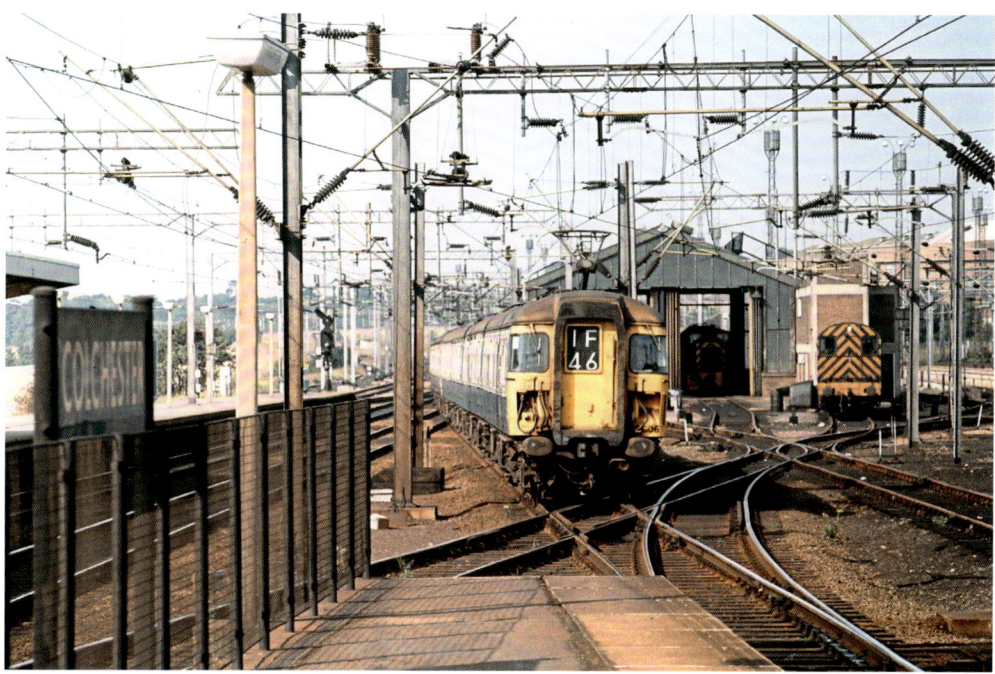

One of the distinctive Clacton sets draws past the diesel depot into Colchester on 20 September 1974. This modernised maintenance building replaced the old steam shed, which closed on 2 November 1959. (Ian James)

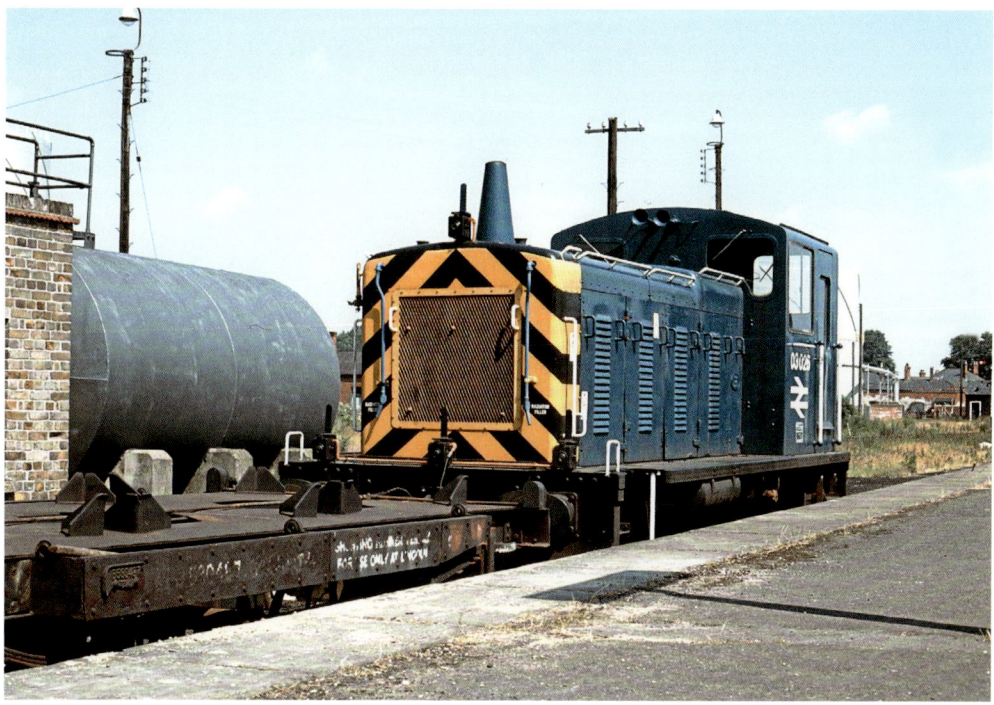

The match truck coupled to Class 03 No. 03026 at Boston in June 1975 appears to be one of the now-redundant Conflat wagons. (Arthur Wilson)

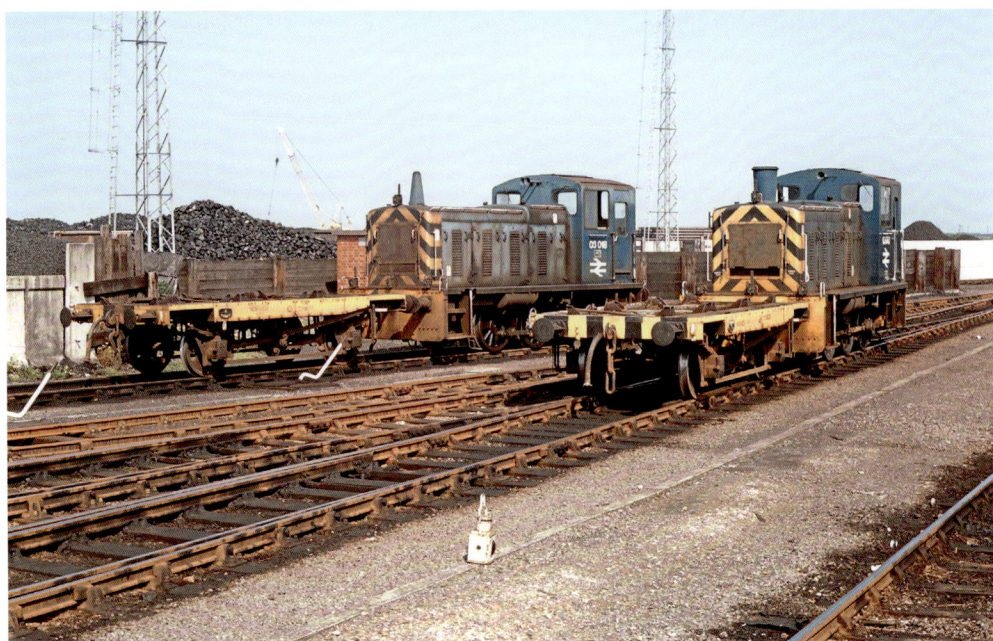

This pair of Class 03s at Norwich in 1975 have yellow-painted running trucks to aid visibility. It also gives us the chance to compare the two styles of exhaust-cowling fitted to the class. The earlier cone gave way to a cast traditional style of flowerpot mock chimney. This modification also helped a little with adhesion at the front of the locomotive. (Arthur Wilson)

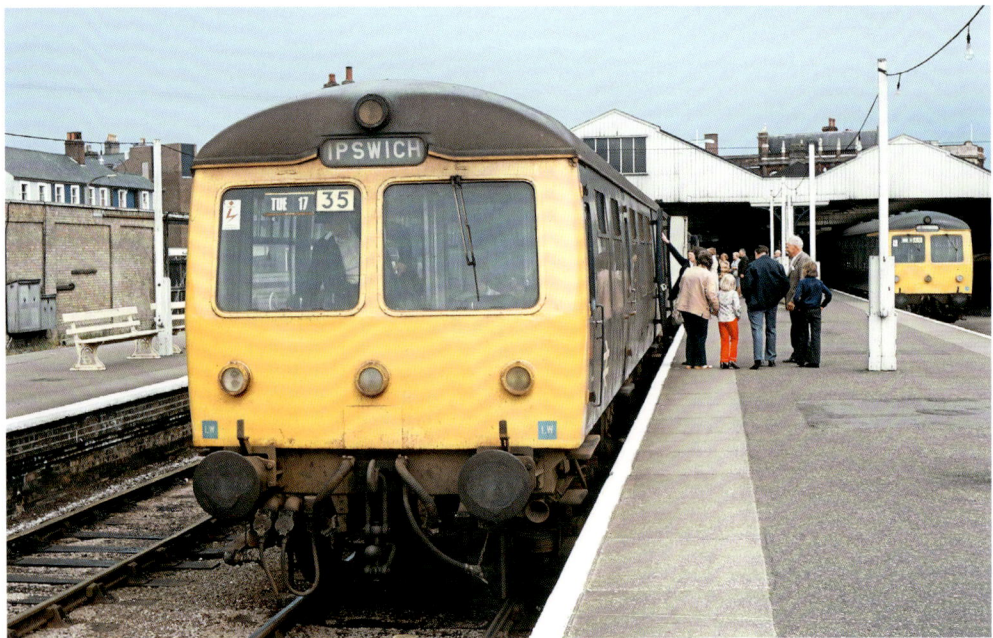

The summer of 1975 saw Cravens DMU sets dominating the local services at Lowestoft Central. The town's other station, Lowestoft North, fell with a number of closures around the Eastern Region in 1970. (Arthur Wilson)

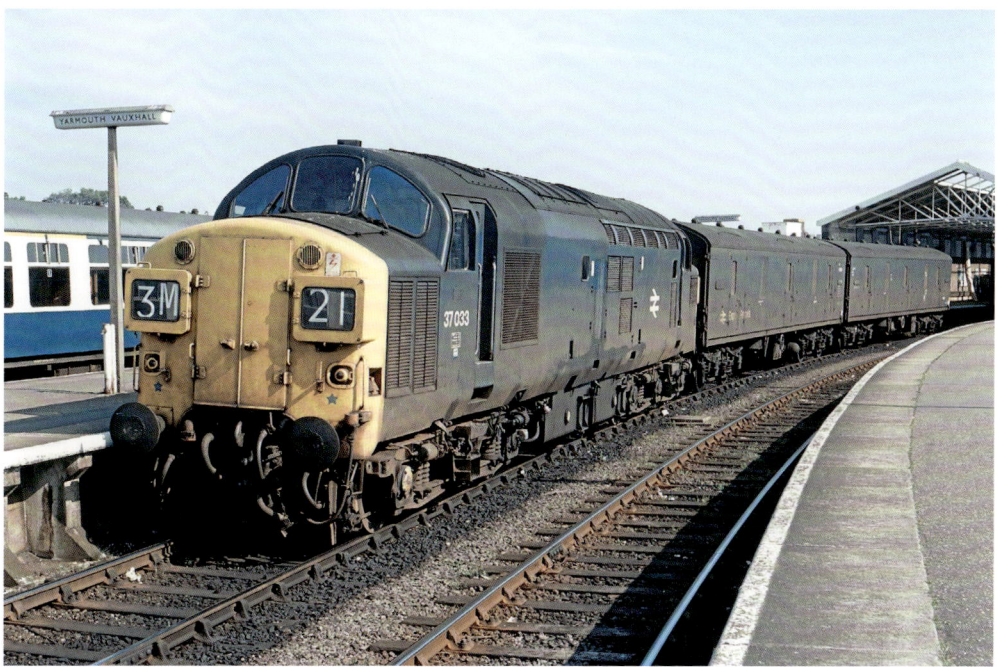

Touring East Anglia in the summer of 1975, our cameraman watched Class 37 No. 37033 shunting a couple of GUVs around Yarmouth Vauxhall. (Arthur Wilson)

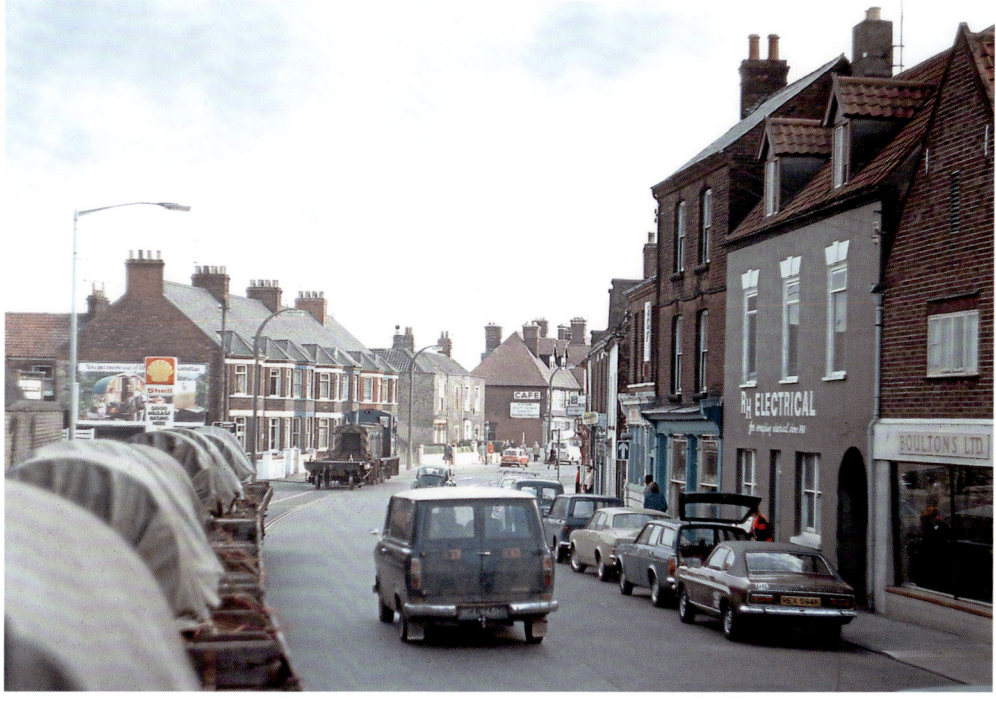

A fascinating street scene along the Yarmouth Quay tramway on 21 May 1974, with a Class 03 shunting its train, while road traffic carries on regardless. (Strathwood Library Collection)

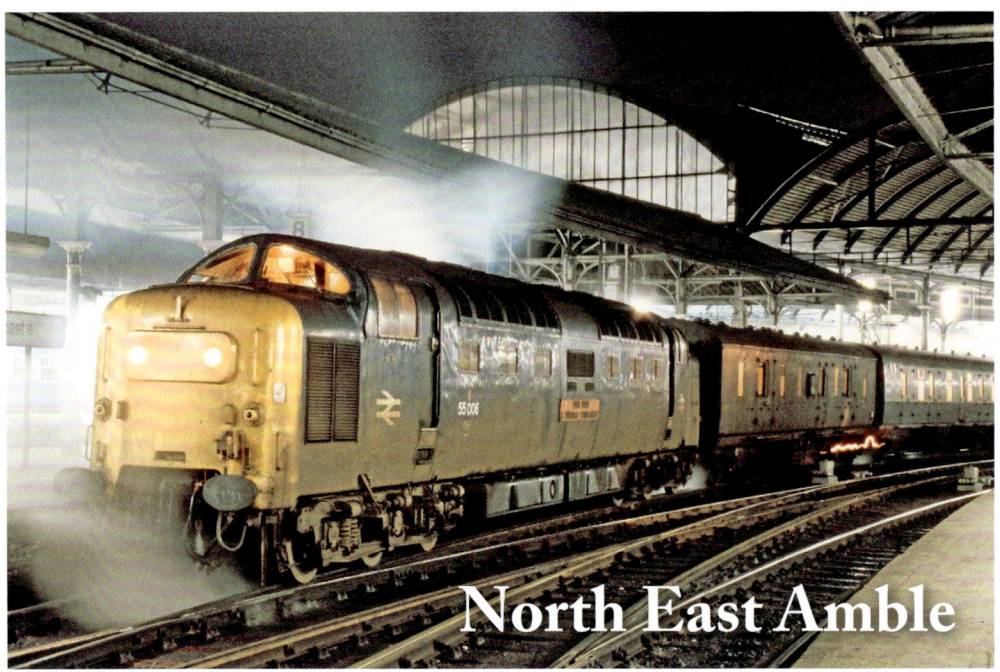

North East Amble

A few days before Christmas and the steam heat is working well from Deltic No. 55006 *The Fife and Forfar Yeomanry* which will take the 20.30 Newcastle–King's Cross on Friday 21 December 1979. (Colin Whitbread)

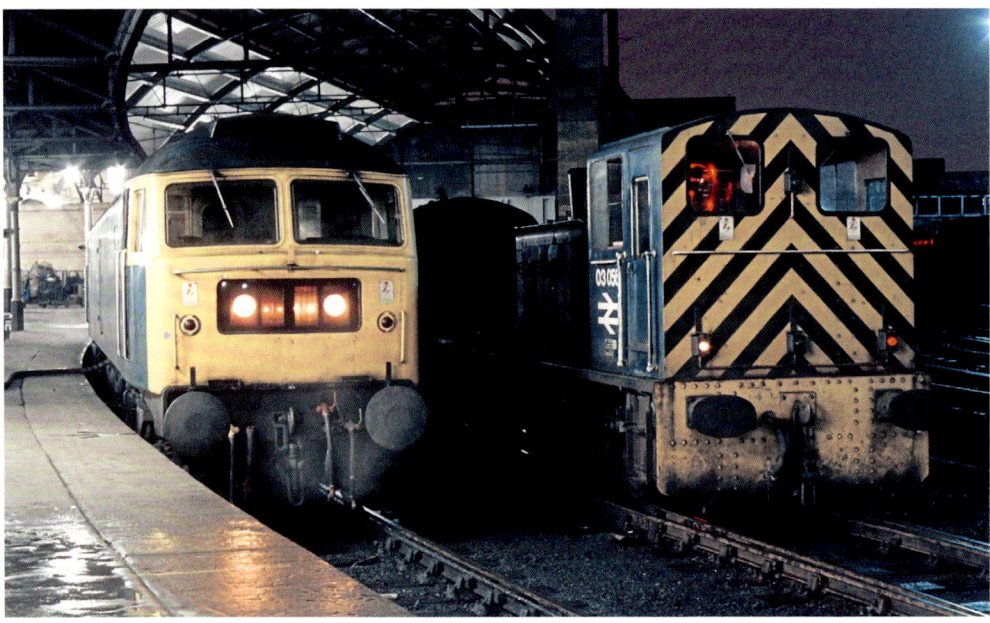

Having taken over from Class J72s in the early 1960s, the Class 03s and Class 04s became the station pilots at Newcastle Central. The Drewry-built Class 04s slipped away at the beginning of the seventies, leaving the Class 03s in sole charge, often with at least three to be found on duty around the station. On this evening No. 03056 is pictured alongside Class 47 No. 47038 pausing with the 19.25 Aberdeen–King's Cross on 20 December 1979. (Colin Whitbread)

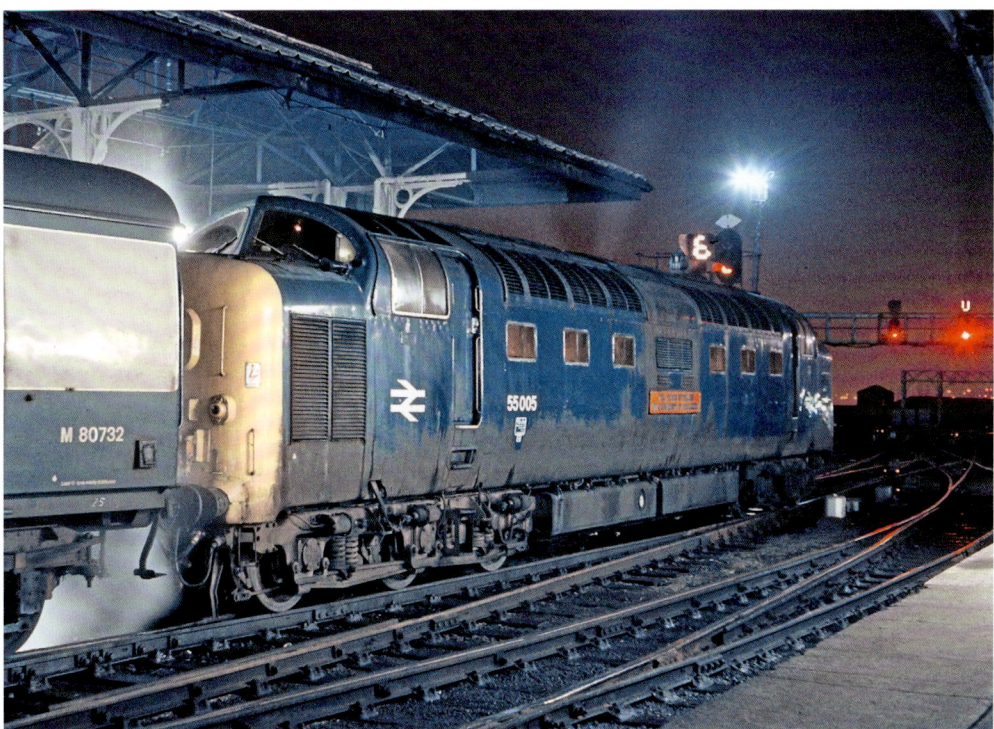

Ready for the off from Newcastle Central is Deltic No. 55005 *The Prince of Wales's Own Regiment of Yorkshire* on 25 May 1979. (Sid Steadman)

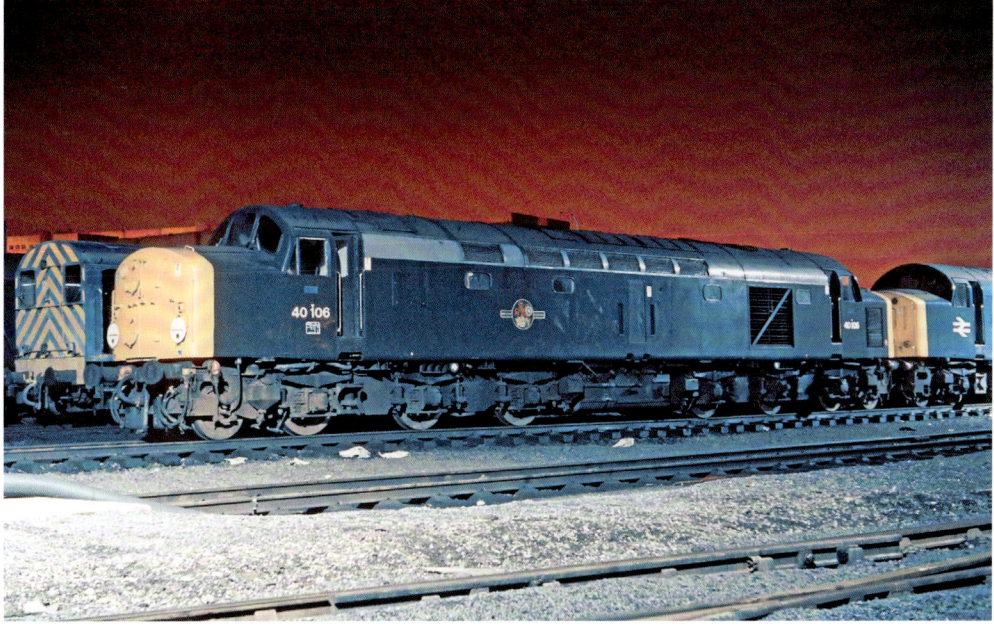

Caught on shed at Gateshead that same evening was the celebrity green Class 40 No. 40106 which appealed to our cameraman, armed with his tripod, against the glow of the city lights in the background. (Sid Steadman)

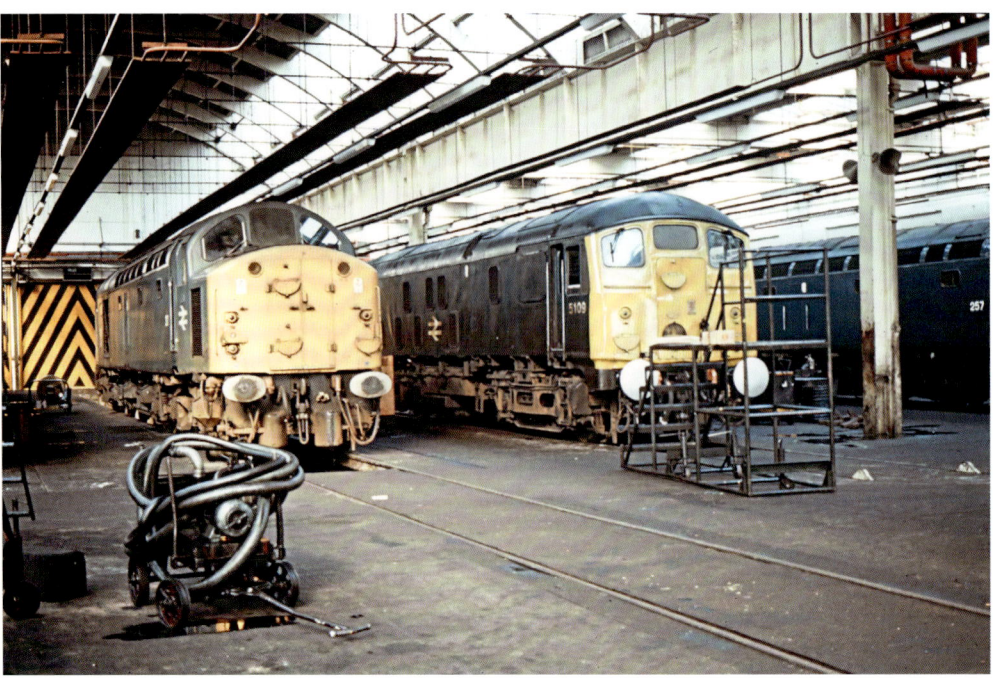

Sheltering inside Gateshead with a pair of Class 40s on 20 May 1972 was Class 24 D5109. These Sulzer-engined locomotives were specially equipped for working the Tyne Dock–Consett iron-ore trains, and could be found doing filling-in turns on coal workings around the north-east. (Frank Hornby)

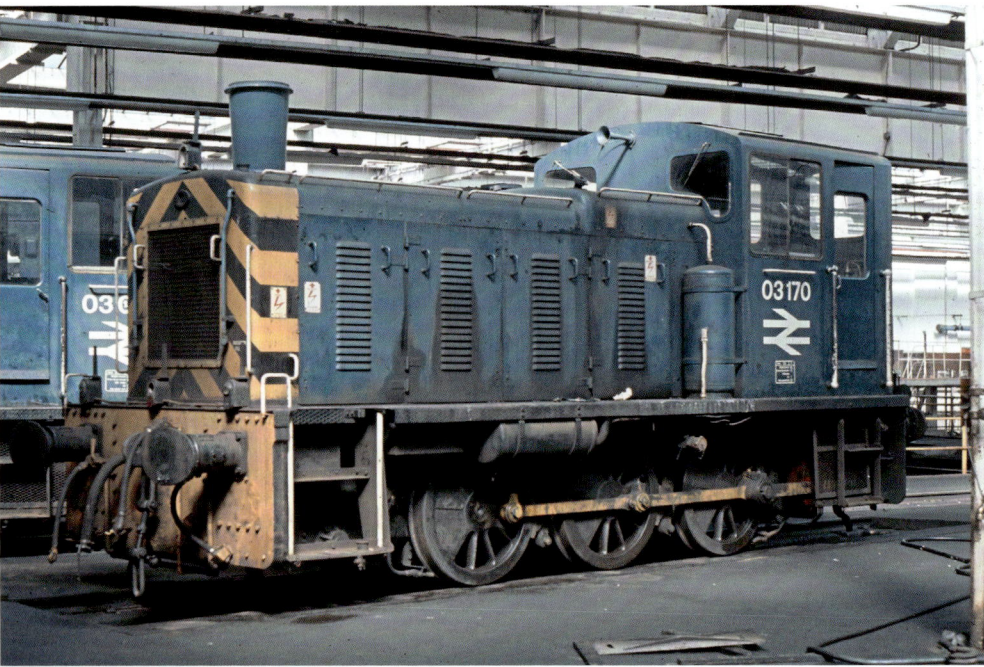

Inside the depot during this visit on 3 September 1977 were a pair of Class 03s. This example, No. 03170, spent all of the decade based here, engaged in shunting and local trip duties. (Aldo Delicata)

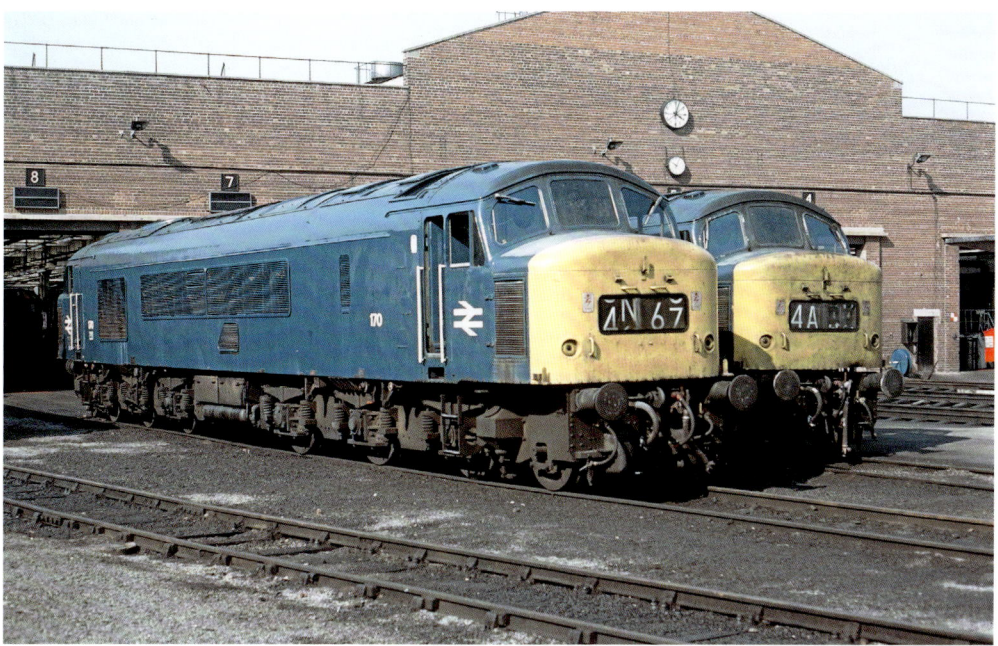

Many Peaks were sent to work from 52A Gateshead from new. Among those early allocations was D170, arriving in June 1962 from Derby Works. Aside from a two-month spell on loan to Edinburgh Haymarket in 1970, this Class 46 spent its entire career based at the Newcastle shed, where we see it alongside a classmate in June 1973. (Ian King)

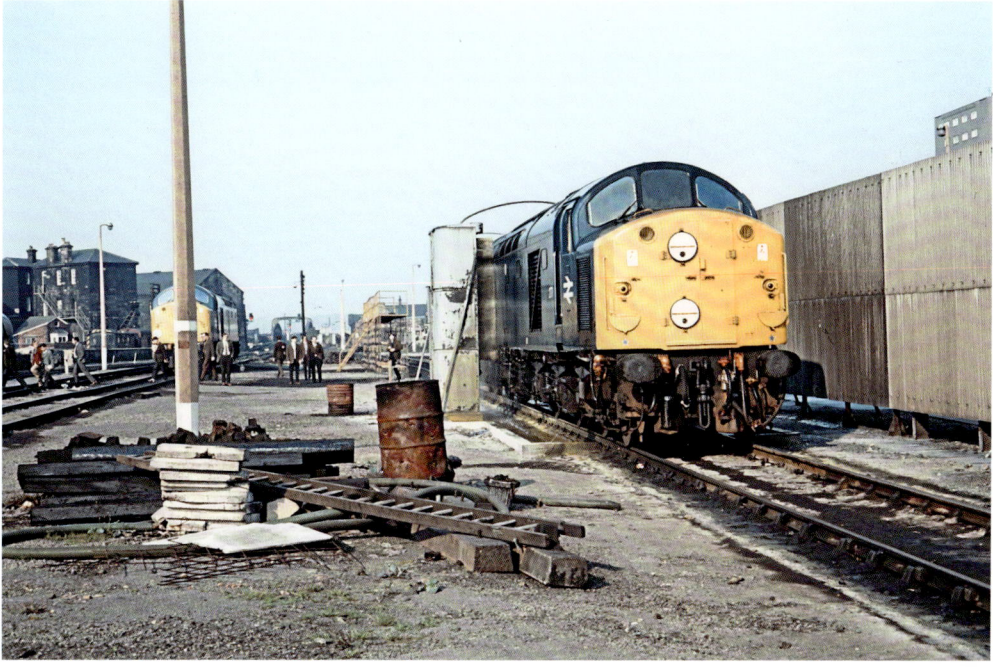

Throughout the sixties and seventies Gateshead also enjoyed a healthy allocation of Class 40s, and often hosted visitors such as No. 277 from 55B York on 20 May 1972 (Frank Hornby)

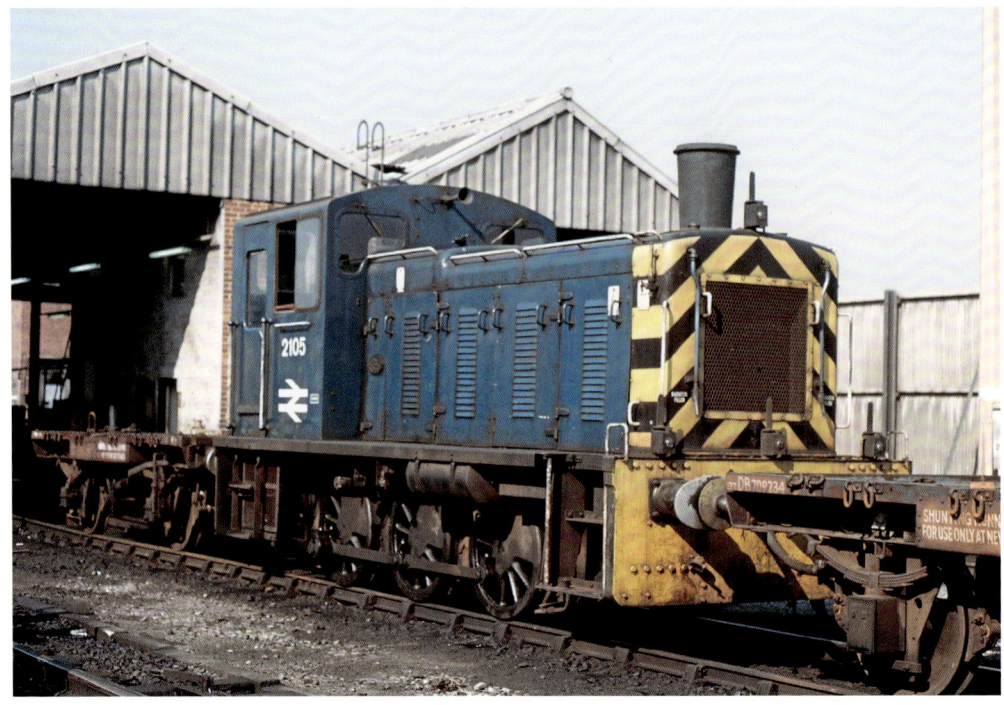

This Gateshead Class 03 was penned in by match trucks in September 1973. As for No. 2105, it would be withdrawn from here on 16 February 1976, and cut up by Cohens of Kettering by that September. (Ian King)

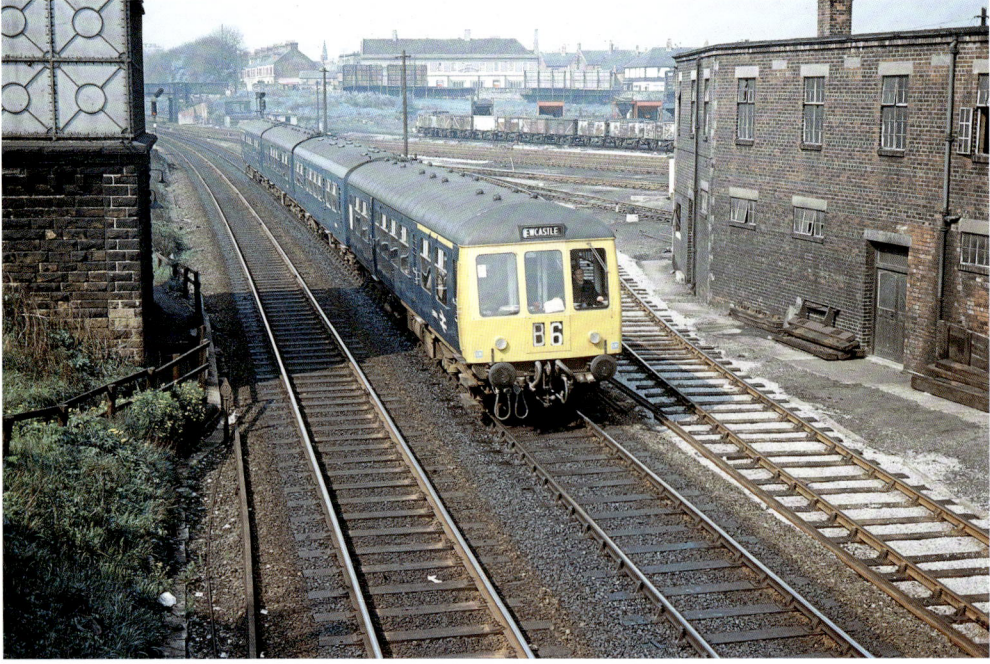

One of the Derby-built three-car DMU sets is augmented by a Metropolitan Cammell trailer past the old steam sheds at Heaton on 20 May 1972. (Frank Hornby)

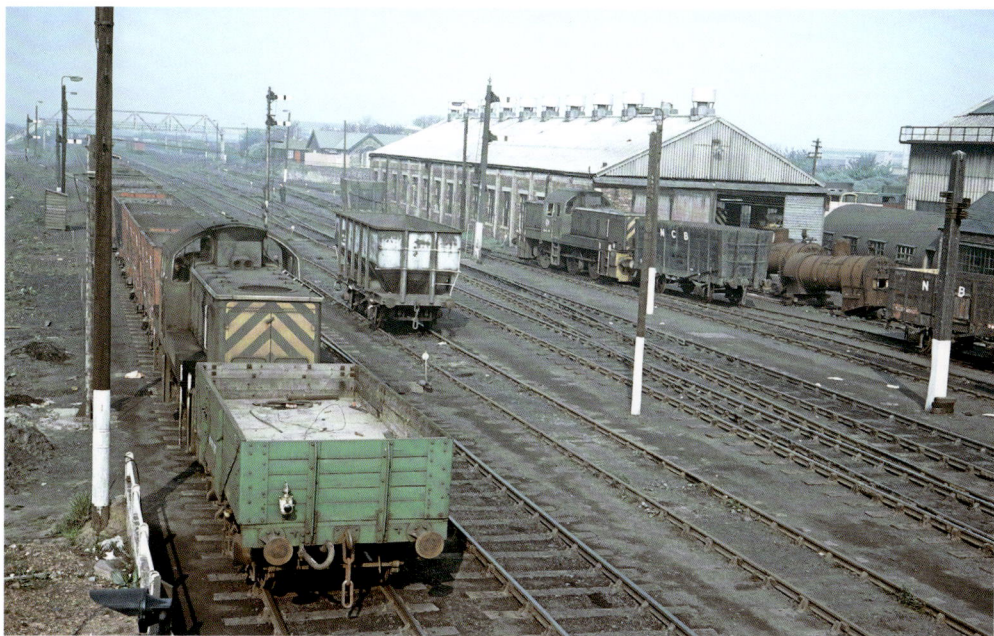

Continuing north the same day to Ashington and the once-vast complex of lines and collieries centred around the workshops here. Two of the bargain-buy ex-British Rail Class 14s are in the yard with D9527 now numbered as NCB 9312/99. Both retained their original liveries at this time. (Frank Hornby)

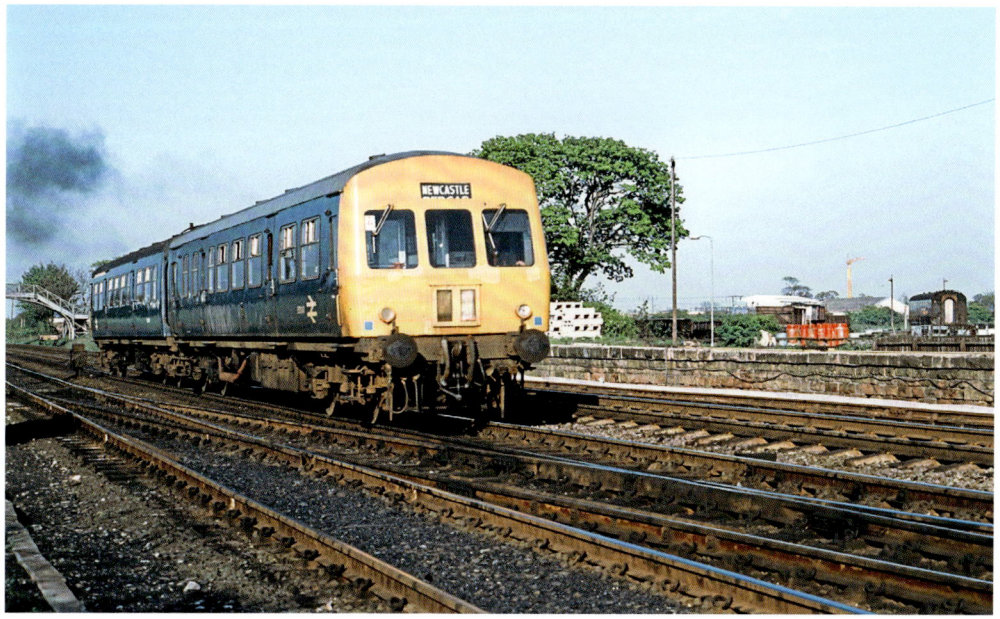

A two-car DMU set accelerates away from Morpeth towards Newcastle with a local service during 1975. The curve through Morpeth has what is reputed to be the most severe curve on any railway main line in Britain. The track turns almost 90° from a northerly to an easterly direction immediately south of the station on an otherwise fast section of the East Coast Main Line. This was a major factor in three serious derailments between 1969 and 1994 in spite of a permanent speed restriction of 50 mph. (Strathwood Library Collection)

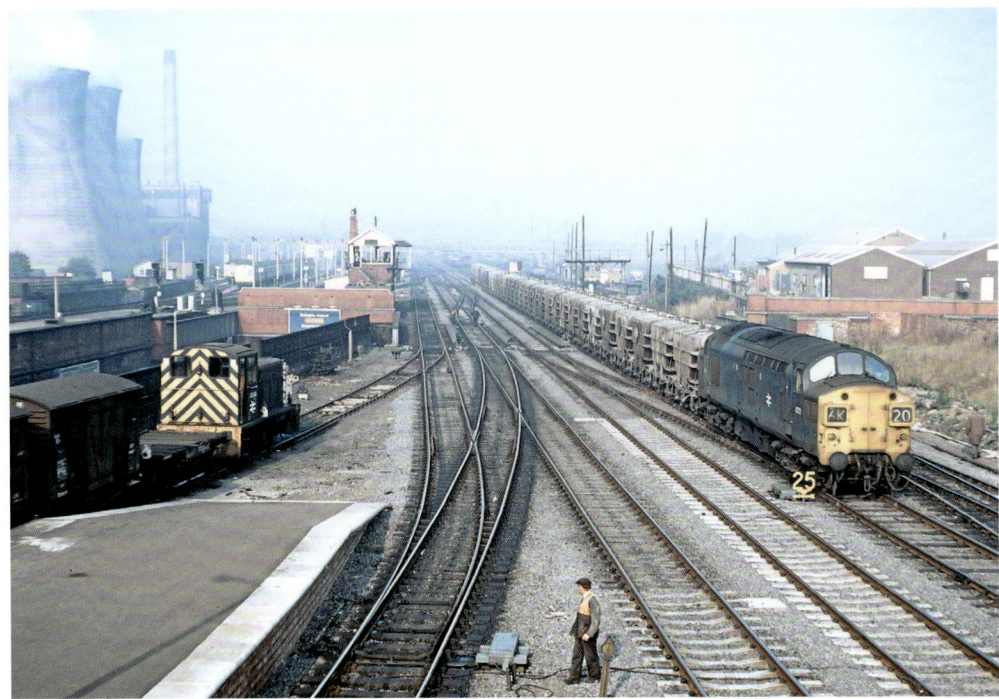

A 25-mph speed restriction can be seen on the crossover at Darlington as No. 6721 passes with a cement working and the once-everyday Class 03 pilot goes about its duties in October 1972. (Arthur Wilson)

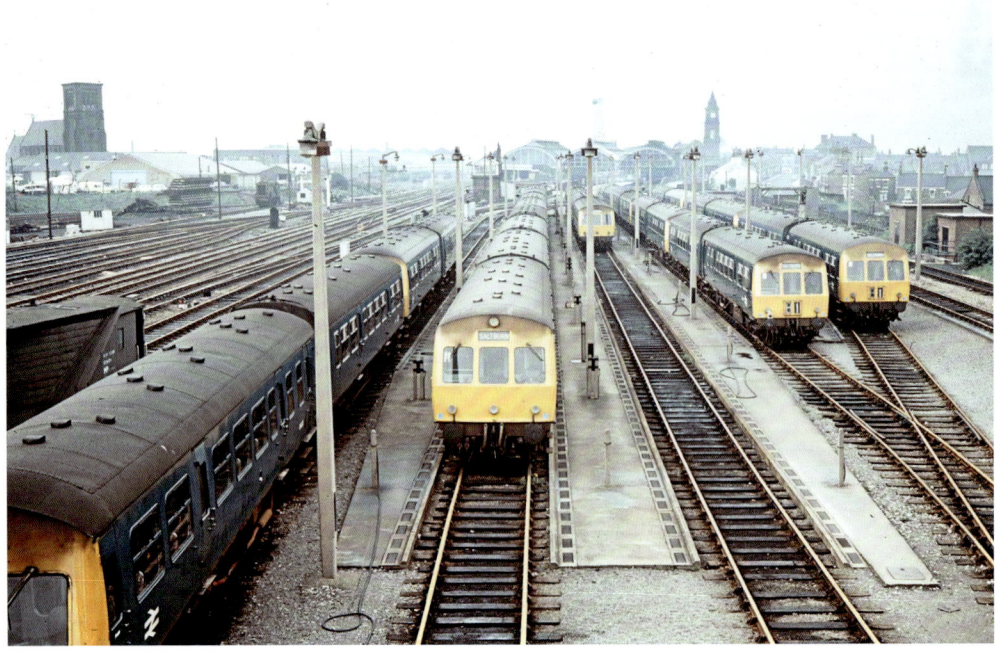

An old North Eastern Railway wooden snow plough can be seen amongst the resting DMUs at Darlington on 21 May 1972. (Frank Hornby).

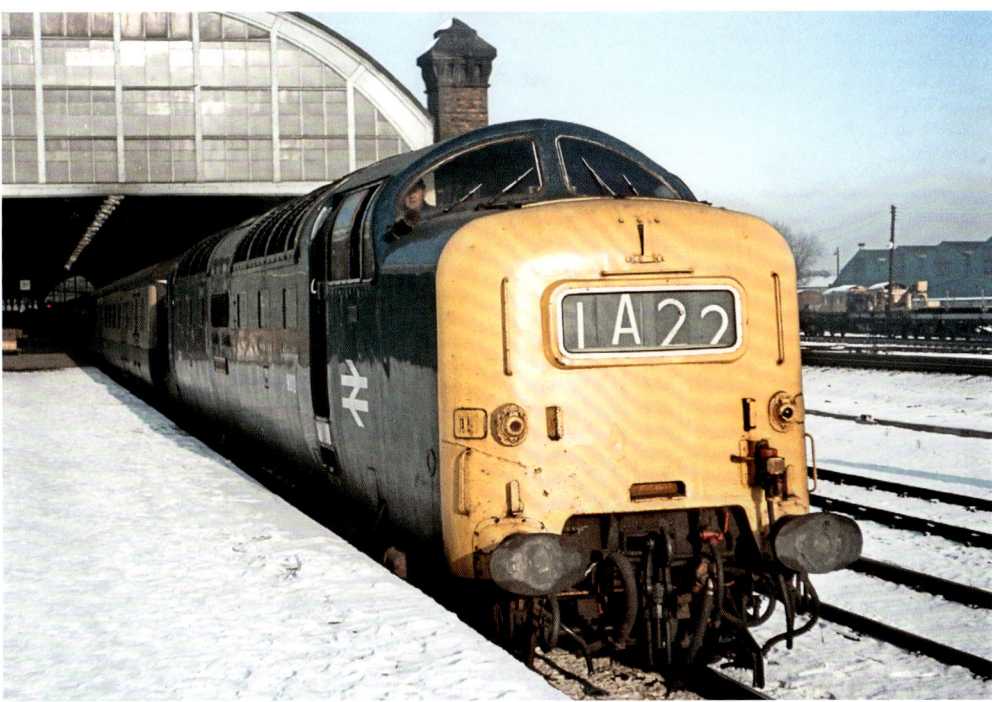

A light fall of snow and the bright sunshine will make spotting signals a little more difficult for the driver of Deltic No. 9012 *Crepello* after the Darlington stop in the winter of 1972. (Don Brooks/Richard Derry Collection)

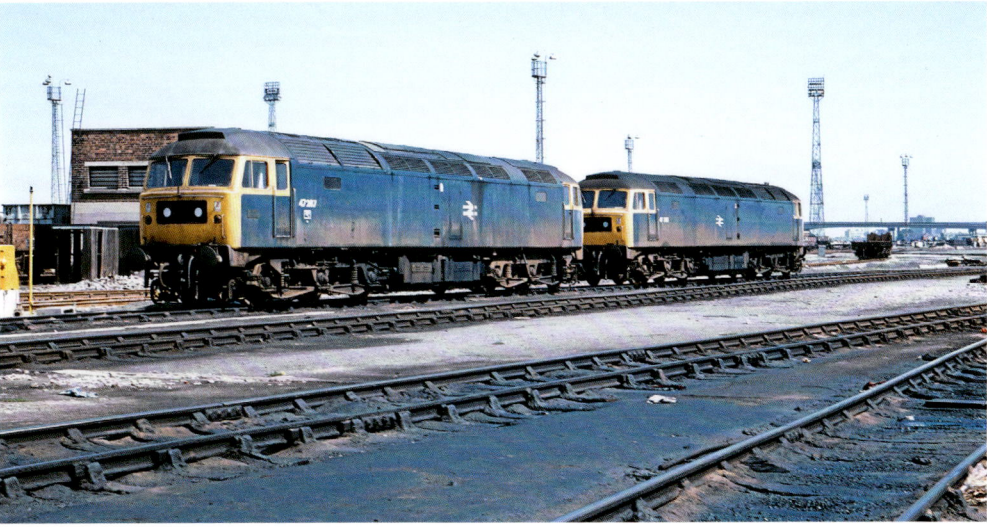

Sharing the open yard at Thornaby with a classmate is No. 47287 in June 1979. The concrete roundhouse here was modernised with steam in mind in 1958 and allowed the closure of more archaic nearby sheds at Stockton, Newport and Middlesborough, concentrating activity on the newly developed freight yards here. Coded 51L, the depot closed officially to steam in November 1964, although steam locomotives were still working into Thornaby from time to time almost to the end in 1967. Along with all of the other active depots and stabling points, Thornaby took on a new alpha-only code in May 1973, which became TE, until final closure in 2007. (A J Halliwell)

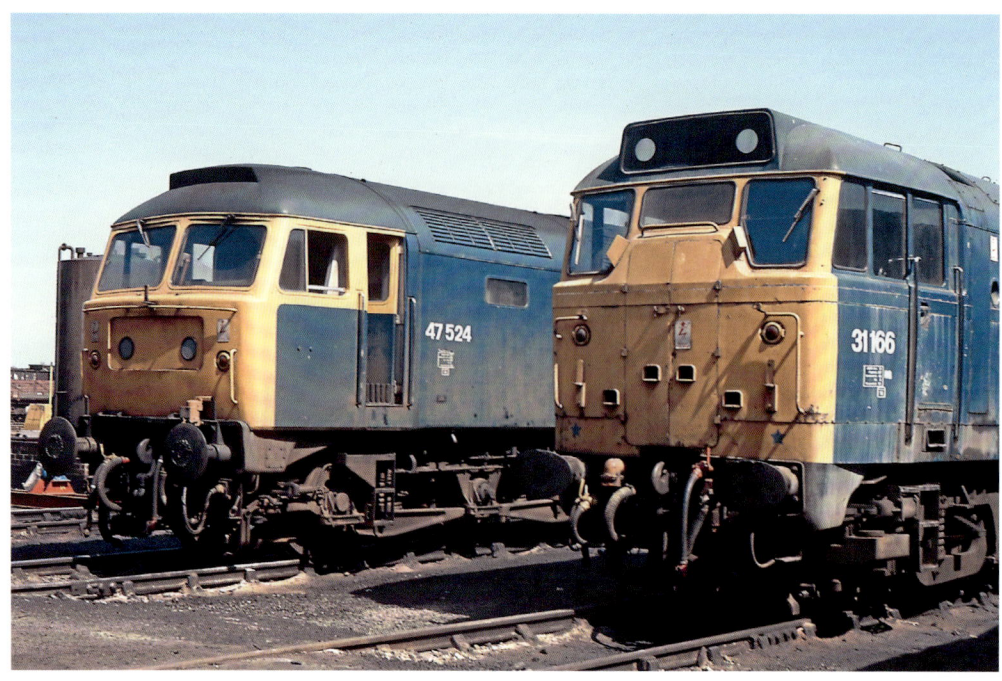

Another Class 47 No. 47524 rests in the sun alongside Class 31 No. 31166 in Tees yard Thornaby during the summer of 1979. (A J Halliwell)

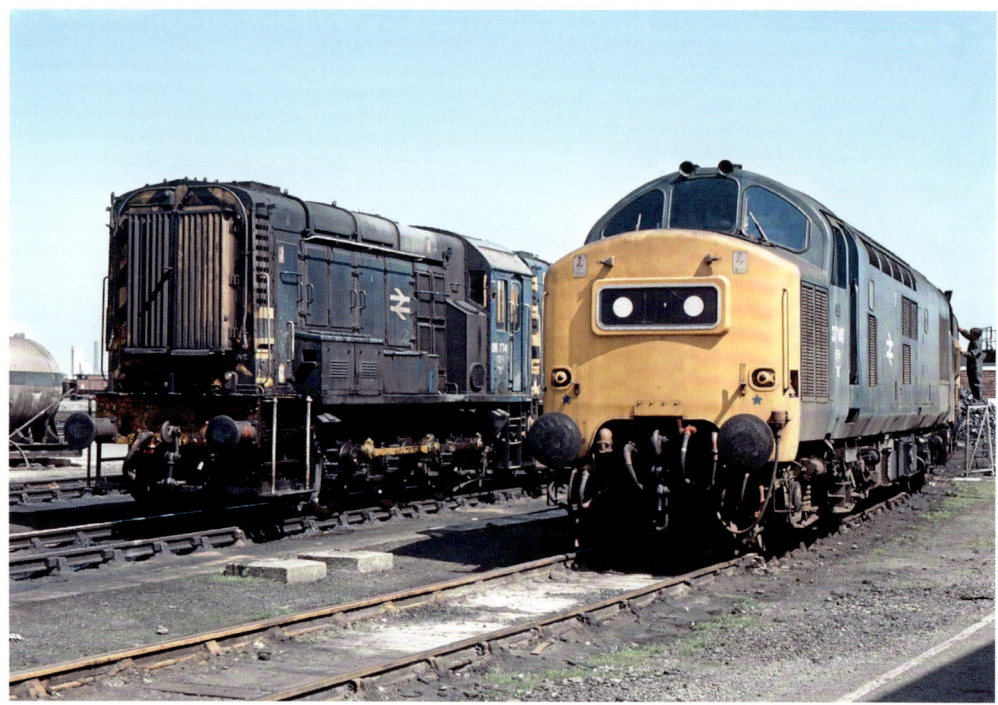

A chance to carry out some light maintenance to Class 37 No. 37141 outside in the yard at Thornaby again in June 1979. (A J Halliwell)

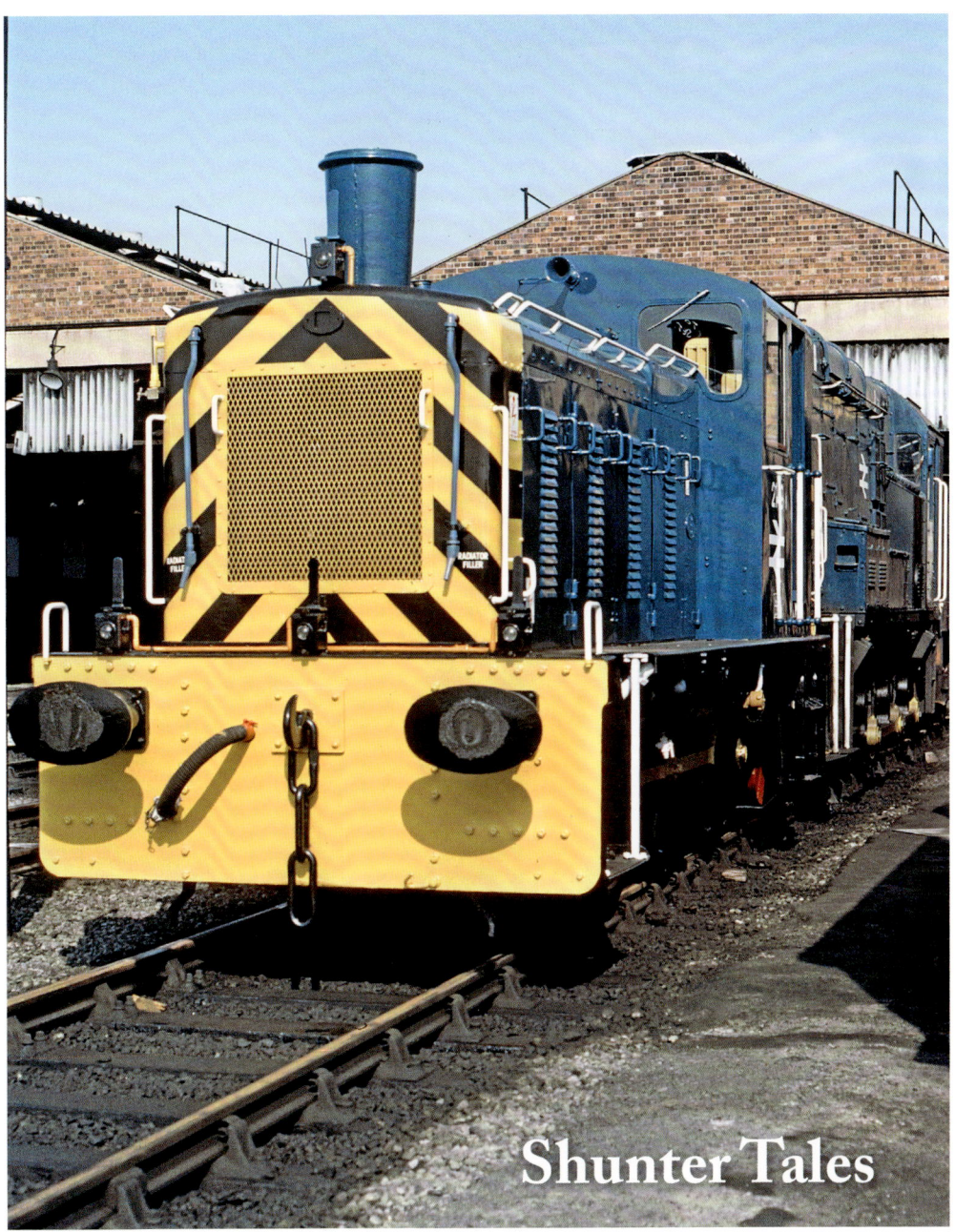

Shunter Tales

Fresh from the works at Doncaster in early 1974 was No. 2149. Renumbering to become 03149 would take place a month or two later in April. Withdrawn from operating stock on 28 November 1982, it came back to Doncaster to be cut up. However, classmate D2148, which had been withdrawn in 1972 and sold to the NCB, had been involved in an accident and needed a new cab. Hey presto and No. 03149 yielded its cab to keep D2148 in operation. (Ian King)

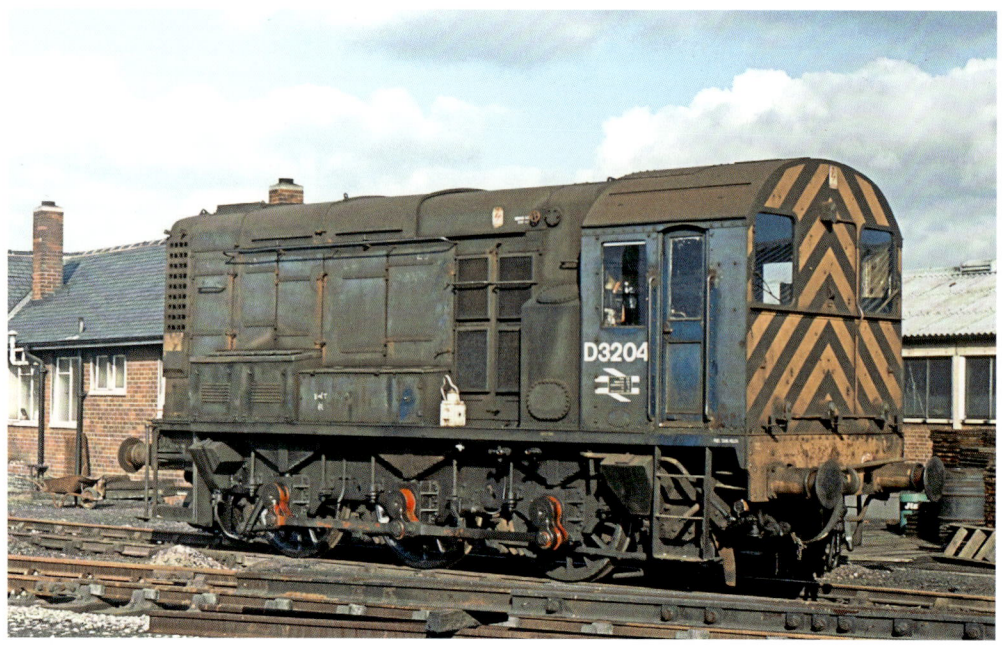

Earlier repaints into rail blue often involved placing the Inter City arrows on the cabside along with the locomotive's number such as here on D3204, now very work-weary at Doncaster on Sunday 21 October 1973. (Roger Bradley)

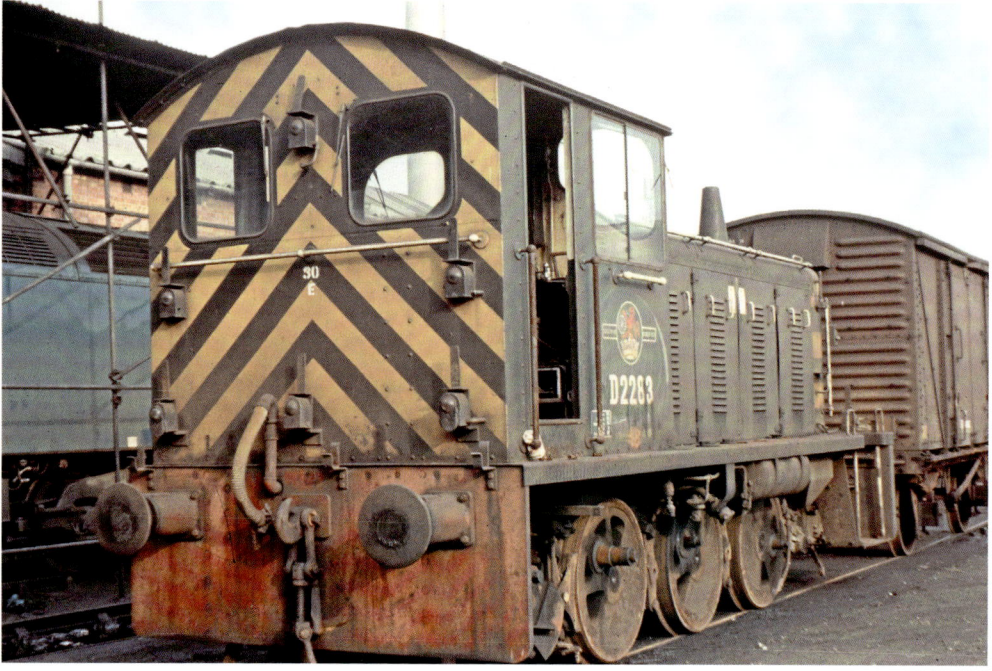

This Class 04 had been withdrawn from Stratford on 12 November 1969, where our unknown lensman recorded this view. A sad-looking D2283 was awaiting the arrival of the flying cutters of Hartwood Finance Co, based in Barnsley, to dispose of the engine on site here at 30A in August 1970. (Strathwood Library Collection)

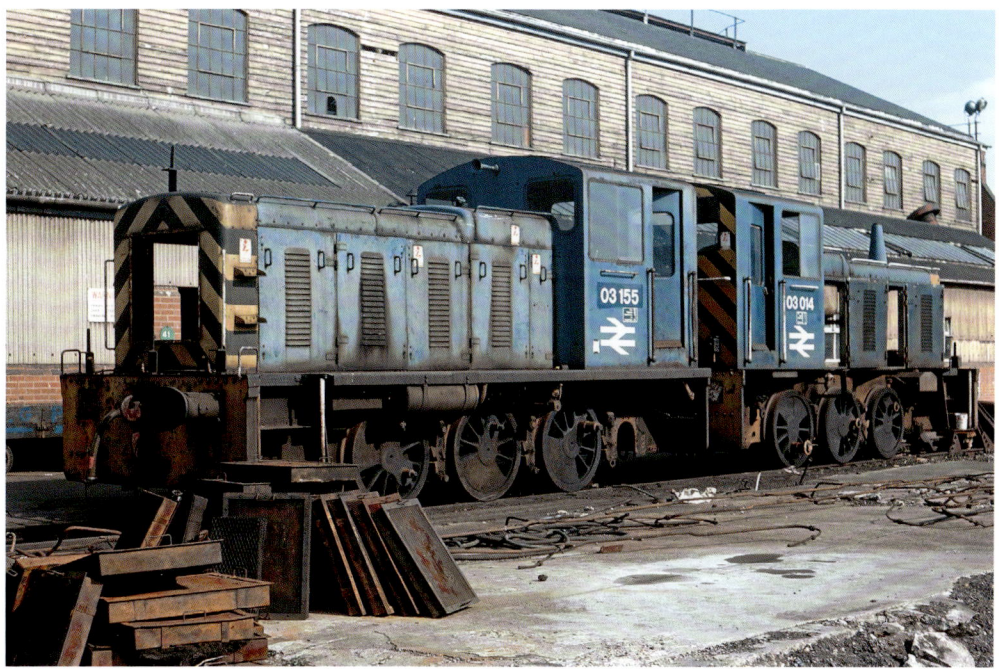

The future is grim for this duet of Class 03s Nos 03155 and 03014, stripped of reusable parts at Doncaster Works in April 1976, as they were cut up here the same month. (Arthur Wilson)

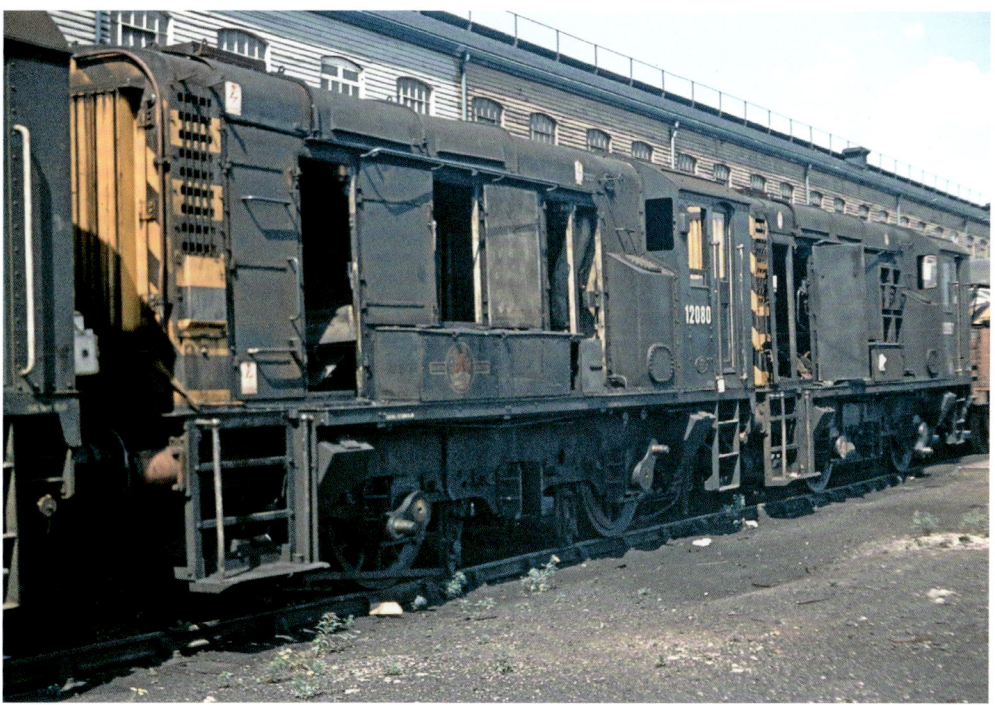

This Class 11 from 1950 has also been gutted of spares and reduced to two axles. Having arrived at Doncaster Works in October 1971, No. 12080 would be finally cut up in March 1972. (Neil Snuggs)

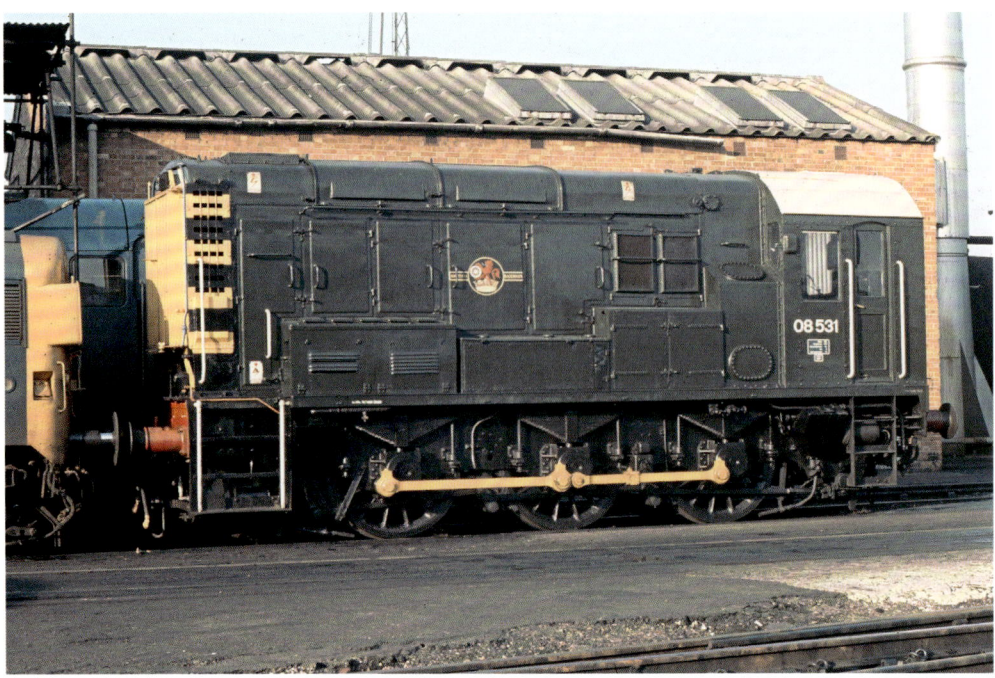

Having been on death row at Colchester and in store during 1971, D3693 was reinstated and came to Stratford where it became a pet and was often to be found as the Liverpool Street pilot, hence the smart green heritage livery now worn as renumbered No. 08531 on shed at Stratford on 4 December 1977. (Aldo Delicata)

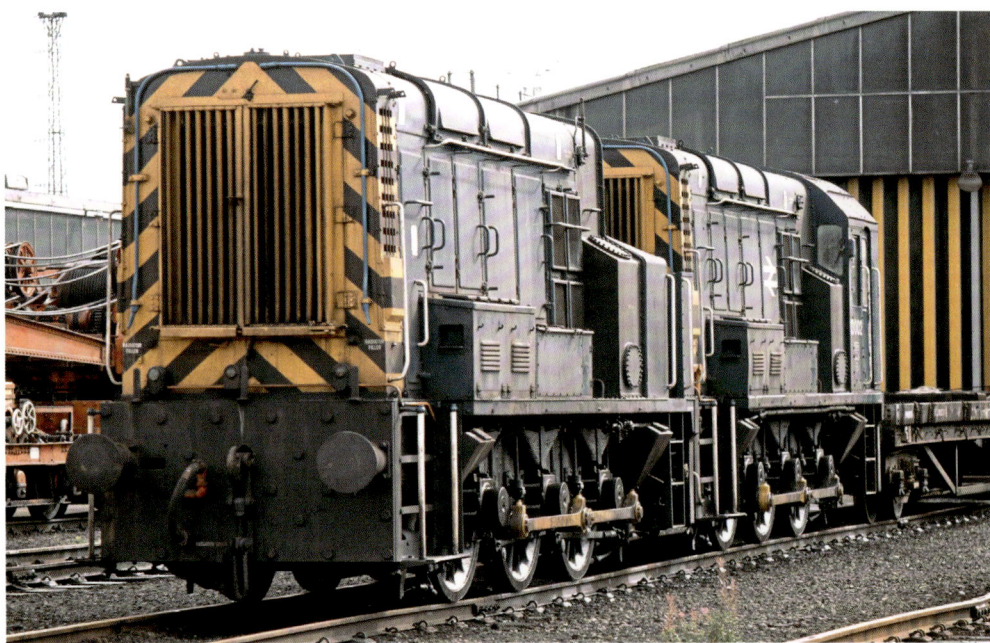

The use of the telephoto lens highlights the almost brutish nature of the Class 13 hump shunters, such as No. 13002 showing the beefed-up buffer beams at Tinsley on 30 September 1978. This one was the first of the trio to be withdrawn in June 1981. (Aldo Delicata)

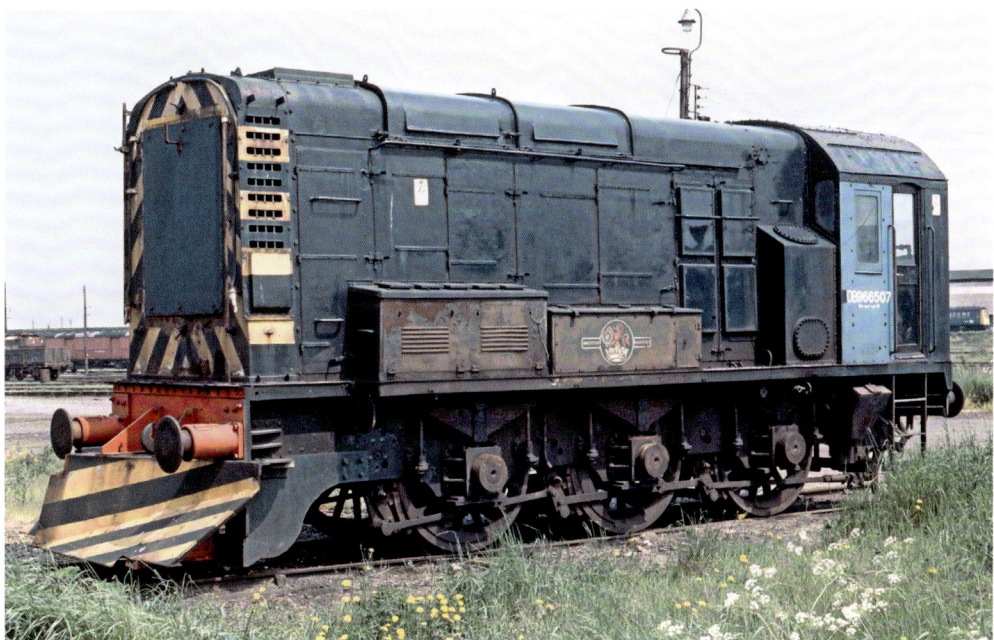

This conversion into a snowplough took place in 1973 at Doncaster Works, using the withdrawn D3006 from Immingham as a basis. Becoming DB966507, it was sent to Lincoln first before arriving at March when seen on 3 June 1978. Withdrawn a year later, it returned to The Plant and was quickly broken up. Did it ever see any use? (Aldo Delicata)

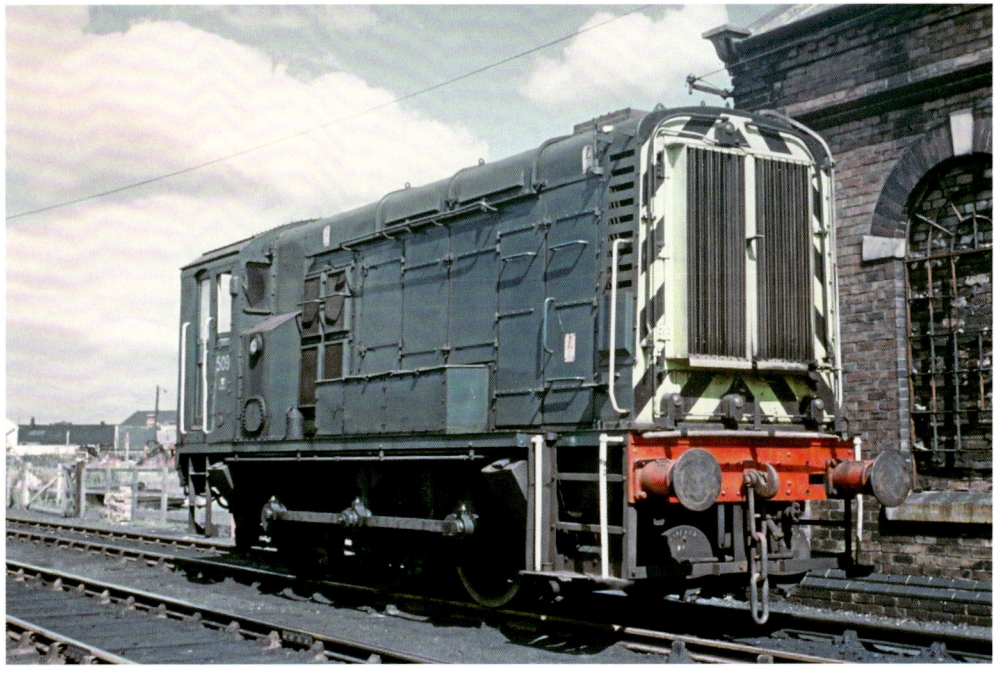

Sold out of service in February 1969, No. 12119 arrived for further work with the NCB at Philadelphia, where it is seen alongside the engine sheds wearing its new number, 509, on 25 July 1970. (Stewart Blencowe Collection)

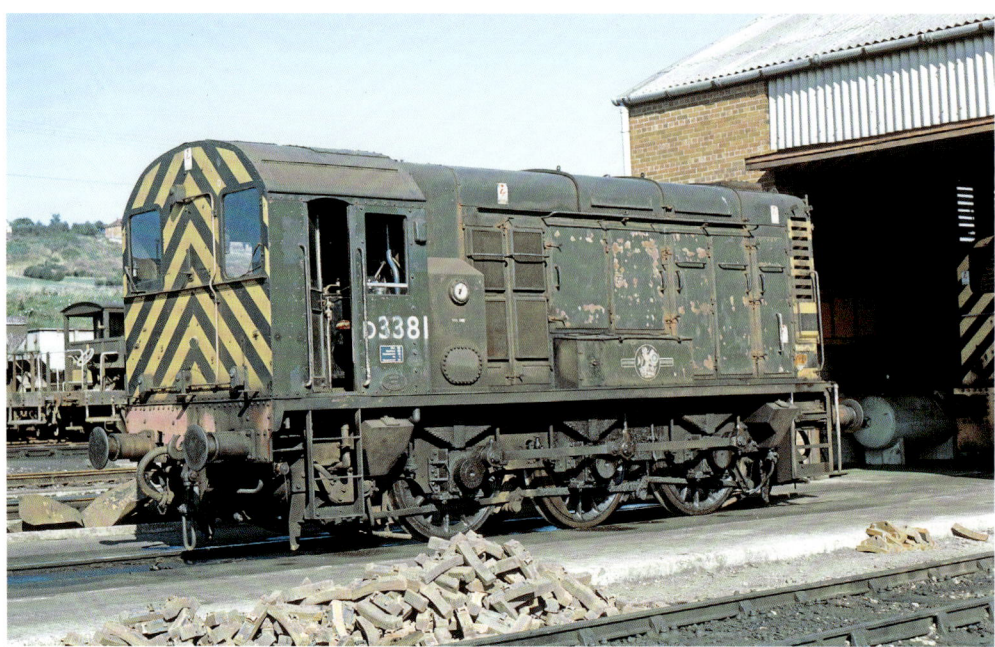

Still adorned with the large style of numbering from steam days and prefixed with a smaller D, this Class 08 was not unique by any means as several examples existed at the beginning of the seventies. This one at Healey Mills in January 1974 would become No. 08311 in April that year as the TOPS renumbering swept the country. (Ian King)

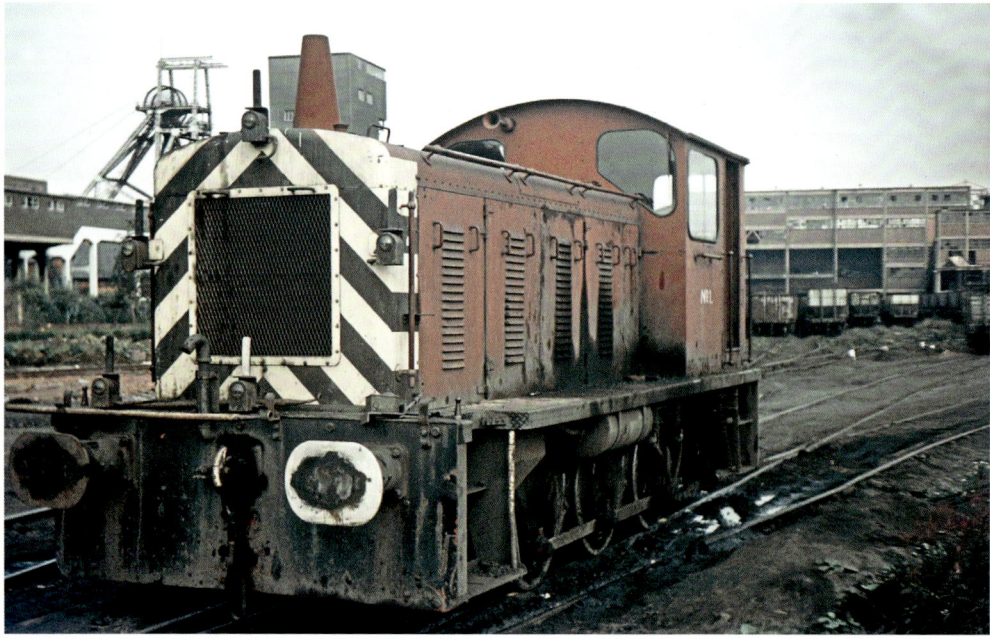

Another engine that did not survive in British Rail stock into the seventies was Class 04 D2274, sold to the National Coal Board and numbered as No.1 at Maltby Main Colliery. The locomotive was dismantled for spares in 1979. (Neil Snuggs)

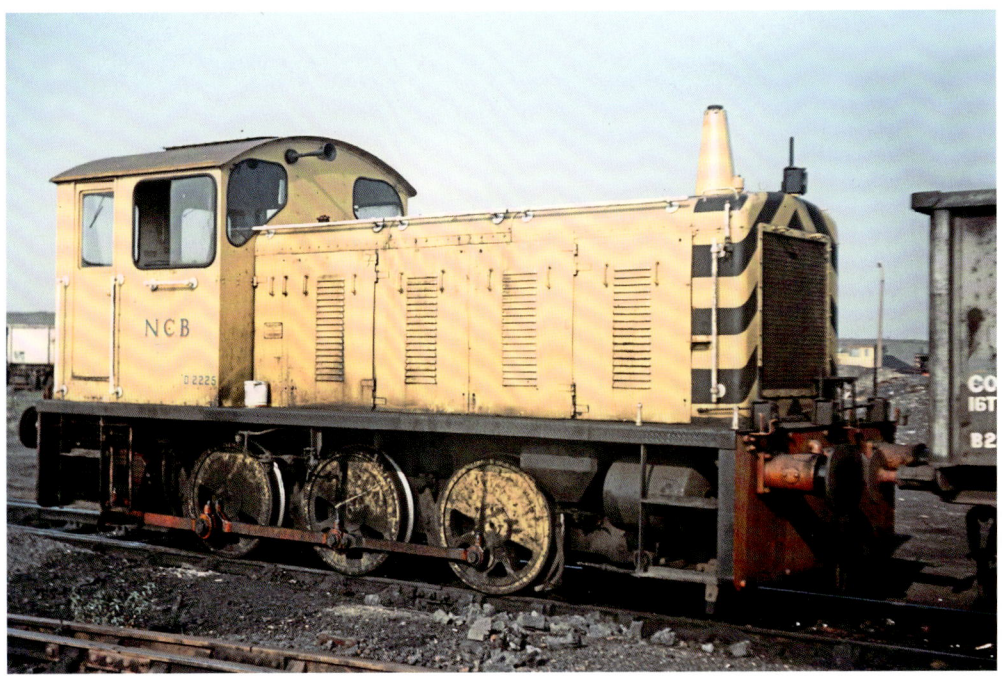

A number of locomotives found their way to Manvers Main Colliery and Coking Plant from British Rail, and among them was D2225. Later it was transferred to the nearby Wath Colliery, where the shed collapsed onto it! (Neil Snuggs)

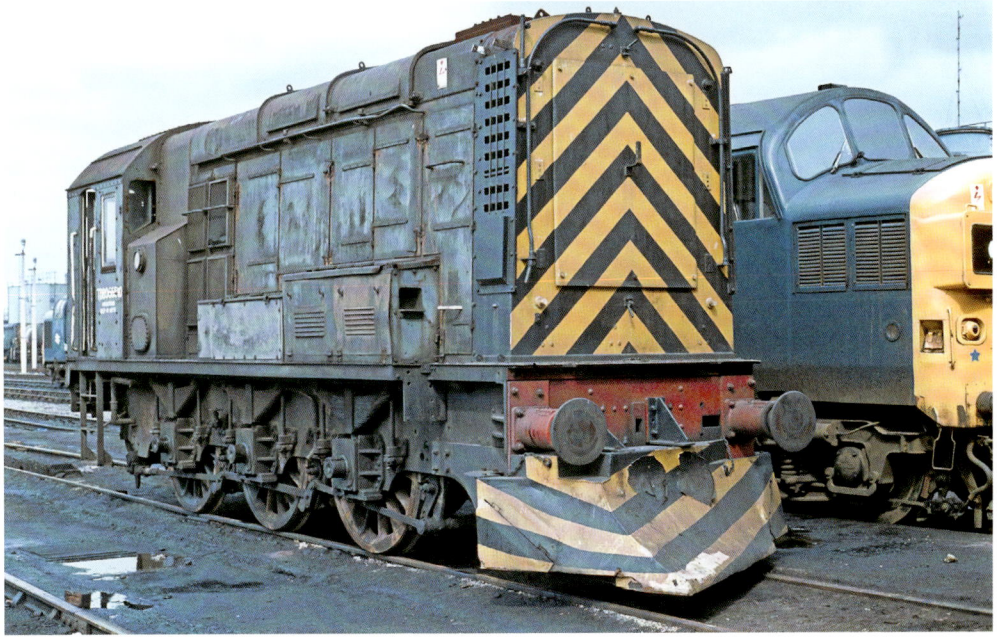

Another one of Doncaster's recycled snowploughs, this time D3037 from Tinsley was the donor, becoming ADB9666510 in 1974. Back again at Doncaster after just four years based at Grantham, it will be cut up in the works during 1979. (Arthur Wilson)

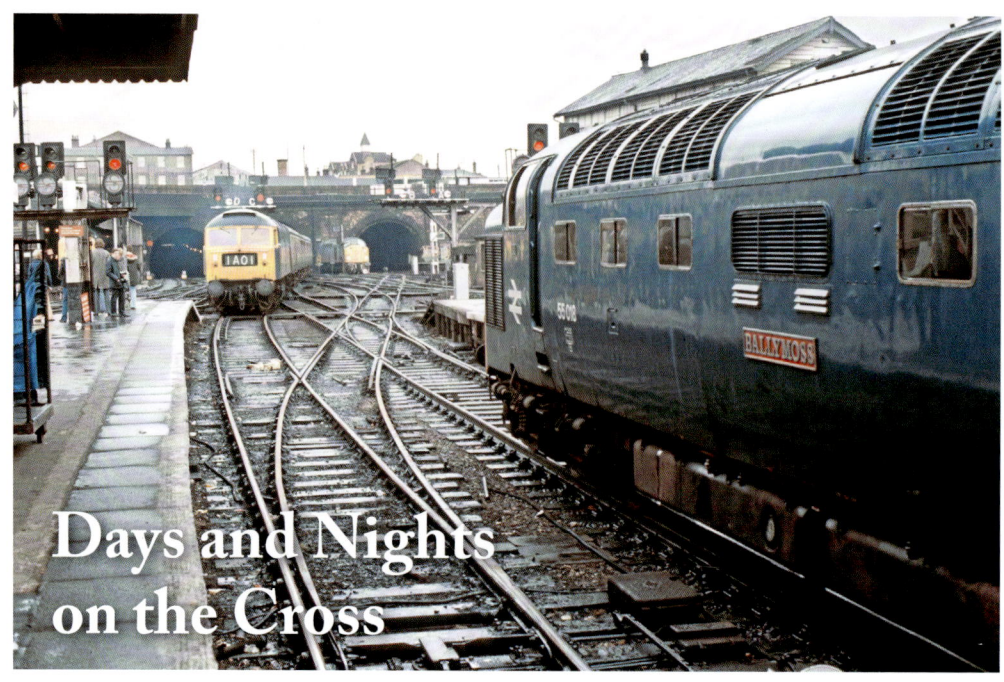

Days and Nights on the Cross

Ready to depart after the arrival of the Class 47 will be Deltic No. 55018 *Ballymoss* while Class 40 No. 40075 waits patiently on the spur in the distance close to the Up Drain platforms in 1975. (Roger Griffiths)

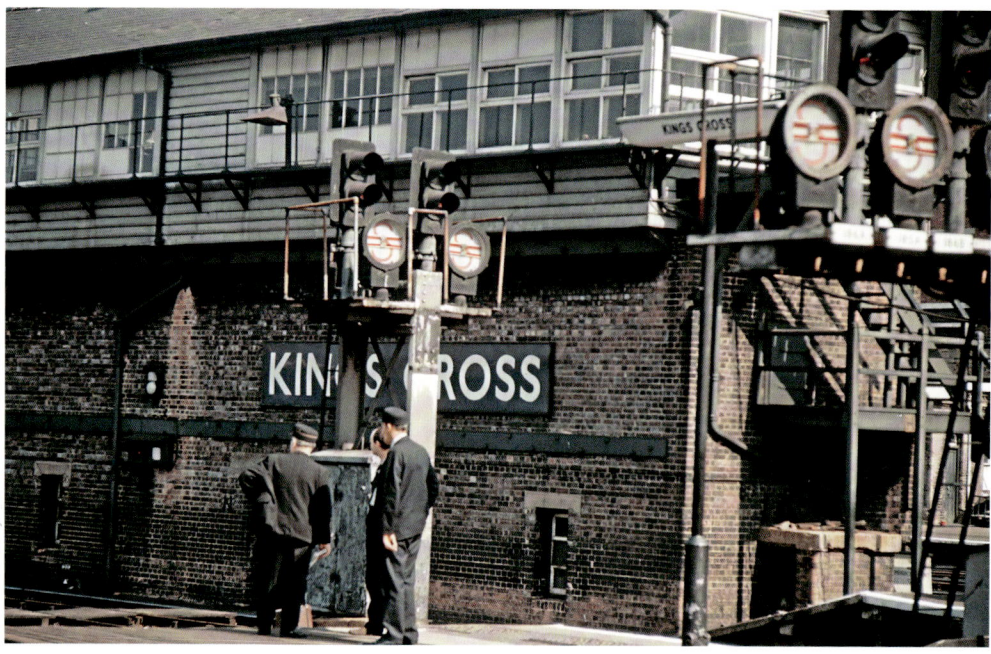

Mud are singing about 'Tiger Feet' at number one, and the general election results in an almost dead-heat. Harold Wilson becomes Prime Minister again, despite his Labour Party having received fewer votes than the Conservatives, who won fewer seats. Something interesting must be happening in the direction of the tunnels in February 1974. (Strathwood Library Collection)

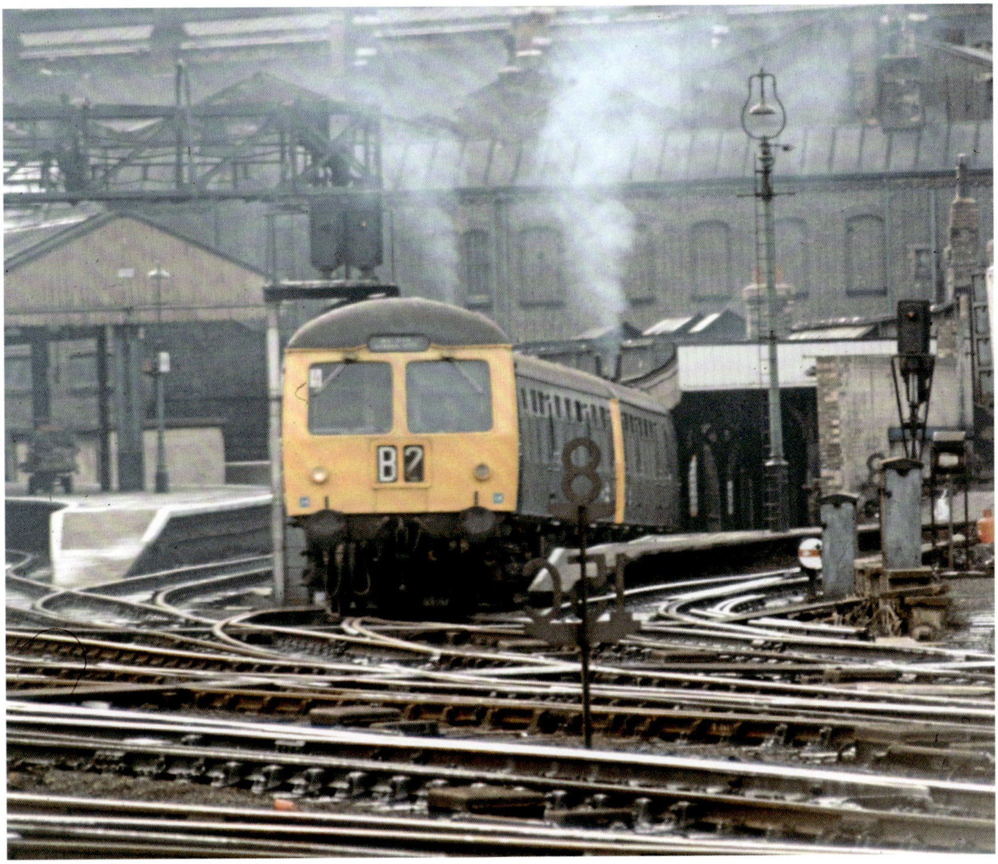

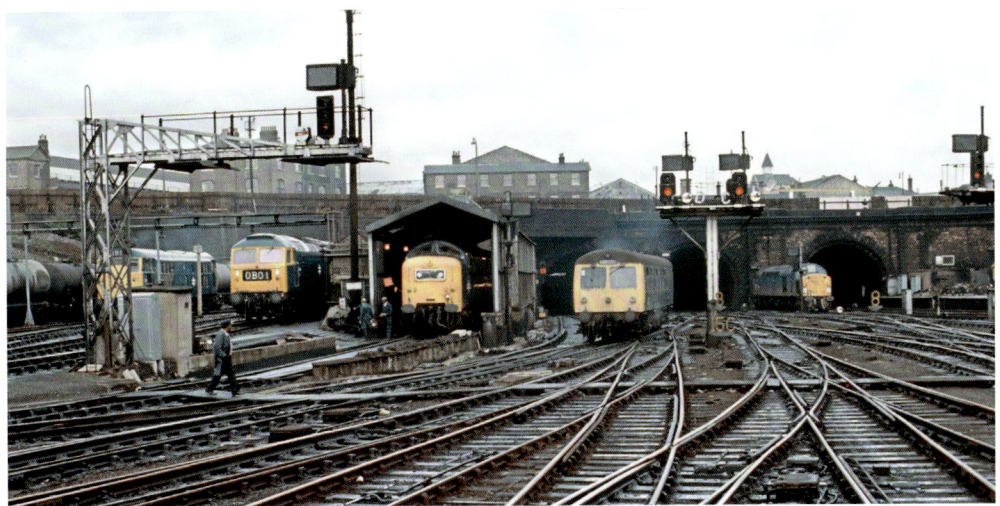

Engines working hard to climb away from the Drain platforms at King's Cross. Having started from Moorgate, this pairing of Cravens DMUs also makes for the tunnels to run under the Regent's Canal in 1975. (Roger Griffiths)

A variety of types for the spotter to enjoy from the platform ends the same day. (Roger Griffiths)

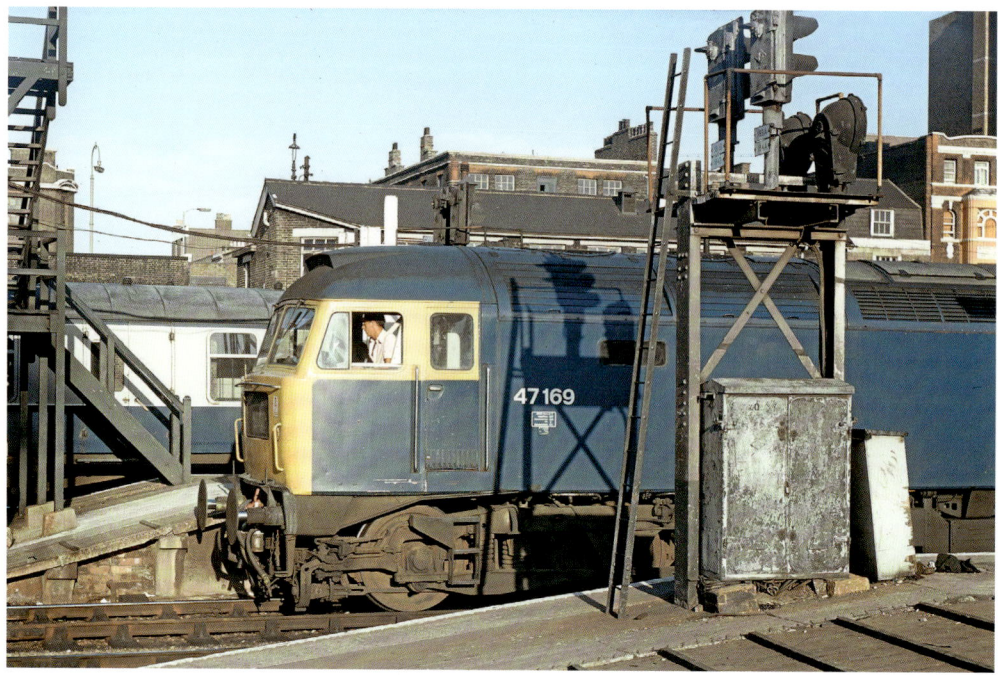

It will soon be departure time for Immingham-based No. 47169 to go back northwards on Saturday 9 August 1975. This Class 47 would be renumbered again before the end of the decade as No. 47581 in December 1979 as a Stratford engine. (Roger Bradley)

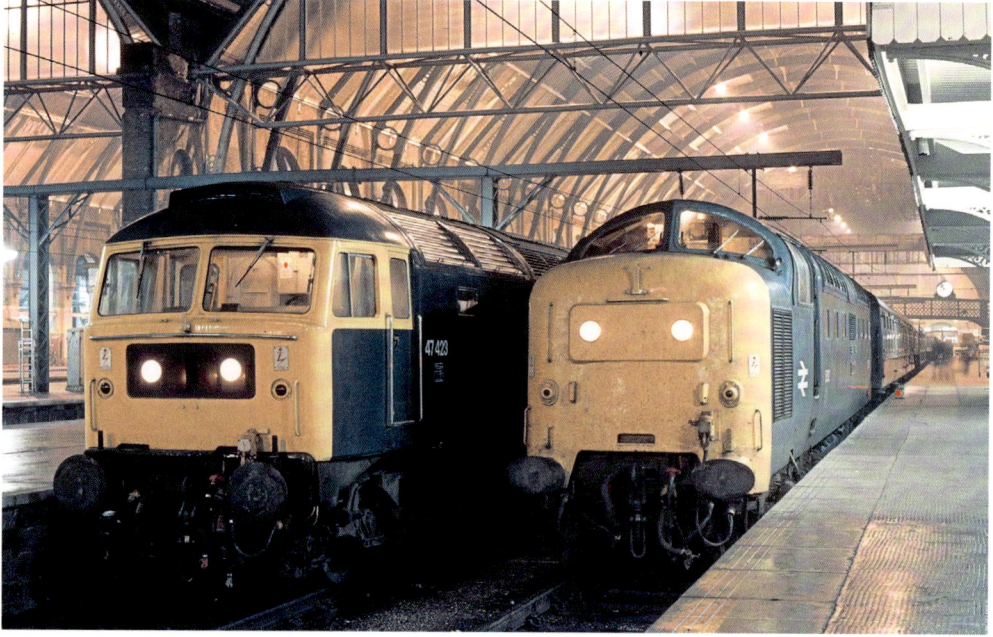

Darkness and light rain have fallen on the station as Class 47 No. 47423 prepares to take the 20.00 King's Cross–Aberdeen and Deltic No. 55012 *Crepello* will follow with the 20.15 departure for Edinburgh Waverley on 3 October 1979. (Colin Whitbread)

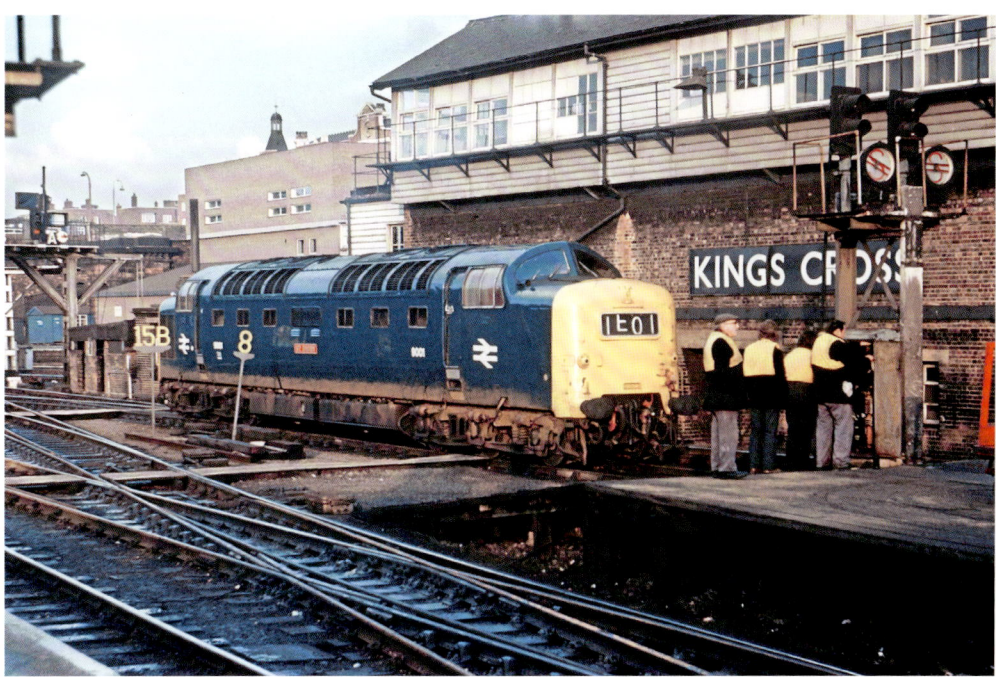

Light-engine Deltic activity on 6 January 1973 as No. 9001 *St Paddy* approaches four track workers. A week later, in a much warmer Hawaii, Elvis Presley plays a concert to a worldwide live television audience of over one billion people. (Ian James)

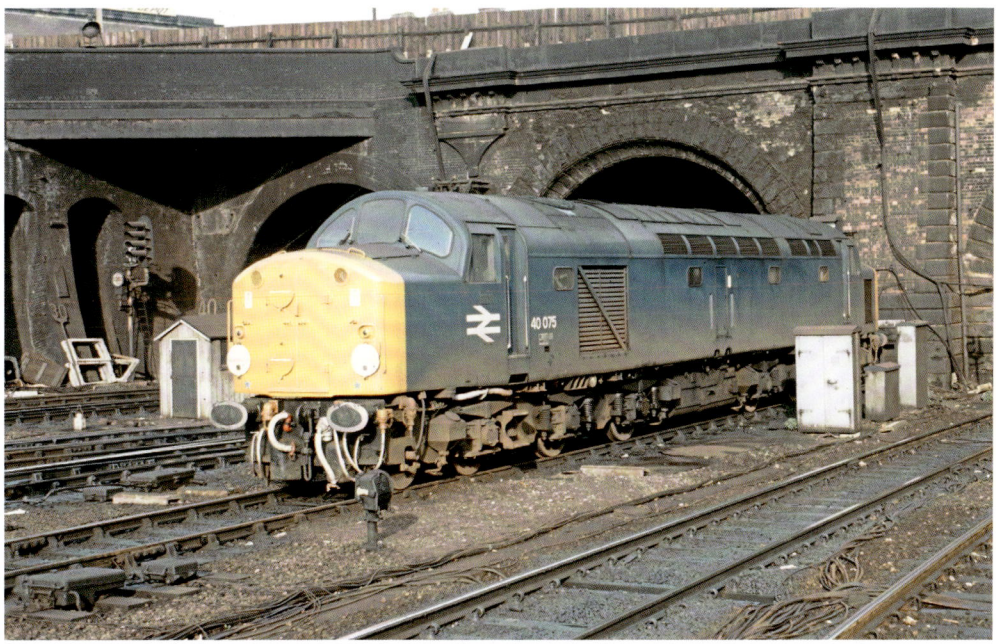

Giving twenty-one years' faithful service to the Eastern Region was Class 40 No. 40075, six years away from being withdrawn here in 1975. Longer spells at York and Healey Mills preceded allocations to Thornaby and Gateshead. (Roger Griffiths)

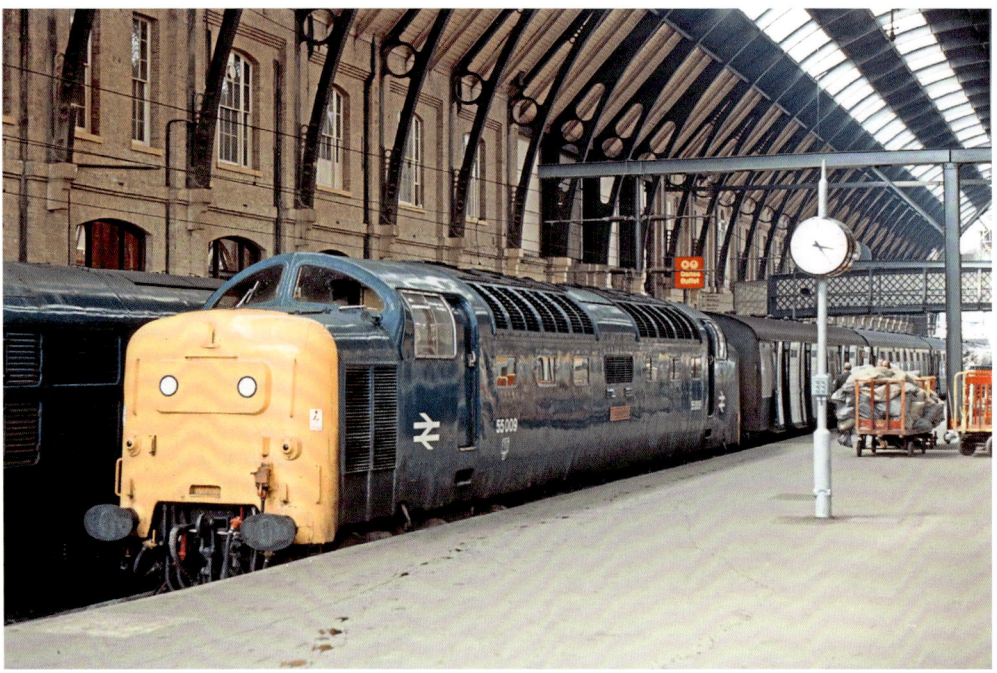

A generous trolley or two of mail has come south behind Deltic No. 55009 *Alycidon* on 18 May 1979. This was less than a week after the FA Cup Final when three goals scored in an electrifying last four minutes saw Arsenal lift the trophy 3-2 against Manchester United. (John Harrup)

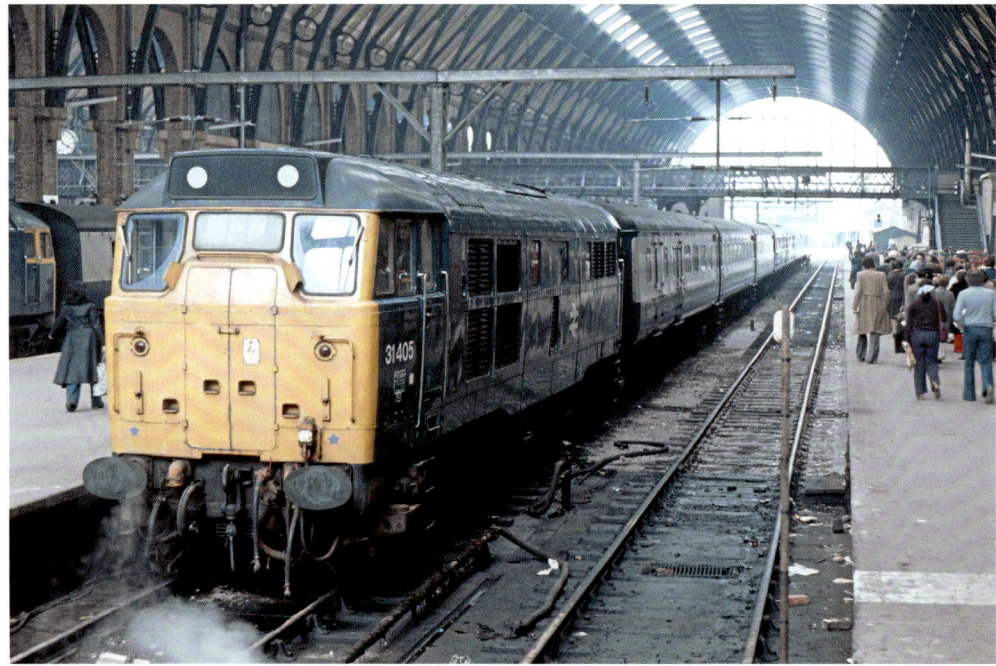

The clock is ticking for many changes as the electrification of the ECML works its way north from the London terminus, where Class 31 No. 31405 keeps the coaches warm at the stops on 12 April 1977. (Aldo Delicata)

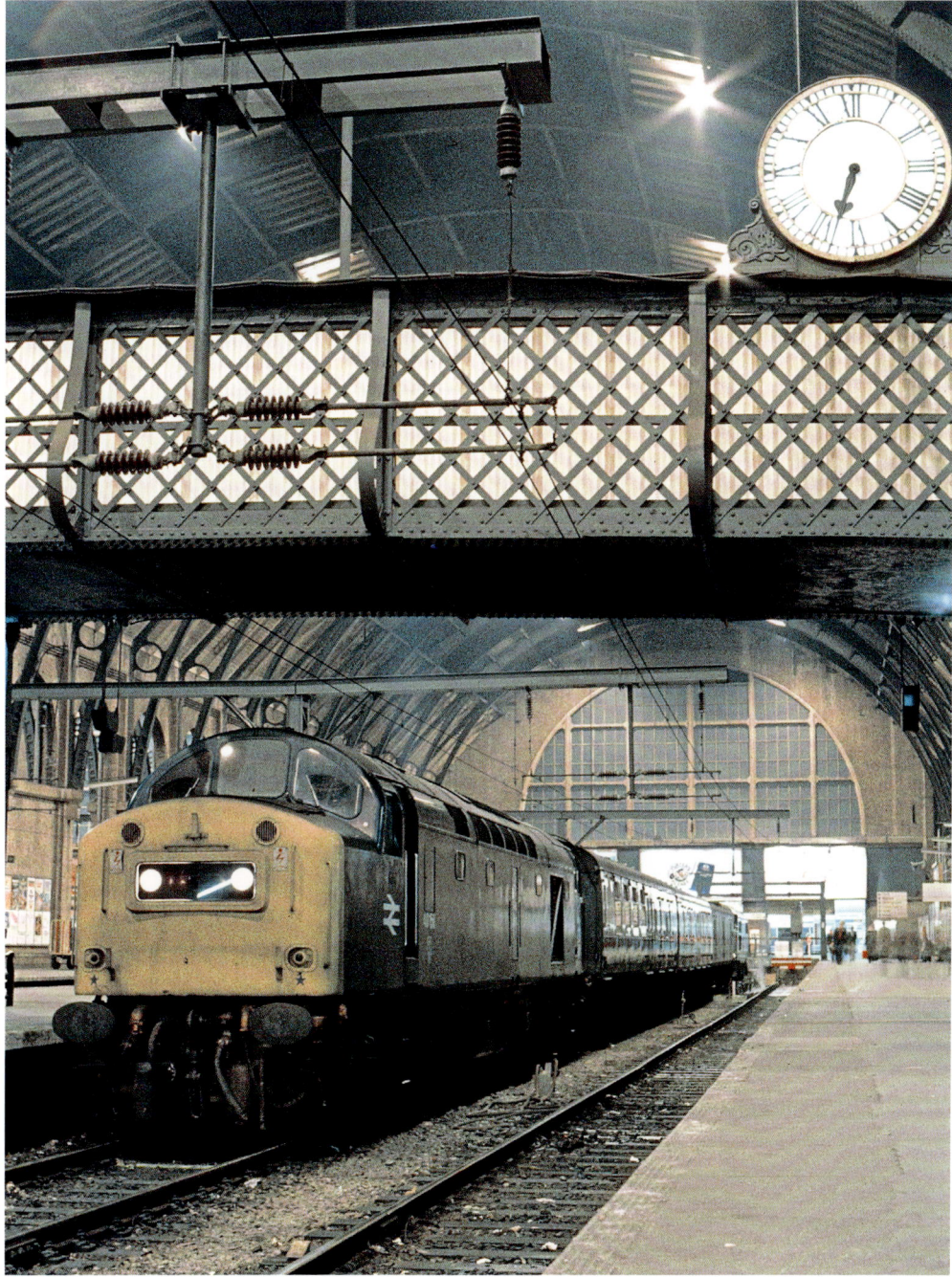

One of the Healey Mills allocation of Class 40s, No. 40156, waits to leave under the clock on Monday 13 November 1978. Time would run out at the end of the seventies for this English Electric type 4, being taken out of traffic on 27 July 1980, with the men of Swindon ensuring nothing was left by the end of the year. (Colin Whitbread)

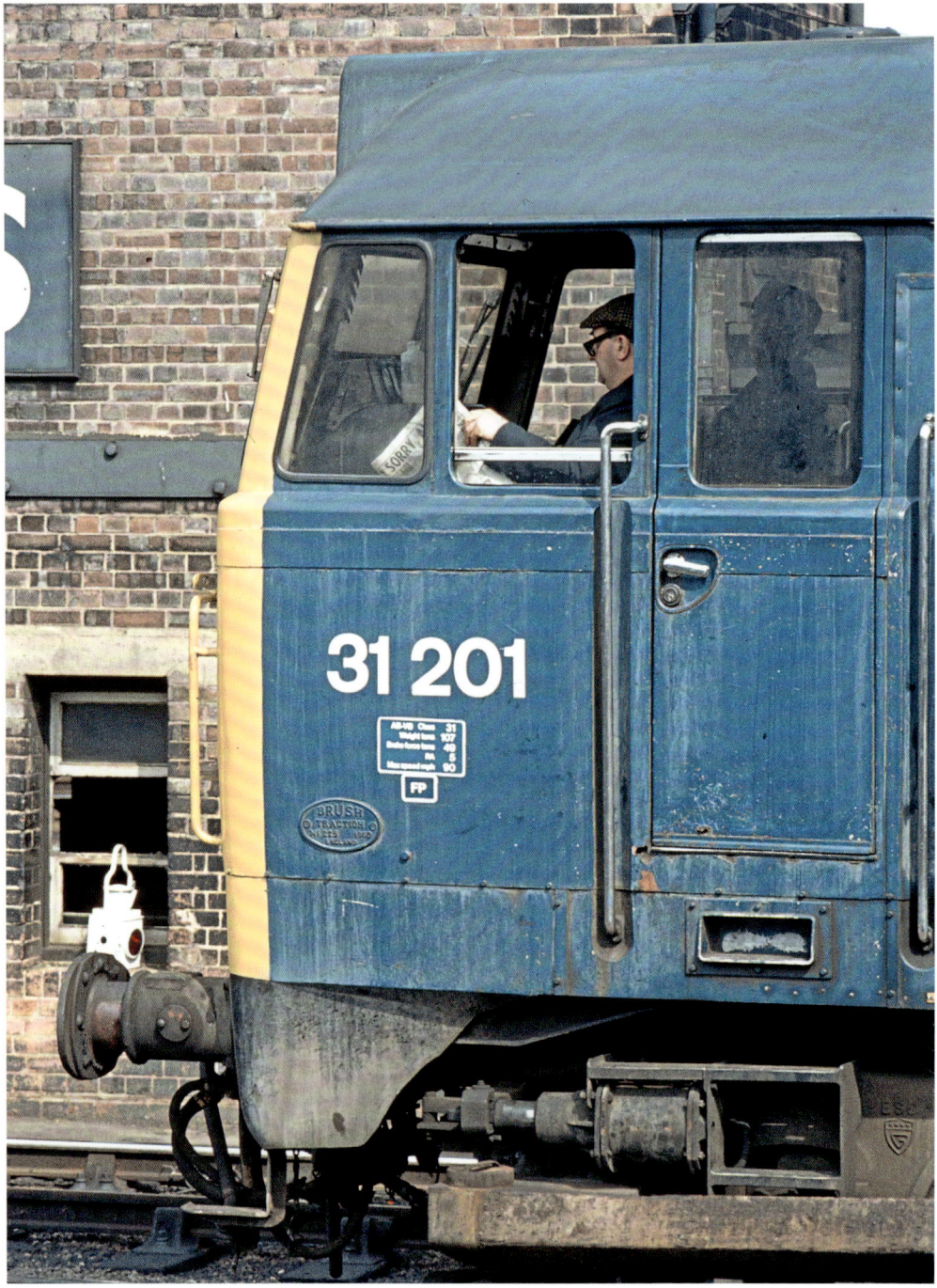

A chance to see what is on television tonight for the driver of Class 31 No. 31201 on 2 May 1975. He does not look the type to be watching the Fonz as *Happy Days* hit our screens, more *Coronation Street* or perhaps *The Sweeney*? (Peter Hallsall)

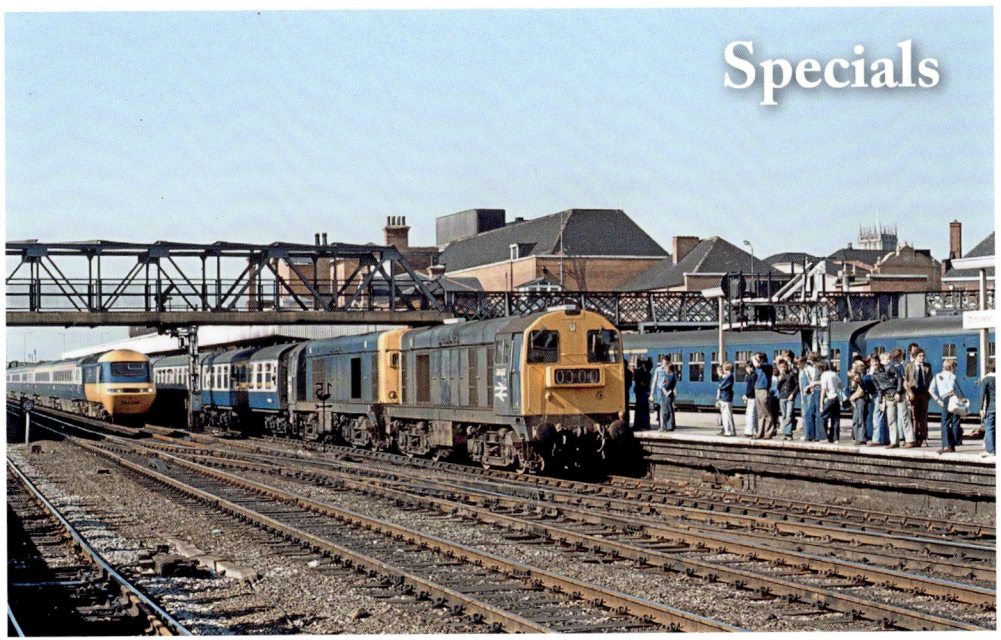

Specials

Run in connection with the Railex 125 event and open days at Doncaster Works, this tour draws into Doncaster behind Class 20s Nos 20186 and 20187 on 18 June 1978. (Strathwood Library Collection)

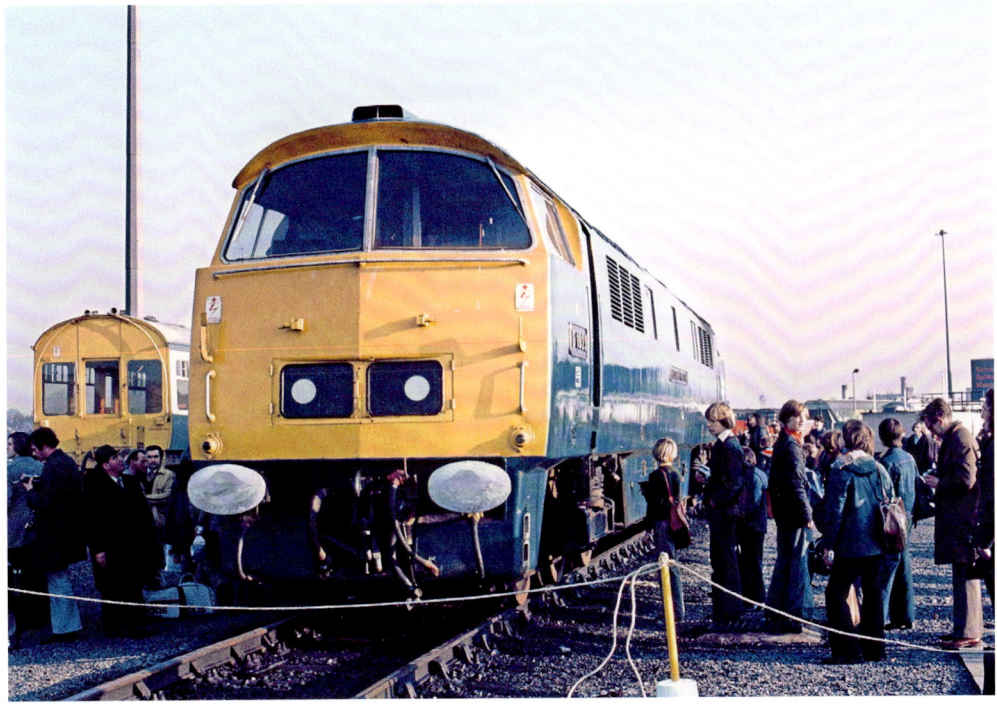

Having brought its train from King's Cross, Class 52 D1023 *Western Fusilier* was put on display at York before the return run south on 20 November 1976. This Western was the only one of the class to receive a black two-dot head-code, as it was an Eastern Region operating requirement at the time. (Strathwood Library Collection)

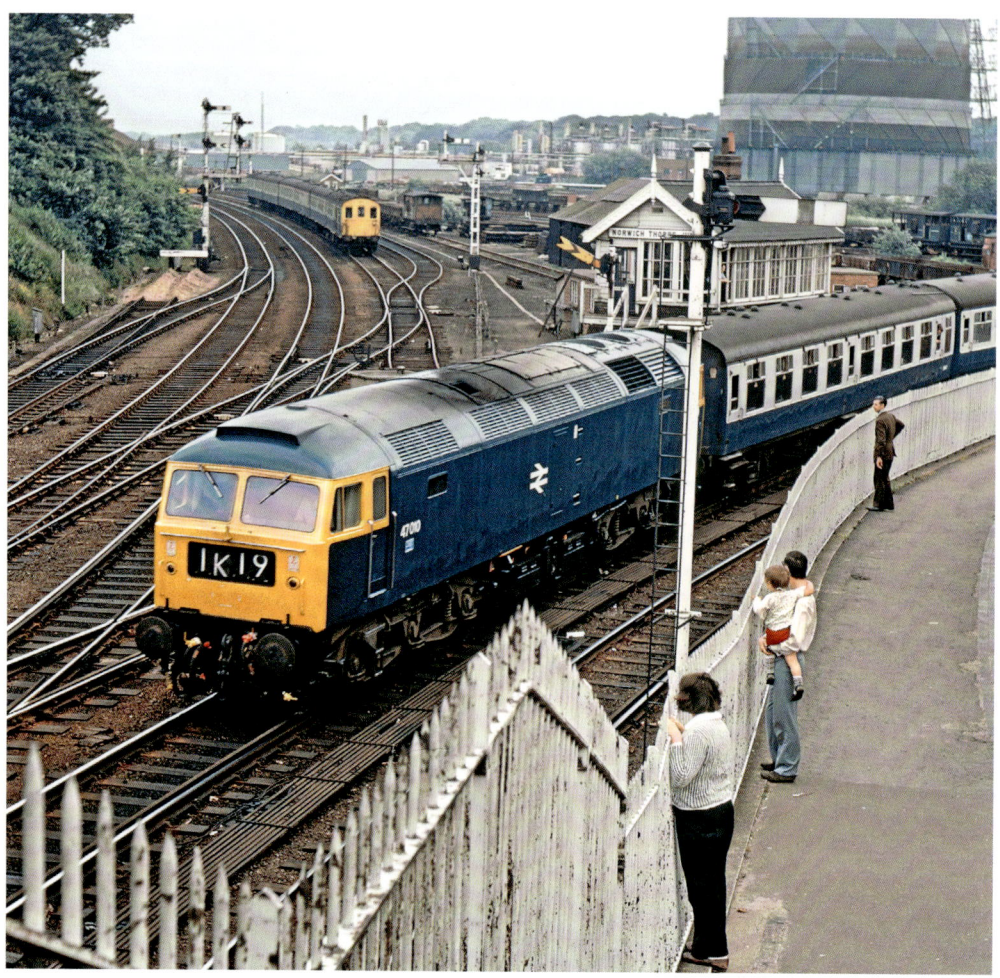

The arrival of Class 47 No. 47010 precedes the passage into Norwich of a Hastings set with a special from the Southern Region in June 1975. These six-car sets managed to get around an awful lot at the time on various excursions away from their home region. After taking television comedy by storm, the Pythons' first film was launched to an expectant fan base in 1975. *Monty Python and the Holy Grail* poked fun at the tales of the knights of King Arthur and medieval chivalry. (Arthur Wilson)

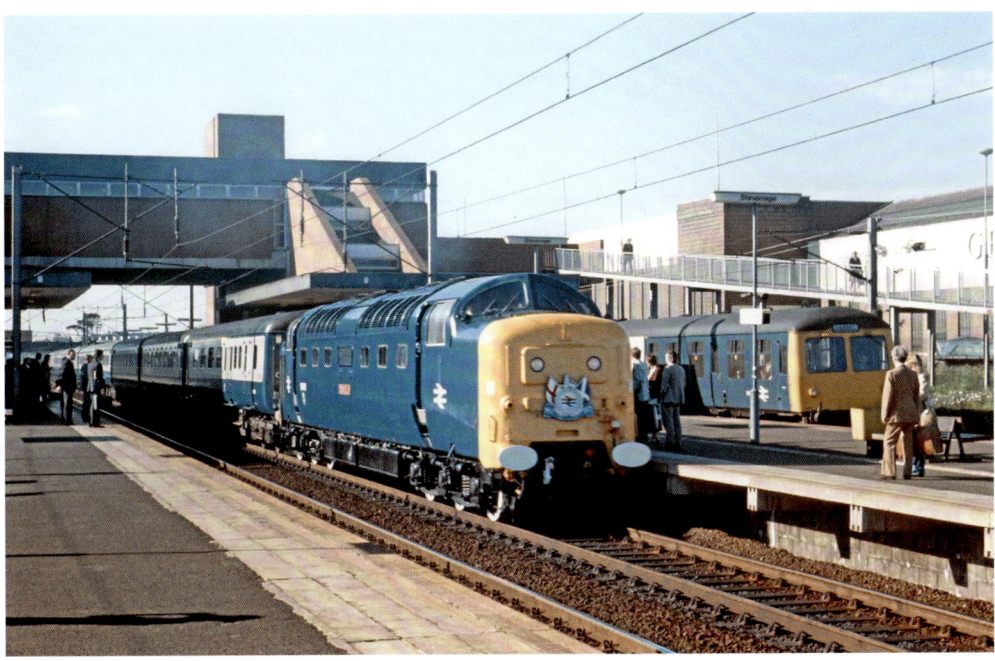

Superbly turned out to work the inaugural run of The Silver Jubilee service on 8 June 1977 was Deltic No. 55012 *Crepello*, seen here coming through Stevenage. In honour of HRH Queen Elizabeth II's twenty-five-year reign as the monarch, British Rail dedicated the 1S12 07.45 King's Cross–Edinburgh and 1E20 15.00 return services as The Silver Jubilee and included a buffet car decked with 1952–1977 memorabilia. Place settings, napkins, destination boards etc all carried The Silver Jubilee motif. This first day's return 1E20 15.00 working saw Haymarket-based No. 55022 *Royal Scots Grey* in charge. (John Dawson)

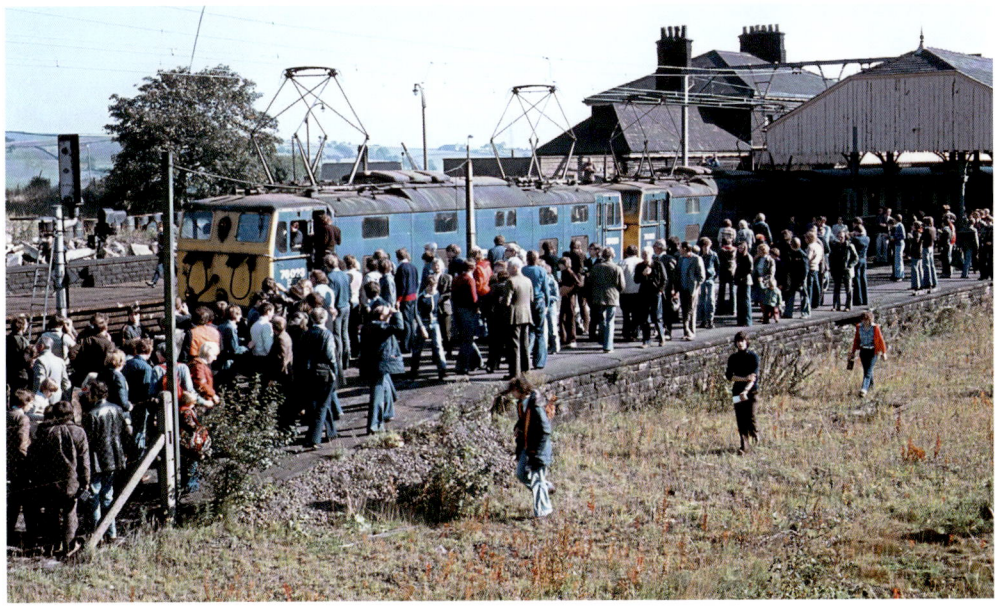

Enthusiasts gather around Class 76s Nos 76023 and 76010 during a pause on the British Rail-organised Pennine Rambler on 7 October 1978 at Penistone. (Trans Pennine Publishing)

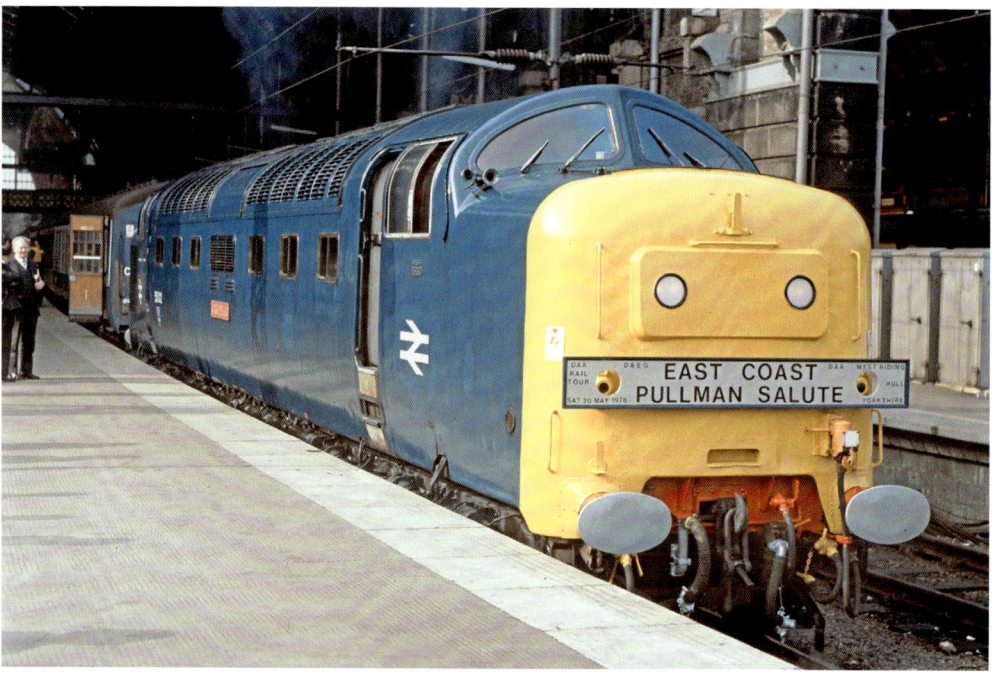

On 20 May 1978, Deltic No. 55012 *Crepello* took the outward leg of this tour from King's Cross to Leeds, being clocked at 99.4 mph at Tallington. A fast return run was also enjoyed behind Class 37 pairing Nos 37037 and 37102, which touched 90.0 mph at Retford and Little Bytham. (Ian James)

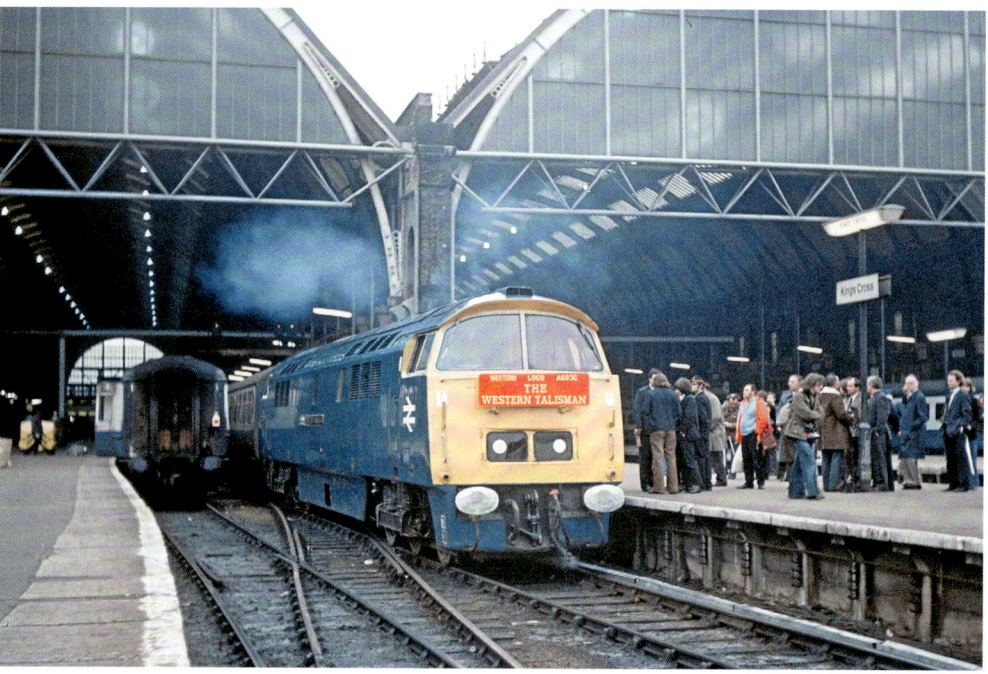

Crowds gathered at various vantage points around King's Cross on 20 November to record the run of Class 52 D1023 *Western Fusilier* in that last full year of Westerns on British Rail in 1977. (John Green)

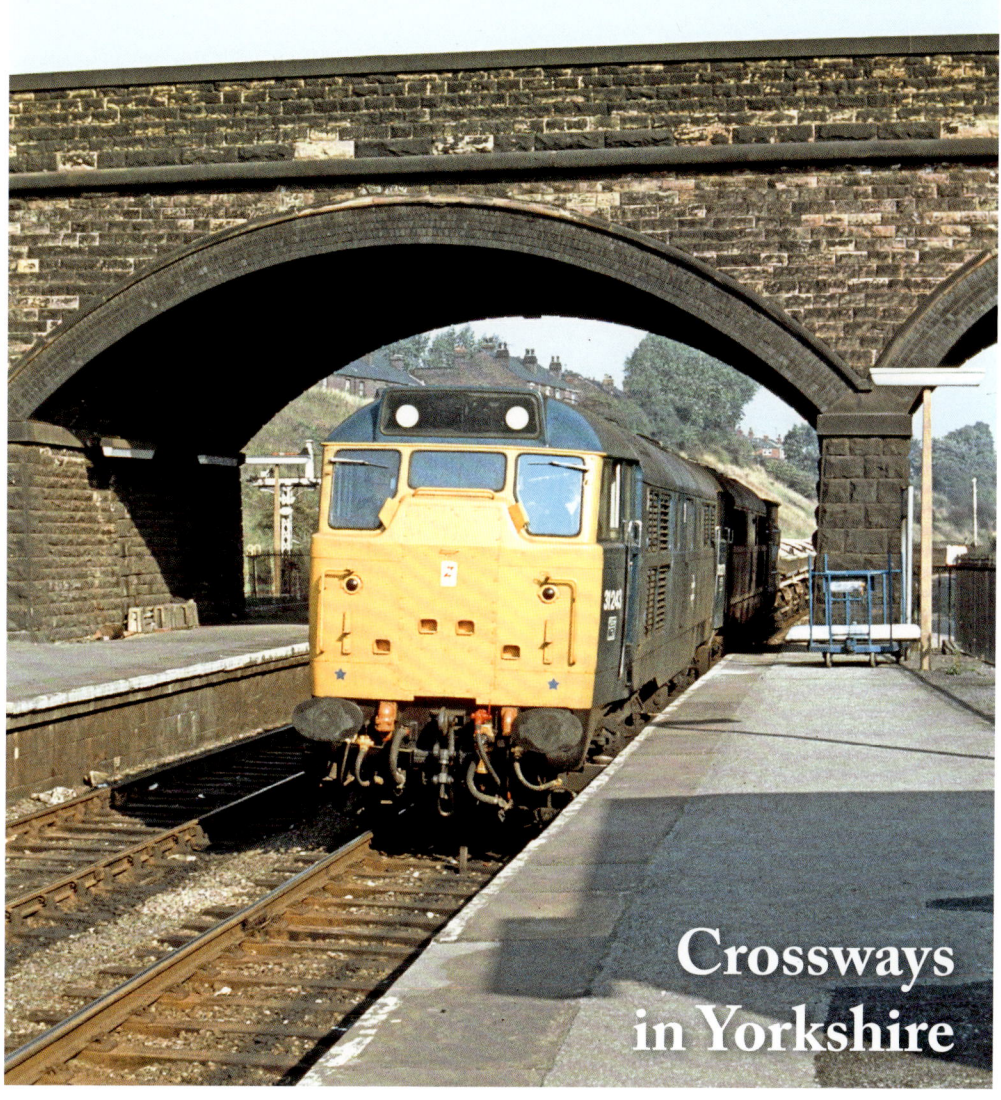

Crossways in Yorkshire

Double-headed Class 31s at Rotherham Masborough for working a ballast train in connection with track relaying, with No. 31234 being the lead engine, on 8 October 1978. Over in Rome, the Cardinals are plunged into turmoil after the unexpected death of Pope John Paul I after only thirty three days of Papacy. Eight days later Pope John Paul II, Cardinal Karol Wojtyla, is announced as the 264th Pope. He is the first Polish Pope in history. (Greg Wyatt)

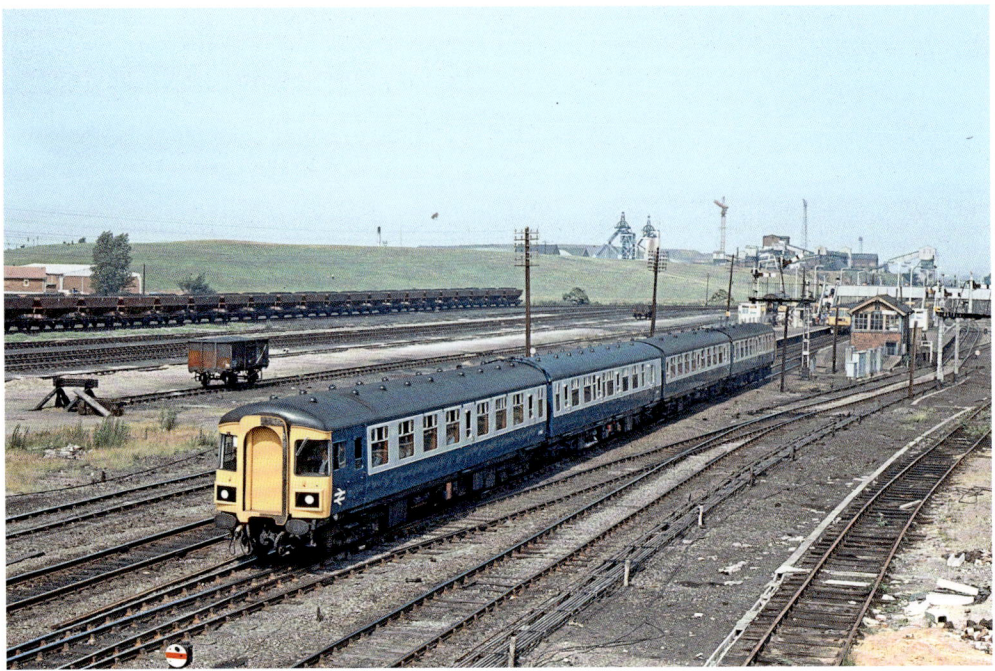

Transferred from the Western Region, these Inter City units were put to work on the same diagrams as the resident Trans Pennine sets. One can be seen in the background as they pass at Hatfield and Stainforth in 1977. (Arthur Wilson)

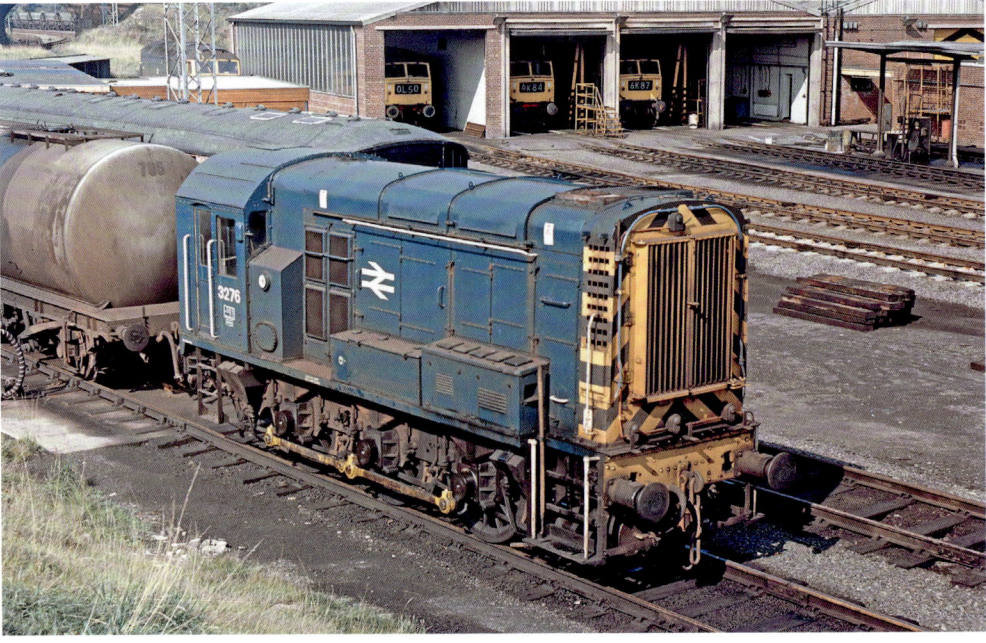

On a Sunday such as 26 August 1973, many of the allocation of Knottingley's Class 47s would be on shed in the days before the arrival of the Class 56s towards the end of the seventies. This Class 08 would move away too in 1978, although only a short distance, to join others at Healey Mills. (Roger Bradley)

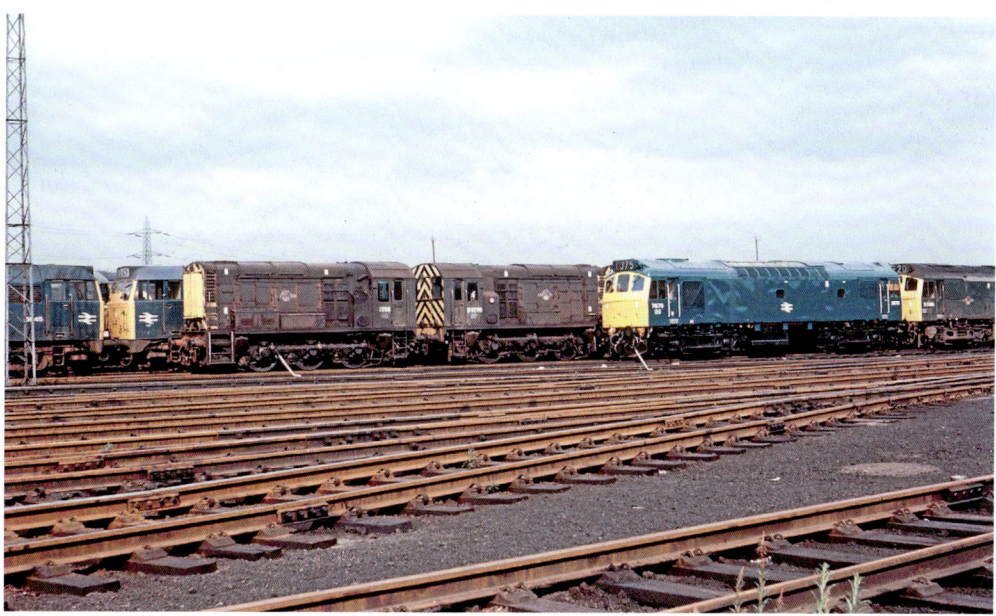

A recently outshopped No. 7673 and another Class 25 are among the usual line-up at Tinsley on 8 July 1972. Always good value for spotters, with a wide selection of classes to be found here throughout the decade. (Sylvester Booth/Strathwood Library Collection)

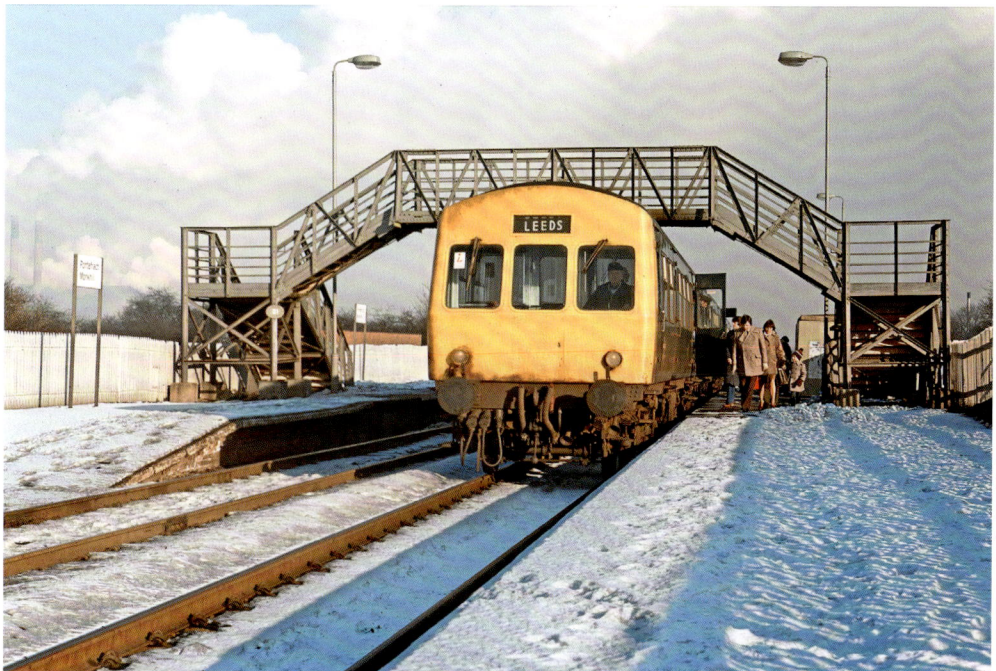

Snow has fallen on Pontefract Monkhill Railways in March 1979. This was the Lancashire & Yorkshire Railways station in the town, while Pontefract Baghill was on the line opened by the Swinton and Knottingley Joint which was to become a joint station for the North Eastern Railway and the Midland Railway soon after completion. (Roger Bradley)

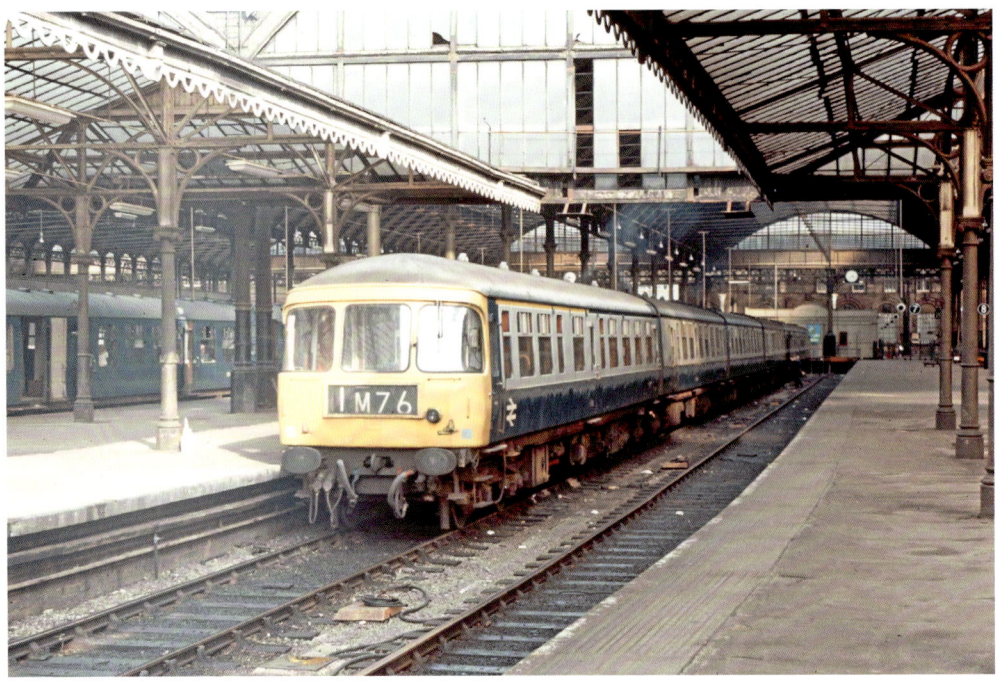

Almost ready for yet another run back across country, away from Hull Paragon, is this Trans Pennine set on 22 September 1973. This same day Dr Henry Kissinger, already the United States National Security Advisor, starts his term as America's Secretary of State. I wonder how many air miles he racked up in the job? (John Dawson)

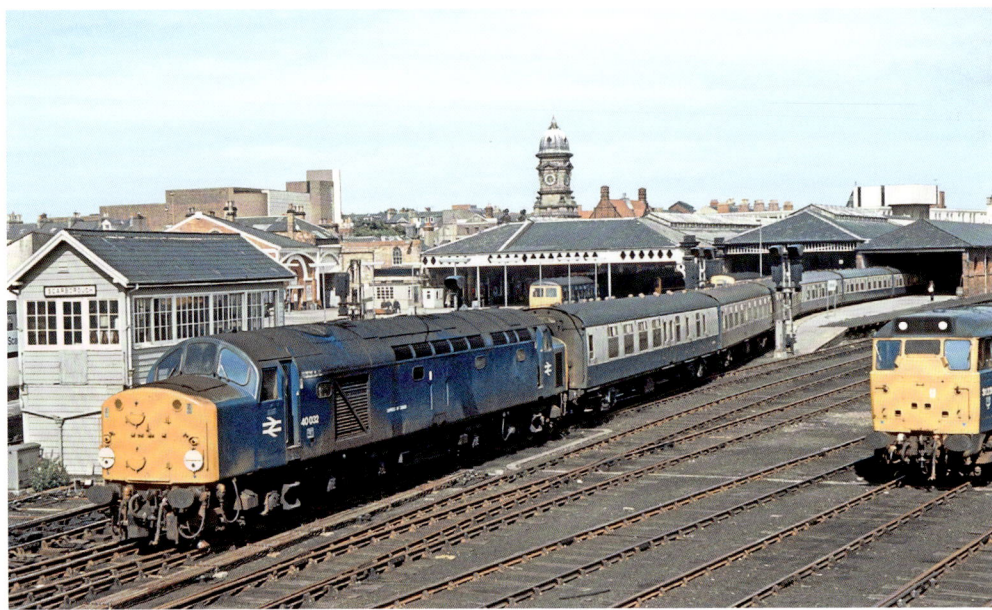

Having a day out at the seaside in the seventies, for many, meant a trip by train to resorts such as Scarborough, where we see Class 40 No. 40032 *Empress of Canada*, now sadly only painted on the locomotive on 27 August 1979. (Sid Steadman)

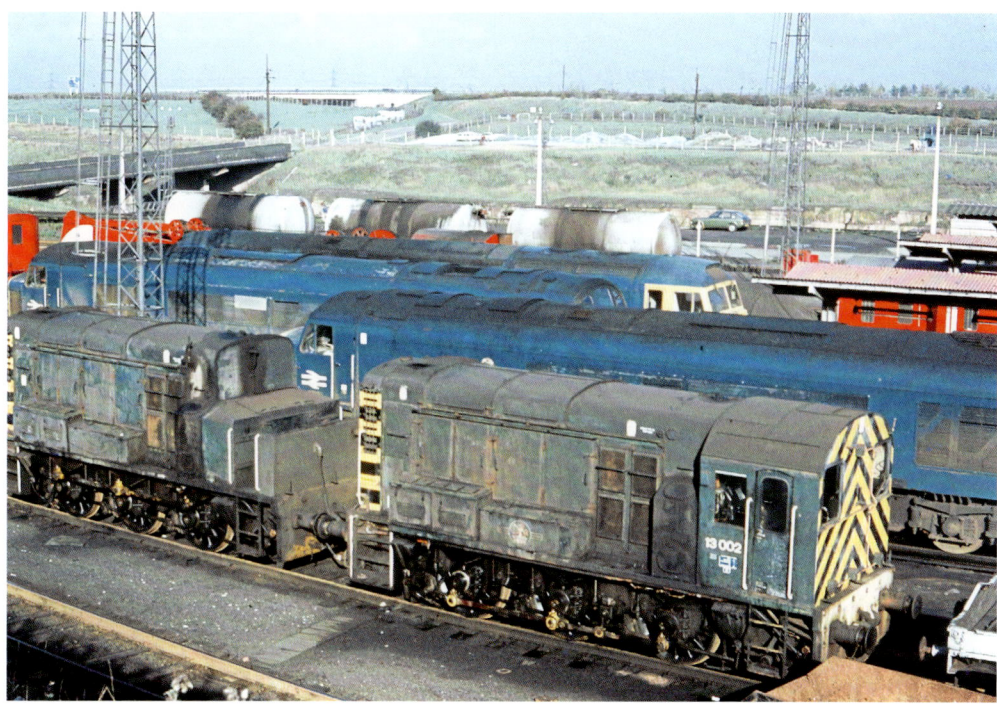

Another view from a different angle of Class 13 hump shunter No. 13002, again at Tinsley around 1974, with the paintwork looking less cared-for than the mechanicals. (Late Pete Walton/Sid Steadman)

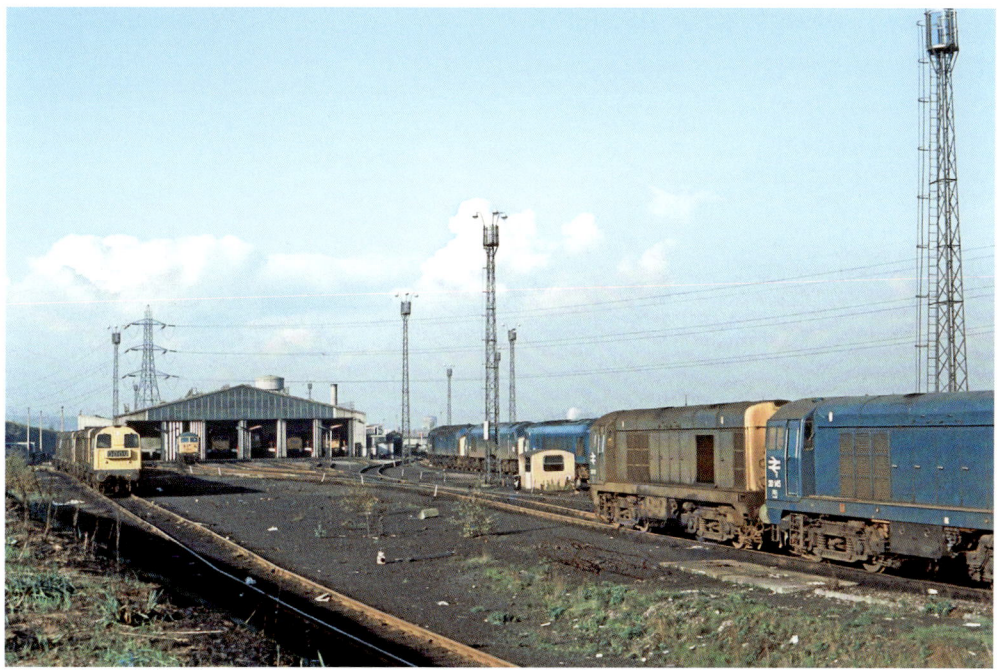

On this return trip to Tinsley in 1977 we can see six Class 20s, two Peaks, a Class 40 as well as a brand-new Class 56 among others on the depot that day. (Late Pete Walton/Sid Steadman)

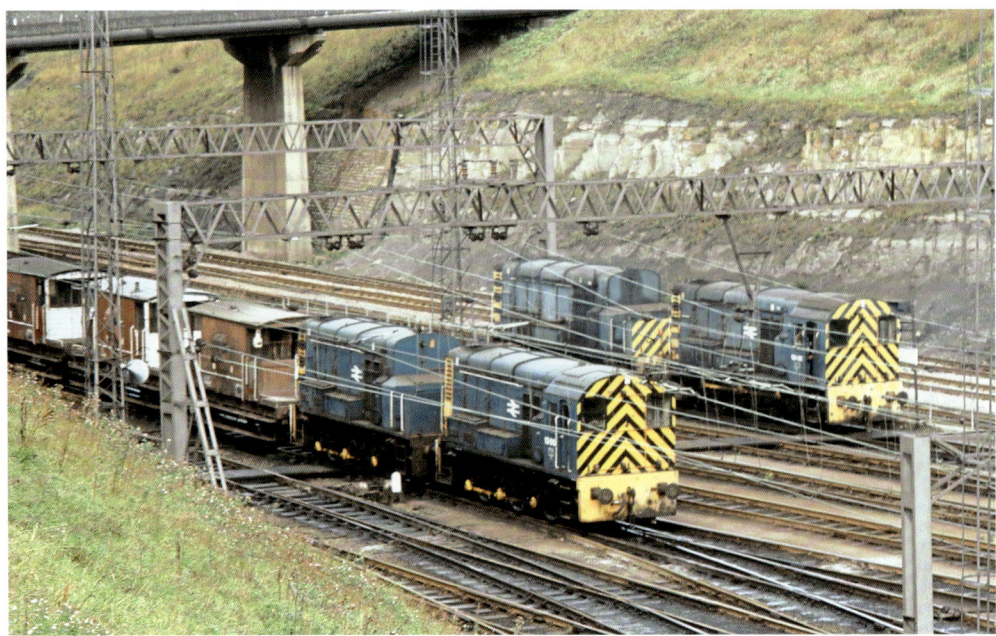

The missing pair of Class 13s Nos 13001 and 13003 is found down in the yard, seen from the depot car park at Tinsley on 30 September 1978. (Aldo Delicata)

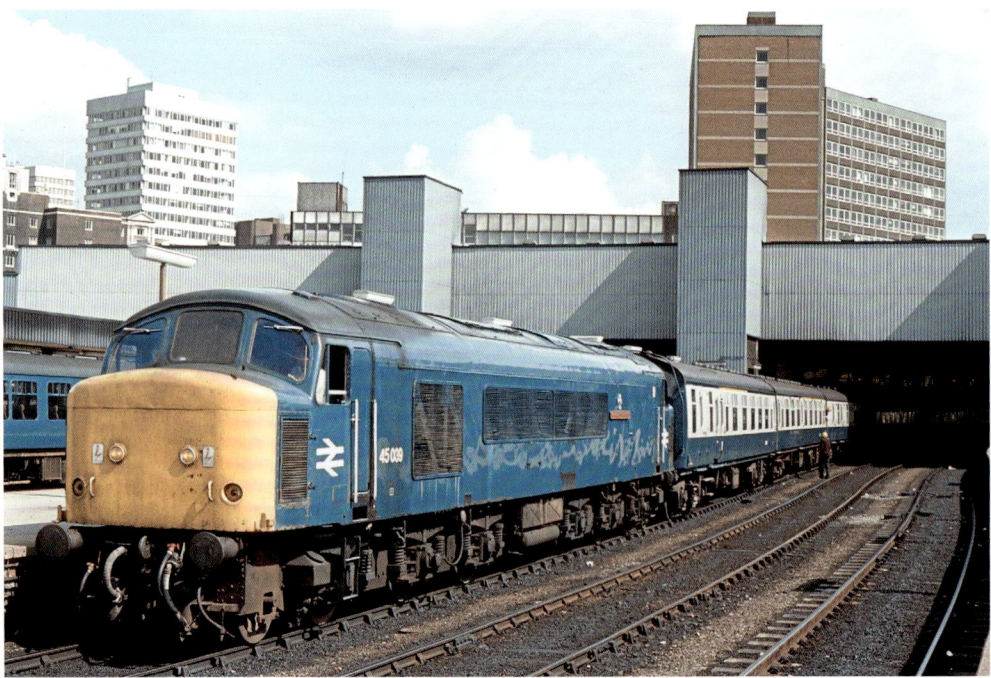

A wheeltapper walks back along the length of the train hauled by Peak No. 45039 *The Manchester Regiment* at Leeds on 25 August 1979. One of the popular television shows of the seventies was of course *The Wheeltappers and Shunters Social Club*, hosted by Colin Crompton, with Bernard Manning, Charlie Williams, George Roper and Jim Bowen among the regulars to make us laugh. (Sid Steadman)

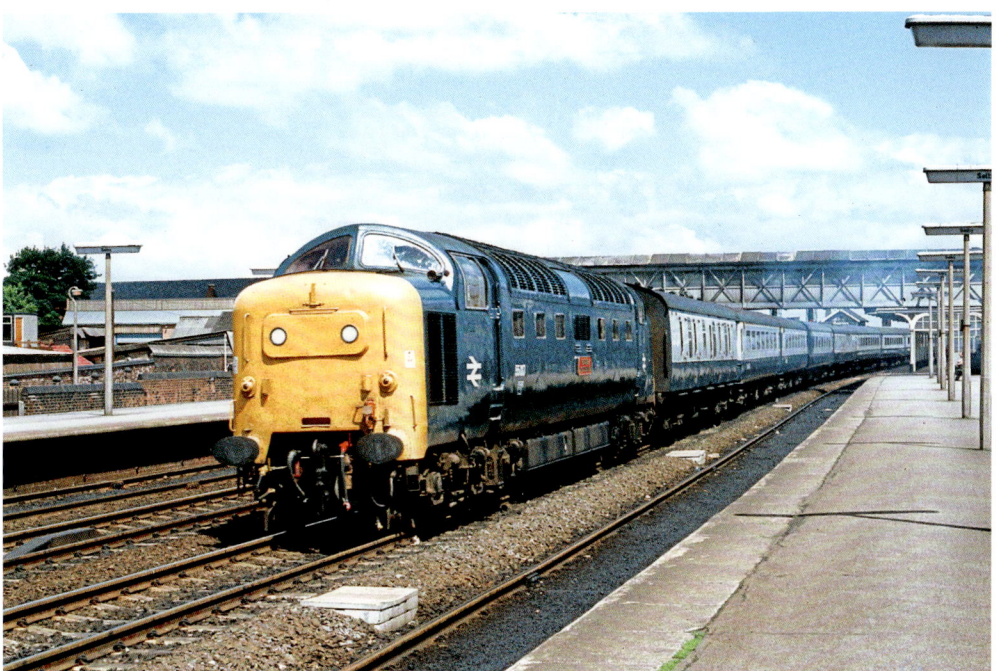

The driver opens up again after the speed restriction across the River Ouse and the swing bridge at Selby with his Deltic No. 55017 *The Durham Light Infantry* with the 09.00 Edinburgh train for London King's Cross on 8 July 1978. (Len Ball)

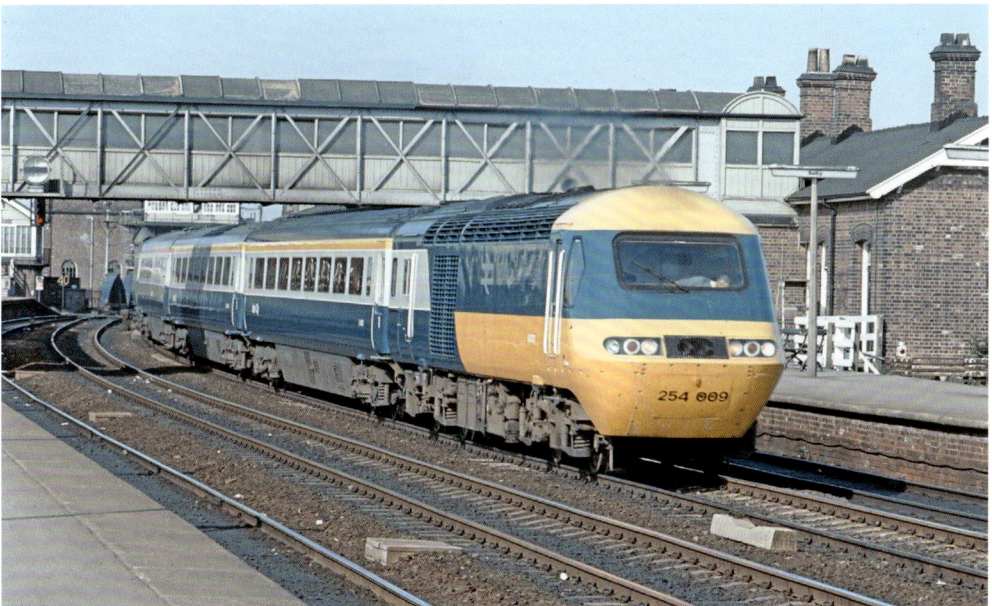

Inroads into Deltic diagrams were being made by recently introduced HSTs such as this set working the 13.10 Edinburgh–King's Cross on 26 August 1978. Thirty years later, and albeit with refurbished sets, HSTs can still be seen running at full line speed across all of the ECML with a daily service from Inverness to the capital covering the 579 miles everyday in just under eight hours. (Len Ball)